15 $\frac{95}{2}$

DISCARDED

Training in Ambiguity

Training in Ambiguity

Learning Through Doing in a Mental Hospital

by
ROSE LAUB COSER

Foreword by
ROBERT K. MERTON

THE FREE PRESS
A Division of Macmillan Publishing Co., Inc.
NEW YORK

Collier Macmillan Publishers
LONDON

Copyright © 1979 by THE FREE PRESS
A Division of Macmillan Publishing Co., Inc.

Foreword copyright © 1979 by Robert K. Merton

All rights reserved. No part of this book may be reproduced or transmitted in any form or by any means, electronic or mechanical, including photocopying, recording, or by any information storage and retrieval system, without permission in writing from the Publisher.

THE FREE PRESS
A Division of Macmillan Publishing Co., Inc.
866 Third Avenue, New York, N.Y. 10022

Collier Macmillan Canada, Ltd.

Library of Congress Catalog Card Number: 78-54109

Printed in the United States of America

printing number
1 2 3 4 5 6 7 8 9 10

Library of Congress Cataloging in Publication Data
Coser, Rose Laub
    Training in ambiguity.

    Includes bibliographical references and index.
    1. Psychiatric hospitals—Sociological aspects.
2. Psychiatry—Study and teaching (Residency)
3. Psychiatric hosptial care.   I. Title.
RC439.C813   363.2'1   78-54109
ISBN 0-02-906580-1

For Steven

Contents

List of Tables

List of Figures

Foreword

by

Robert K. Merton

As everyone knows, a foreword should be restrained in tone and cautious in praise; else it runs the distinct risk of defeating its purpose. With that precept firmly in mind, I merely suggest rather than insist that Rose Laub Coser's *Training in Ambiguity* bears comparison with such classical monographs in organizational sociology as *TVA and the Grass Roots*, by Philip Selznick; *Patterns of Industrial Bureaucracy*, by Alvin Gouldner; *The Dynamics of Bureaucracy*, by Peter Blau; and, most particularly, the classic in the same substantive domain, *The Mental Hospital*, by Alfred Stanton and Morris Schwartz.

Like those celebrated studies, Professor Coser's five-year longitudinal study of psychiatric training and practice in a mental hospital puts basic sociological ideas to effective use in the course of sensitive and detailed participant observation in a particular organization. Like them also, it extends and deepens these ideas for use by others. And like some of them, it skilfully combines qualitative and quantitative analysis, with each mode of inquiry serving to illuminate results obtained by the other.

The attentive reader will soon detect three planes on which this book makes its contributions. Most generally, it fortifies our sociological understanding of the structures and social processes at work in formal organizations. More specifically, it clarifies the interaction of social structure and therapeutic practices in the mental hospital, conceived of as a particular kind of organization. And most specifically, through its focus on the workings of apprenticeship in psychiatric training, the book advances our understanding of how professional socialization takes place.

On the first, most general, plane, Professor Coser exhibits the

theoretical versatility of structural analysis. This theoretical orientation proves to be as effective, for example, in working out the social
dynamics of mutual trust and cooperation between members of
subsystems in the organization as in working out the social dynamics
of mutual distrust and conflict between them. With the seeming ease
that is usually the result of a lot of hard analytical work, the study
moves back and forth between the analysis of key statuses and their
role-sets in the organization, on the one hand, and variations in
modes of role-performance, on the other. Even as the participants,
staff and patients alike, are shown to be greatly and often
unwittingly affected in their behavior by the local social structure,
they emerge not as passive puppets manipulated by that structure
but as active individuals diversely trying to negotiate their way
through it and at times actually managing to change it. The analysis
thus succeeds in taking account of both the constraints introduced
by structural contexts and the variability of individual behavior
within those contexts.

Even an abbreviated catalogue of sociological problems and concepts pivotal to the study should give some idea of its wide-ranging
scope. Consider only the analysis of social control systems, bases of
consensus and dissensus, contending systems of authority, status-sets
and role-sets, the social contexts of attitudinal as distinct from
behavioral conformity and nonconformity, and mechanisms of social
defense. I should add that no other empirical study known to me
makes better use of that pair of complementary concepts which
some of us sociologists take as basic to an understanding of systems
of social control: the long-familiar concept of *visibility* (the extent to
which status and role behavior are open to notice) and the less
familiar companion concept of *observability* (the extent to which
various positions in the social structure afford differing vantage
points for the observation of status and role behavior). But no more
about the contributions of this book to organizational analysis
generally.

On the second plane, centering on the mental hospital as a particular kind of organization, Professor Coser consolidates vivid you-
are-there depictive accounts of life at "O'Brien Hospital" with
imaginative sociological formulations of what is going on below the
surface. As a result, we come to know and increasingly to understand
the cast of principal characters: the resident psychiatrists, the clinical
administrators, and the chief reason for their organizational existence, the patients. To a less but still significant degree, we also come
to know the nurses, with their distinctive and often latent functions
for the medical staff and the patients. I found especially instructive
the sociological interpretation, developed with Simmel-like subtlety,

of the treatment triad of patient, psychotherapist, and clinical administrator. Basic structural arrangements have evolved that evidently serve to reduce the extent of sociological ambivalence (in which antithetical behaviors are expected of the *same* role-partner). Thus, one psychiatrist ordinarily engages the patient in therapeutic sessions (these calling for the full expression of the patient's inner dispositions) while another psychiatrist ordinarily manages the patient's life on the ward (this calling for the control of acting-out impulses and fantasies). This analysis incidentally illustrates Professor Coser's theoretical orientation to the concept of social mechanisms. She sees them not as operating to preclude the everyday troubles that stem from contradictions in the formal and informal social structure of the hospital but as serving to lessen the extent of these troubles below the level that would presumably obtain in the absence of such mechanisms.

Throughout the book Professor Coser tries, so far as is possible, to present a sense of what this one hospital probably shares with other hospitals and what is probably idiosyncratic to it. This discrimination is plainly required if case studies of organizations are to be assigned general significance. A special effort along these lines appears in the dramatic chapter 9, a sociological cameo devoted to an interpretation of the two waves of suicides that occurred at O'Brien Hospital within a fairly short time. In a fashion complementing the memorable analysis by Stanton and Schwartz of how socially patterned conflict among staff in a mental hospital affected individual and collective disturbance of patients, this chapter ingeniously works out the apparently sociopathic consequences of sharp declines in rates of social interaction in the hospital.

As for the third plane on which this book makes its contributions, these prefatory remarks can close much as they began. With all due restraint, I suggest that in this book Professor Rose Laub Coser just may have given us a prototypal field study of apprenticeship as a form of professional training and socialization.

Preface

This book is about the psychiatric staff of a mental hospital. It discusses how problems of treatment affect the social organization of its staff and, in turn, how interaction patterns among the psychiatric staff seem to impinge upon at least some aspects of patients' behavior. The focus is on residents, the recruits to psychiatry who come from medical schools, medical internships, and sometimes medical practice to obtain training in the psychiatric specialty.

The emphasis of the analysis is on contradictions in values. What may seem to be a "total institution" from the vantage point of patients is from the point of view of the participants, and of the social scientist, a heterogeneous group of people whose interests in patients and in one another differ, and whose alliances as well as conflicts crisscross one another. The title of this book, *Training in Ambiguity*, has been chosen so as to convey a dual meaning: the ambiguity inherent in the training situation and the ambiguity inherent in the psychiatric practice for which residents are being trained. The focus is on the residents' simultaneous tasks of learning and treating, the ambivalence inherent in the dual tasks of custody and treatment of patients, and the ambiguities pertaining to staff relationships.

It took a long time to write this modest book. Lack of funds and lack of time were the more obvious reasons; a less obvious reason is a reluctance to write about one's colleagues. The hospital staff was much involved with the research on which this book is based, and I was much involved with them. I hope I am permitted the audacity to say that some of them are among my best friends! I am indebted to all of them for their unflinching cooperation, and to the psychiatrist-in-chief and the hospital's director for welcoming my intrusion and giving me full access.

Many colleagues took an interest in my work. Alfred H. Stanton, coauthor of a book written many years ago on a similar hospital, gave me invaluable assistance. Long conversations and conferences with Merton J. Kahne helped me focus on problems that otherwise would have escaped me. Richard Longabaugh and Robert Schnitzer were not only most stimulating but helped in some aspects of the research design. Robert K. Merton was a superb critic of some of the work included in this book. Patricia Kendall was an invaluable consultant on research design and procedures, as was Stanley H. Eldred on matters pertaining to the practice of psychiatry. Michael McGuire and Richard Sens provided information and ideas concerning residency. Each of them read some chapters of the book and made important comments. None of them is, of course, responsible for its many shortcomings.

Without the help of research assistants, who by now are my colleagues in academe, the work for this book could never have been done. Janice Stroud was much involved in the early stages of planning and data gathering; Rachel Kahn-Hut was involved for several years with data gathering and organization; Natalie Allon, Hedy Miller, and Andrea Carr were devoted and able assistants; and William Stanton worked on computer programming far beyond the call of duty.

Thanks also go to Kai Erikson, Donald Light, and Gerald Platt, who all read one or the other chapter and made valuable comments. Finally, whatever readability this book has is due to the fine pen and careful attention of Gladys Topkis of The Free Press.

The research on which this book is based was sponsored by the National Institute of Mental Health, Grant No. M-3534, and in part by the Commonwealth Fund. One chapter (chapter 10) was written in conjunction with a seminar I was invited to hold at the Institute for Advanced Studies in Vienna, Austria. My thanks go to my colleagues at this institute, especially to Helga Nowotny and Jürgen Pelikan. Also, part of the work on the book was done while I was a visiting professor at the Langley Porter Clinic at the University of California, San Francisco, where I enjoyed the hospitality and support of Majorie Fiske Lowenthal of the Adult Development Program and of its research team.

Fieldwork in Norway (NIMH Grant No. M3534-C1S1) made it possible for me to gain distance and to obtain a more general view of universals and particulars in mental hospitals. Thanks go to Dr. Harald Fröshaug of Dikemark Hospital and to Åsi Gausted, who was an invaluable interviewer and interpreter. I enjoyed hospitality at Oslo's Institute of Social Research, and am grateful to its then director, Johan Rinde, and the other colleagues for letting me collect my thoughts and test them with their help.

Lewis Coser provided all the encouragement I needed. He not only suffered with good humor through the ups and downs of my efforts all through the years of data gathering and analysis but he read, evaluated, and discussed every line I wrote—and many that I didn't. Ellen Coser Perrin showed a lively interest in this work whenever she was home from school or work, and Steven Coser helped punch cards and tabulate when he was still in junior high. Ellen and Steven will have much to tell about what it means to have a working mother.

In short, this book is not my work alone. Those I have named, and many I have not, can claim some share in it.

Training in Ambiguity

1
Introduction

This is a book on social structure. It is addressed to sociologists who enjoy doing sociological analysis. It is also addressed to those professionals in the health field, in academia, and in administration who recognize that ambiguities cannot be avoided but that mechanisms exist to cope with them, if only in some small measure.

The setting is a mental hospital, an organization where mentally ill patients are being treated and psychiatric residents are being trained. Yet, the book is about much less but also about much more.

It is about much less than mental hospitals in general because it is concerned with one very special institution: a teaching hospital on the Eastern Seaboard affiliated with a major medical school, which treats patients mainly from the upper and upper-middle classes and from academic and professional circles, and which specializes to an important extent in psychoanalytically oriented psychiatry.

It is about much less than mental hospitals in another way: it deals only with selected problems, and not with all aspects of the organizational or professional life of the hospital; nor does it deal with the lives of patients. For the purpose of making abstractions, nurses' aides, social workers, and group and recreational therapists have been left out of the picture except in the first, explanatory chapter, where some of their relationships with psychiatric residents are described. Similarly, patients are considered (mainly in chapter 3) only to the extent that their care affects the interpersonal relations among the psychiatric staff in some aspects that have been selected for scrutiny.

However, the book is also about much more than just one mental hospital. Unique as O'Brien is, it provides the opportunity to pinpoint some of the basic problems confronting the treatment of the

1

mentally ill; and although it is specifically a training center for psychiatric residents, it provides the opportunity to confront some basic problems of professional socialization. Further, in spite of its uniqueness or perhaps because of it, it provides the opportunity for analyzing social processes endemic to all sorts of organizations, for the dramatic nature of its problems brings into visibility, and hence allows analytical access to, problems that often remain hidden or dormant in organizations that are less socially tense.

Hence, this book deals with some problems that occur both in mental hospitals generally and in organizations generally. It deals with the multiplicity of goals that are not always compatible, with ambiguities and vagueness in interpersonal relations, with contradictory values, human errors, and anomie. An attempt is made to determine how structural arrangements contribute to such problems, compounding or alleviating them. It is hoped that the analysis will demonstrate the fruitfulness of sociological concepts in discovering structural sources of ambiguities and failures and in implying remedial action through organizational change.

The book started out as a five-year longitudinal study of professional socialization. But the initial focus had to be shifted to some extent to social structure and the impact of unanticipated events. One of the problems in conducting research in an active organization is the unpredictable and unmeasurable effect on attitudes of unexpected dramatic events such as deaths and departures. Not only do status occupants come and go, signaling organizational changes, but their arrivals and departures also signal unrest and have unanticipated consequences for attitudinal changes. Not only is the life of an organization affected in a patterned and predictable manner by the goals and the life of other organizations with which it is affiliated; in addition, there are unforeseen changes in relations with outside organizations that lead to changes within. The impact of some changes and events can be best illustrated in conjunction with the description of the research plan.

The Research: Plans and Vicissitudes

The initial purpose of the research reported in this book was to study the process of acquisition of professional values among the psychiatric residents of one training center, here called O'Brien Hospital. This teaching hospital, affiliated with a medical school of high prestige, had at any one time approximately 200 patients and 50 psychiatrists; about half of the latter were residents. It seemed small enough for study in some detail, yet large enough to yield some generalizable insights about the process of the absorption of values by new recruits to the profession. It was hypothesized that such values are transmitted through mediators—that is, by those mature psychiatrists who have a permanent position in the hospital (henceforth referred to as "senior staff.")

The data gathering took place over five years, from 1960 to 1964. Nine series of semiannual interviews were conducted with residents, a total of 260 interviews. Most questions were asked each time, some were asked once a year, and some were asked only once. In order to ascertain some of the dominant values prevalent at O'Brien Hospital and some of the predominant attitudes, the senior staff members were also interviewed at regular intervals. Yearly interviews with them yielded a total of 109. In addition to providing data about the attitudes of the normbearers, these interviews yielded an additional advantage: it was possible to use the responses of the senior staff as controls for changes that would appear in the residents' interviews. If senior staff had also changed their opinions and beliefs, a similar change among residents could not be used as evidence for the socialization process; changes of all that staff would then be due to some other factors. (The research design is shown in appendix A. Appendix B presents the interview schedule for residents. With minor changes, essentially similar questions were used with supervisors and administrators and with incoming residents.)

Some findings about changes of attitudes over the five years of the research illustrate this point. An attempt was made to ascertain whether, according to their own reports, residents became more or less restrictive of patients over the years of training. Yet, no linear trend in changes of attitudes could be discerned over the five years (measured from one half-yearly period to the next), either for the same cohorts followed over time or for a comparison of all residents by length of training. It turned out that the senior staff also changed their attitudes between one yearly interview and the next in regard to their willingness to restrict patients. Indeed, the two trends were more or less parallel over time. This called my attention to the events that had taken place during these years. Among the events that stood out in everybody's mind were suicides of patients. The staff's willingness to restrict patients "to prevent harm to themselves and others" (as the question was worded) increased after some patients had committed suicide and decreased in periods in which no suicides took place. (See figure 21 in appendix A.)

An example of how changes in the organization are likely to affect the findings is provided by another attempt to ascertain changes in respondents' judgments over time. I set out to determine whether a progressive self-appraisal by residents is related to the progressive appraisal that their supervisors make of the residents' skills, and whether such a consensual judgment is being established between teachers and students.

After the first year of the research the data showed a trend of increased consensus between residents and their supervisors about the residents' ability to treat patients. Yet, this trend did not continue beyond the first year of the research. It is possible that changes in consensus are so irregular that they do not show a linear trend, or that the instrument used was inadequate to measure them. Yet, it is also possible that the events that occurred after the first year of the research, and changes that took place in the residency training program, accounted for the lack of any significant trend.

Again, suicides of patients must command attention. One major suicide wave remained in everybody's mind for years: this was a series of six suicides that ended toward the end of the second year of the research. Even though my field notes include observations about much unrest, there is no way of knowing for certain whether this series of events produced such disarray among the staff that the relationships between seniors and residents were significantly affected. A second major suicide wave occurred after the data collection for the research had long been terminated, so that a comparison was no longer possible.

Among the organizational changes that took place during the second year of the research were important changes in the leadership of the hospital. In addition, and of direct concern to this research, was a change in the training program that altered the length of stay of most residents. When the study was begun, all residents entered O'Brien at the beginning of their first year and were expected to stay for three years. A year later, O'Brien and University Hospital, the large general hospital of which O'Brien was a part (administratively speaking, not geographically), reached an agreement to allow residents to benefit from each other's programs. Residents who had spent two years at O'Brien could take their third year of training at University Hospital. In turn, University Hospital's first-year residents had the option of joining O'Brien for their second year of training. While residents who left O'Brien after their second year could be followed up in the research because they remained in the same city and because they remained part of O'Brien's staff by continuing to do psychotherapy with some of its patients, residents who entered in their second year had not been part of the interview procedure during the first third of their training. This change also meant that some residents would be at O'Brien for one year only, some for two years, and some for three years.

It is quite possible that such dramatic events as a suicide wave, changes in leadership, and the reduction of the residents' stay at

O'Brien combined to help cancel out the consensus residents seemed to have been able to form with their supervisors during the first year of the research.

There is a structural property of the mental hospital and of psychiatric training that would seem to have a strong restraining impact on any possible linear development in the socialization of psychiatric residents. This property refers to contradictory values and contradictory expectations inherent in the nature of modern psychiatry generally and in the nature of the modern mental hospital in particular, as well as in the nature of on-the-spot training in the field. In all these areas there exists what Robert K. Merton and Elinor Barber have called "sociological ambivalence,"[1] that is, a condition in which status holders are expected to live up to values and expectations that are contradictory.

Sociological Ambivalence in Psychiatric Practice and Training

One source of ambivalence consists in the nature of modern psychiatry, which, as Harvey Smith has pointed out, has become more medical by becoming more social.[2] A second source of ambivalence lies in the nature of the modern mental hospital, which has the dual mandate of controlling the behavior of its patients, a task based on the use of authority, and giving the patients treatment, a task based on trust between patient and practitioner. The third source of ambivalence comes from the contradiction of having to behave as a professional while learning to become professional, a difficulty extant in all medical residencies but exacerbated in psychiatric training because of the relative lack of preparation psychiatric residents received during the prior five years of medical studies.

Psychiatry, Medicine, and the Nature of Mental Illness

Psychiatry's integration in medicine took place in large part through the acceptance of psychoanalysis by American psychiatrists.

As psychoanalysis developed farther in the social than in the biological direction, it made private practice for psychiatrists possible and developed an elite clientele—two conditions that helped integrate American psychiatry into the medical prestige structure.

As long as psychiatrists could not have private patients, they could not command prestige from the public, for they were seen as "employees" rather than as "free professionals." Also, psychiatrists could not have prestigeful patients as long as their practice was limited mainly to state hospitals, where inmates came from lower social strata. The relatively few private hospitals for the wealthy served primarily as kinds of nursing homes where the rich could store disruptive relatives. The fact that some private hospitals today pride themselves on having hosted some great American figures in the past proves the importance of highly placed clients for the prestige of the institution.

Prevailing ideology in American society has it that private practice assures the safeguarding of individual interests of patients or clients. The ability to pay is seen in our society as the ability to exercise a measure of control. To be sure, this function is poorly served because individual rewards may foster greediness at least as much as devotion. Yet, in American culture generally, and in American medical culture in particular, private practice, for whatever it is worth in fact, has been a symbol of the professional's personal dedication to the individual client.

Hardly able to have private practice in the past, psychiatrists were often seen as violating an important value of the medical profession: the devotion to individual patients. Nor could they gain prestige from titles and positions at medical schools, at least not in any significant number, as long as the field could not boast of having much knowledge or important techniques to teach.

The breakthrough for psychiatry came with psychoanalysis, in part because this approach helped bring about the conditions that would lead psychiatry into the core of professional life. It provided a specialized technique for dealing with mental disturbances on an individual basis. Because it was usable primarily for nonhospitalized patients, psychoanalytic technique broadened the field of psychiatric practice by creating a consumer market. And because of the high cost of one-to-one treatment, the market was among the elite, and this furnished the means for prestige grading in the psychiatric profession. Psychoanalysis made it possible to treat respected and upper-class members of the community, thereby enhancing the prestige of psychiatric practice. At the same time, it fostered the opportunity for treatment in a private doctor's office, the symbol of a physician's devotion and service to patients. It is not exaggerated to say that it is largely thanks to psychoanalysis that psychiatry has "made it," both within the medical profession and with the "respectable" public.

The rapprochement between psychoanalysis and psychiatry had begun in the twenties and thirties, but it was not until World War II, and especially during the postwar period, that psychoanalysis helped American psychiatry to become an integral part of medicine. Already with the work of Adolf Meyer in the twenties service to the client had become an achievable goal, at least as a normative guideline.

Meyer centered his attention on the life situation of the individual and set the stage for studying the person within an interactive system.[3] He stressed the patients' relationships in their communities and made their social involvements the source of clinical data. Although he himself was not a follower of Freudian psychoanalysis, his theory prepared the ground in psychiatry for a gradual acceptance of Freud's theory, in which unconscious processes are related to the interactive system in the history of the individual.

The success of modified psychoanalytic techniques during the war years helped make psychiatry into a psychological and social discipline and contributed toward the view of mental illness as part of the human condition instead of a departure from it.[4]

Other treatment techniques, such as electroshock and especially drug therapy, have made mental illness amenable to treatment and, most important, to treatment in private practice, and hence have helped integrate psychiatry into medicine.[5] Yet, this also adds to the confusion in attempting to delineate mental illness.

This confusion about the medical nature of psychiatry finds expression in everyday talk or in jokes. For example, at a case conference a psychiatrist reported having told a patient who had developed a pain in the chest, "You are *really* sick." Although this remark apparently was made in all seriousness, it is remindful of the jocular expression frequently used by O'Brien's psychiatrists when someone had physical symptoms: "You ought to go see a real doctor." The following humorous exchange highlights the ambiguity of the rapprochement between psychiatrists and other MDs:

> *Resident* [during presentation of a case]: Patient's father tried to get help for the mother. He was told there was no psychiatric help available [at the time], he should read Freud. So he took a course in do-it-yourself psychiatry. [Laughter]
> *Senior member* [interrupting]: Are you going to leave us in the lurch as to how it worked? [Laughter]
> *Resident:* He did as well as most MDs; his wife is still unhospitalized and still has many complaints. [Laughter][6]

When asked, "Do you think mental illness is an illness like any other, or is there a difference between mental and other types of illness?" O'Brien's staff included moral and social criteria in their definitions, yet revealed in their responses vagueness, hesitation, and confusion, as in the following answer by one of the hospital's leaders:

> I don't know what "an illness like any other" means anyway. I fussed over this [question] once before. . . . Is it an illness such as, for instance, pneumonia? Well, it shares certain characteristics certainly, and there are certain other

characteristics it doesn't share. . . . For my money, I like to include in mental illness mental defect, the mental phenomena that accompany brain tumors, the hysterical overvaluation of pain on the operating table, obsessive neurosis, psychopathic personality, etc., huh? It's a very broad term.

Or take the following uncertain answer from another psychiatrist who had been in practice for many years:

That's almost a silly question. . . . It's an entirely different category, and as functions, they have an entirely different ideology, although I'm a firm believer that there are certain constitutional elements . . . that it is obvious that it takes all kinds of factors, but the primary factor is functional, environmental, and as such, then, it has to be influenced by entirely different factors.

The author of the following statement recognized the uncertainty of the nature of the illness but sees it from the point of view of the patient:

Mental illness . . . has psychological as well as biological, as well as genetic and hereditary factors, depending where your emphasis is. . . . It's something rather frightening, intangible that patients can't get hold of. They can't grasp it. So it's quite different than trouble with the heart.

Thus it seems that what psychiatrists are supposed to treat is to some extent social in nature, has moral implications, and beyond that is uncertain to the point of eliciting confused responses on the part of practitioners who are devoting their lives to the treatment of this "disease."

Respondents apparently did not acknowledge the fact that uncertainties, as well as social elements, are present in all illness. As most physicians will agree, not all medical illness is as clearly definable as a broken leg or heart failure—examples my respondents liked to mention to highlight the difference between mental and physical illness. In some sense all medical training is training for uncertainty, as Renée Fox recognized years ago.[7] Uncertainty and certainty in medicine are not dichotomies. They are two ends of a continuum with psychiatry at one end and surgery close to (though not entirely at) the other end. This is why a psychiatric setting promises to teach us something that is relevant for other medical specialties as well: in every specialty the practitioner learns to act in the face of some degree of uncertainty; in psychiatry, the uncertainty can hardly be ignored.

The consideration that psychological and social factors are the basis for psychiatric judgment and treatment applies to some extent to other medical specialties as well. The wide use of the term "psychosomatic" amply indicates awareness that social, emotional, and moral factors may precede or accompany physical symptoms. Yet, the difficulty this fact presents for medical treatment can be, and often is, ignored. In psychiatry, the ambiguity is part of every-day practice.

For this reason, among others, there is a sharp discontinuity between medical and psychiatric training although psychiatric residents are reminded of the medical model at the same time that they are encouraged to abandon it.

At O'Brien, residents are discouraged from relinquishing their claim to membership in the medical fraternity. Senior staff make it their task to keep the medical model alive in the residents' con-sciousness. For example, residents are required, in spite of their occasional protests, to be present at autopsies. More effective than this ritual as a reminder of owed allegiance is the vocabulary of everyday life. Terms such as *illness, hospital, patient, admissions, discharges, and clinical procedures*—to name a few—make O'Brien part of the medical culture. This vocabulary helps put the daily tasks of residents into the framework of medical practice, as when decisions about patients' freedom of movement are considered part of *clinical management.*

O'Brien remains an integral part of the medical world through the affiliation it maintains with University Hospital and with the presti-gious medical school, where most of the members of the psychiatric staff have appointments. They take part in the medical school's faculty meetings, and several of O'Brien's staff members have been called upon to teach medical students. The medical school, as well as University Hospital, is important for the training of O'Brien's staff, especially since these organizations have considerable power and authority in determining policy that affects this mental hospital. In short, the medical school and University Hospital are important foci of orientation for residents who hope to further their careers through future appointments in these high-prestige organizations.

While the medical model is adhered to and reinforced at O'Brien, much of what has been learned in medical school has to be unlearned in training for psychotherapy. The dual aim of both maintaining and dropping part of the values that were taught in medical school can be read from the interview with one supervisor, who said: "I explain to the residents that psychotherapy is a social engagement of a different kind than the ordinary one. If I tell the secretary that it is a nice day, and she tells me, well, it isn't such a nice day, I say she's all wrong. . . . But if a patient asks me how are you today, I ask him: why do you want to know? This is a *medical model.*"

In psychotherapy, just as in medicine, the practitioner must never take anything for granted in order not to miss the hidden reasons underlying a symptom. However, when this supervisor continued to explain what he thought was the most important thing to learn in psychotherapy, he pointed to its discontinuity with medicine: "They learned in medical school that waiting could be death. . . . The first notion in medicine is 'I'm going to treat.' I say to them, 'Never mind, it took twenty years for the patient to get that way.' " Implicit here is the notion that psychiatric residents have to unlearn the medical attitude that decisions must be made quickly and that action must be oriented toward a short time perspective.

The difference in time perspective alluded to here does not only distinguish psychiatry from medicine. Within psychiatry itself, and especially in the psychoanalytically oriented mental hospital, two time perspectives exist side by side. The psychiatrist-in-chief at O'Brien believed that "the unconscious is timeless." Yet the director of the hospital exclaimed: "Time is running on at $40 an hour, and the family wants to know if the patient is getting better." This summarizes one of the differences between psychoanalytically oriented psychotherapy and ward psychiatry. Not only do residents have to learn that treatment of mental patients is based on a different time perspective than other medical treatment; in this hospital they must have a long time perspective in psychotherapy and a short time perspective on the ward when making assessments of patients' behavior. This raises the question of the heterogeneous value system in this psychoanalytically oriented hospital.

The Dual Mandate at O'Brien

The practice of psychoanalytically oriented psychotherapy is an important element in O'Brien's value system, at the same time as there is strong commitment to what at O'Brien is called "clinical management of patients."

To most residents entering O'Brien from the "aseptic" environment of medical school and internship, the Psychoanalytic Institute and its representative members become important foci of reference in regard to future career. Most of O'Brien's psychiatrists are members of the institute or are candidates there. Although residents cannot apply to the institute for training at the early stage of their training, they can orient themselves toward one general hospital in the area (other than University Hospital) in which the department of psychiatry is run by psychoanalysts and where residents can go for their third year of training. Moreover, they can, and often do, after being so counseled by their elders, go into personal analysis in preparation for future psychoanalytic training. During their last year of residency they can apply for admission to candidacy at the Psychoanalytic Institute. And rejection by the institute is considered by the applicants a major blow to their career aspirations.

Some prestigious members of the Psychoanalytic Institute have clinical staff appointments at O'Brien and exercise their influence on the hospital in this indirect way. They are usually supervisors of therapy, in addition to being readily available consultants. They may relate to O'Brien in still another way, as one supervisor explained: "I have a great deal of knowledge about many of the residents—maybe more than most people at [O'Brien], because I hear about them when they apply to the institute." The fact that this supervisor is not a member of the permanent staff and comes to O'Brien only rarely lends further weight to his assertion that as a leading member of the Psychoanalytic Institute he knows the residents "maybe more than most people" at the hospital. This type of loose yet important relationship with residents, in addition to the fact that most of the residents' supervisors of psychotherapy are psychoanalysts, makes psychoanalysts in the community generally, and the Psychoanalytic Institute in particular, important reference groups for O'Brien's residents. We recognize here the operation of a "social circle" as defined by Charles Kadushin, that is, a network of people who share common interests and who can be mutually influential without well-specified organizational legitimation.[8] The psychoanalytic model of treatment is an important part of residency training at O'Brien.

Psychiatric residents are less prepared for this kind of training than medical residents are for most other medical specialties. Medical schools in general have lagged behind in the recognition that psychiatry relies heavily on the psychosocial definition of mental illness. In most medical schools in the country, there is little preparatory teaching of the techniques that future psychiatric residents will need. This contrasts with the preparation medical students get in most other specialties.[9]

In addition to being trained in psychotherapy, residents at O'Brien are being trained in "clinical management of patients"—that is, in the supervision of patients' behavior and their treatment programs on the wards. However, for this task also residents have been little prepared in medical school. This aspect of their training leads to the second difficulty they have to deal with in the hospital, namely the task of supervising patients.

Mental patients differ from patients in general hospitals in at least one important way: their behavior is much more closely controlled. This is because, by the definition of mental illness, their behavior is expected to be more unpredictable as well as potentially more disruptive.

In general hospitals, physicians do not exercise direct control over the behavior of patients. To be sure, some restriction of patients is part of the pattern, accepted by the public and hospital staff. A patient who is hospitalized is defined as needing bed rest. That the medical soundness of this practice has been repeatedly questioned by at least some medical authorities[10] is beside the point here. What is at stake is that confinement to bed, with the concomitant removal of street clothes and restriction of movement in general, is considered legitimate by all concerned, including the patients, and is enforced by the nursing staff. It does not need a special use of medical authority. It would not usually enter a patient's mind to go exploring the building, let alone to leave the premises for a stroll or an errand. The word *escape* is not part of the vocabulary in a general hospital because the concept does not apply. If it will be objected that the notion of "escape" is used in other than mental hospitals—for example, in TB hospitals—this proves the point that is stressed here: restriction of movement beyond what is routine in a general hospital takes place in hospitals in which (a) patients are defined as being potentially harmful to self or others and (b) patients' movements are not routinely controlled through around-the-clock bedrest and removal of street clothes.

If a mental hospital is defined as being therapy- rather than custody-oriented, control of patients must be legitimized by being assigned to the medical staff. In a modern, treatment-oriented mental hospital, the amount of freedom patients enjoy is decided individually and almost day by day, and this is considered to be the result of a clinical decision by a psychiatrist. Making patients' freedom dependent on clinical decisions helps de-emphasize the custodial nature of mental hospitalization and also helps keep psychiatric hospital practice in the realm of medicine. But it puts the burden of using control, and coercion if need be, on the psychiatrists' shoulders. Paradoxically, psychiatric practice is considered *more* medical when it takes upon itself a form of control that is usually *not* part of the medical tradition.

Residents who begin their training at O'Brien have not learned to exercise the type of authority that is required for the management of a ward of mental patients. When they first come to O'Brien, psychiatric residents are usually surprised to find how much emphasis is placed on "clinical management of patients"; and some of them feel that, in the words of one resident, "the use of authority over patients" is the hardest to learn. He added: "I was not prepared for this at all."

The use of authority to sanction the behavior of patients "for their own protection" or "for the protection of the public" is often incompatible with the immunity that must be granted to patients in psychoanalytically oriented psychotherapy, which is expected to help them gain insight so that they may change their outlook on themselves and society. Chapter 3 describes and analyzes the complex organization of treatment at O'Brien.

The social complexity that arises in a system that sets itself the dual goal of resocializing its patients and controlling them is analyzed in chapter 2. The various relationships residents must maintain with role partners differently placed in the organization are described in chapters 4 and 5, which deal with the ambivalent relationships that residents must enter and maintain in the course of their hospital training. The ambivalence is further enhanced when these activities are carried out by residents who themselves are in the process of professional socialization.

Learning through Doing

The lack of preparation for psychiatric residency during medical training highlights an ambiguity present in all *learning through doing*—that is, when a student has to perform as if already having the qualifications that are to be learned. In some respect psychiatric residents share this plight with their status equals in other medical specialties. These trainees have a double role. Insofar as they are learning, they are students; insofar as they are doing, they are professionals. Their doing is not only *as if*, it is for real. They are physicians to the patients but advanced students in relation to the senior staff; thus they face different expectations from their various role partners. This ambiguity exists in most types of apprenticeship and certainly in every type of medical residency, yet it is more pronounced at O'Brien because of the lack of preparation residents have for the dual tasks that have been described. For this reason, the senior staff is even more alerted to the residents' student status than is the medical staff of a general hospital, and this leads to a reinforcement of this status ambiguity: residents at O'Brien are not given full authority over their ward patients but are merely assistants to the psychiatrists who are the clinical administrators of the wards.

As a result of the residents' lack of *de jure* authority, the patients' fear of being treated by students is further reinforced. While patients are supposed to expect residents to behave as full professionals, they know at the same time not only that the young psychiatrists are still in training but also that they have little leverage for the exercise of authority on the ward, because they are not as yet fully trained and because they are not given a position that legitimizes the use of authority. The ambiguities inherent in the student-practitioner status are discussed in chapter 6.

The contradictory values of the profession are faced differently by psychiatrists who occupy different positions in the hospital. Among the senior staff, those who are more directly involved with controlling the behavior of patients tend to be more conflicted than those whose position permits them to remain aloof from everyday decisions. All psychiatrists at O'Brien share the values of psychoanalytically oriented psychiatry, yet some of them are not as much as others in a position to practice psychotherapy. The ways in which various staff members see themselves in relation to expressed ideals are explored in chapters 7 and 8.

Reference has been made earlier to the occurrence of dramatic events. Chapter 9 explores the qualities of interpersonal relations in the hospital in relation to suicide waves among patients. While the relation between suicide waves and conditions of anomie in society in general is among the few propositions tested in sociological theory, the opportunity is afforded here to spell out in some detail the probable impact of anomic conditions in one organization.

The final chapter discusses some structural conditions that do and some that do not enhance solidarity and a feeling of competence among a young psychiatric staff. O'Brien presented the strange paradox of a centralized form of organization and a more or less unified view of what constitutes good psychiatric practice, with a structure that made the treatment of patients a lonely and to a large extent individualistic affair for the young practitioners. In order to understand the functioning of a mental hospital and the practices of its professional staff, it is not sufficient to recognize the hospital's nature as a "total institution," in Goffman's term.[11] Goffman, deliberately writing about mental hospitals from the perspective of patients, emphasizes the functioning of solidary teams of staff members for the total control of inmates. To be sure, this is how the staff often appears to patients. Yet, at O'Brien, patients differentiated between psychiatrists. They knew who had authority and who did not. They knew that residents were there to learn, and that the senior staff was not. They would call one psychiatrist a "baron," another one a friend, and at one time they picketed the administration building when they heard of the resignation of the clinical director. They also made use of the diversity among the staff as leverage for their own ends.

This book deals with patients only tangentially. It deals primarily with the psychiatric staff, whose control is in no way "total." I intend to show the conflicts and the diverse socially structured and often antagonistic interests of psychiatrists differentially positioned in the organization, as well as some of the unanticipated irrational consequences of rational, and not so rational, attempts on the part of administrators and clinicians to do a good job.

2
Psychiatric Residents at Work

Residents at O'Brien are involved in several areas of activities: admission of new patients (in rotation); a three- to six-week workup of new patients; "on-call" and night duty; clinical management of patients on the halls where they are hospitalized; group psychotherapy; individual psychotherapy of patients; and academic exercises and other formal teaching situations.

Some of these activities are more salient than others. The two major areas of training are individual psychotherapy and clinical management of patients on the wards (called "clinical administration"). The bulk of this book will deal with these two activities. Yet, it is useful to give a brief and necessarily partial description of the other activities as well in as far as they contribute to the complexity of the residents' relationships.

In each of their activities, residents can be viewed as occupying the center of a web of social relations in which they are in direct or indirect contact with several role-partners. The areas of activities will be described in turn with special attention to the following questions: Whom do the residents observe and by whom are they observed? With whom do they communicate and in what capacity? Who is in a position to control their behavior, and what are the standards underlying expectations for conformity?

Admissions Procedures: The Social Worker

While the social service is in charge of scheduling and organizing admissions, psychiatric residents do the actual admitting and report

their admissions at the all-staff meeting called "the morning conference." They don't rate this activity highly as a source of learning. In
the eight consecutive interviews in which they were asked to check
the comparative usefulness of thirteen learning situations, residents
ranked admission procedures last or next to last. The senior staff also
ranked them last the first time they were asked this question, in year
2 of the research. Subsequently, in years 3 and 4 of the research, the
senior staff raised their perception of the importance of admissions
for the residents' training to the eighth and sixth place, respectively.

In admitting patients, residents are often under stress because they
have to deal with the situation without a supervisor (though a senior
person is always on call in case of need). They have to act quickly,
they cannot stall decisions, they have to relieve the anxieties of
patients and of the caller's relatives as well, and they have to take
care of formalities swiftly and accurately. The relatives are usually at
a pitch of anxiety; for them, the physician is the most important
person they have to see, yet they are at the same time suspicious of
his or her competence, especially when they find out that the
admitting physician is "only" a resident.

The chief social worker controls preadmission procedures and is in
charge of setting up the roster for the rotation of residents in regard
to this service. The task of dealing with relatives of patients and with
referring physicians gives the social worker a particular interest in the
reputation of the hospital on the outside, for relatives might communicate their experience with the hospital to other people in the
community. This concern seems to be justified, because patients at
O'Brien are likely to come from influential families or organizations.
Many of them belong to the upper social class or are connected with
the prestigious academic community of the area. Referring physicians also are likely to come from the top rung of the prestige ladder
and to be affiliated with the medical school or the Psychoanalytic
Institute. Belonging to the same social milieu as the psychiatric staff,
patients' relatives and referring physicians tend to be considered
important transmitters of gossip and information about the hospital.
By becoming the spokesperson for these important members of the
community, a social worker assumes some part in controlling residents in their work with patients and relatives.[1] The following report
by a social worker illustrates her informal power.

It was after 5 o'clock, the admitting resident was gone, and the patient was
standing there with his father and [another resident]. The father asked, "Who
is going to talk to me after I straighten out about the baggage?" so it was
obvious that one of us had to talk to this man. [The resident] said, "I will."

*He saw the look on my face and rose to the occasion. . . . * I thanked him the next day.

Social workers are significant role-partners of residents in admissions procedures for another reason as well. They are in a good position to observe the residents' behavior and hence can exercise some control over them. The contradictions in the relationship between residents and social workers are similar to those between an intern and the head nurse in a general hospital.[2] Residents are higher in authority than social workers both because of the doctoral title and because residents act in their anticipatory role as psychiatrists. Most social workers, however, and especially the chief of the social service, can boast many years of experience with psychiatric patients and also seniority in the hospital, with whose welfare the chief social worker identifies strongly. Social workers repeatedly remind the residents of their responsibilities toward patients' relatives. Although they have no direct authority over residents, they exercise some power indirectly, as in the anecdote reported above. Moreover, if a resident's behavior seems unacceptable to them, they can, and often do, report it to higher authorities. Some of the high-status social workers periodically report their opinions about residents to the psychiatrist-in-chief or the hospital's director.

A contradiction in status relations of this kind creates tension, yet they are so structured that the tension does not paralyze the residents in the articulation of their roles. This is because a social worker's power is not legitimized by position of authority. If this were the case, residents would be much restricted in their freedom when dealing with incoming patients, and criteria stemming from outside the hospital—namely from relatives and referring physicians—would threaten to dominate in-hospital norms. Since social workers, both because of their lack of academic or medical title and because of their structural position, have no legitimate authority over residents, the latter find themselves insulated from social service's authority over their work even though they are in the social worker's sphere of visibility. This constitutes a safety valve: the person best placed to observe and know about a certain area of the residents' work is least equipped to shape their behavior directly.[3]

Workup of Patients

Residents conduct diagnostic interviews with new patients about three times a week for a stretch of three to five weeks. They report to a "workup supervisor," who is either a member of O'Brien's staff or an outside psychiatrist especially invited to come to the hospital for that purpose. During the period of the research there were usually two such supervisors. During the time of the workup, residents continue to interact with the social workers who see the patients' families—an interaction usually initiated by the social workers. In this relationship residents continue to experience the stresses that started during admission procedures, but the relationship loses in intensity as the weeks go by.

Residents find this activity useful. In the third year of the research and onward, they ranked it third of thirteen actual or potential learning situations. In earlier interviews it was ranked fifth, fourth, and eighth. The senior staff always thought highly of this activity, ranking workups third in usefulness among the thirteen learning situations they were supposed to rate.

The organization put much effort into these workups, not only providing supervisors but conducting workup conferences with all those who dealt with a patient (except nurses and recreational and occupational therapists). That is, these conferences included, in addition to the workup supervisor and the working-up resident, a high-level psychiatrist, the social worker who interviewed the relatives, the psychologist who had done the testing, and the patient's clinical administrator and assistant administrator (a resident). In these sessions residents had the experience of being part of a process of collectively arriving at consensus.

There is no necessary continuity between admissions procedures and workup, which may or may not be done by the admitting resident. Nor is there continuity between the workup and later therapy—a situation often mentioned as being undesirable at the meetings of the Residency Education Committee. Since it was organizationally difficult to establish such continuity, and since residents themselves generally did not press for it as a principle, no policy change was ever made. However, if residents were much interested in continuing therapy with patients they had "worked up," they often succeeded in doing so without much difficulty.

Workups afford an opportunity for residents to learn about mental illness without much stress—a rare opportunity in the daily life of residents. They can study thoroughly the history of a patient's illness without being responsible for treatment or for the patient's condition; they can bring their questions to a supervisor, listen to the supervisor's comment, and yet not be under the latter's authority for any considerable length of time. It is not surprising that residents value this activity highly.

"On Duty": The Night Nurse

There is always one resident on duty during the night at the central administration building, and a second resident, called the "second on duty," is available if need be. In this capacity residents deal with all the halls. More than any other task, night duty is unanimously considered "service to the hospital" and not part of training, although some residents say that they may gain experience unexpectedly by being given the opportunity to see some patients who would otherwise escape their attention. (This can also be a cause of embarrassment if a resident on night duty is obliged to make decisions in regard to a colleague's patient.)

The residents' main contacts during the night are with nurses on the wards on which emergencies occur. Only rarely are emergencies considered to be of such extreme nature that the "senior on call" is notified at home. In spite of this, the topic of night duty calls forth strong feelings among residents. Especially during their first year, they feel that they are exposed to serious situations without adequate supervision and yet will hesitate to call for help except in dire emergency, for fear of exposing their own inadequacies. While some experienced residents say that the senior on call is readily available and graciously gives advice when awakened during the night, a senior who has to be awakened is certainly not "readily available," much less gracious, and even older residents are reluctant to disturb their seniors.

The tension that develops during the night finds expression in the elaboration of magical formulae—for example, "the first hour in the early evening always tells me what kind of a night it's going to be, it's amazing but I can always predict."

With the exception of the patient who constitutes the "emergency," the nurse who calls the resident on duty to the ward during the night is the only available role-partner at that time. Hence, she is the one who is likely to be held responsible for the disturbance. Residents like to tell about the trivialities that nurses consider important enough to warrant calling them, and some even claim that "this is the way nurses get back at residents." Some residents also seem to feel that "nurses get back at them" during the daily morning reports by describing the night's events in such a way as to shift responsibility from the nurses to the doctor on call. For example, in reading her morning report a nurse may say, "Called doctor on call at 1 A.M. Doctor arrived at 2 A.M."

This is one of the ways in which nurses, who see themselves as defending "the needs of patients," are in a position to influence the behavior of residents. Nurses know more about the patients' daily behavior than almost anybody else in the hospital, and they are more involved than anybody else with the details of the immediate ward situation.

Clinical Administration: The "Preceptor"

Most of the residents' time and energy is spent in what is called clinical administration and in psychotherapy. Residents do not treat in psychotherapy patients whose lives they manage on the wards. There, a resident is an assistant administrator to the psychiatrist who is in charge.

The psychiatrist who is responsible for the ward and for the management of patients and personnel on that ward is called the clinical administrator. He is assisted in this task by one and in some cases two residents. The duration of a resident's stay on a ward varies somewhat from year to year, but usually rotation of residents takes place every four to six months. While on the ward they are in daily contact with the administrator. The relationship is considered to be one of apprenticeship. It has often been called "preceptorship" at the meetings of the Residents' Education Committee.

The word *preceptor* seems to have been chosen for two reasons. One is to upgrade the prestige of the clinical administrators, in line with the philosophy of the hospital's leadership at the time: to make clinical administration a less "intellectually and scientifically arid field" and to elevate it to a status closer to that enjoyed by "its glittering brother, psychotherapy."[4] The other reason for trying to institutionalize the title of preceptor was the training director's concern for giving primacy in ward assignments to the learning needs of residents over the practical needs of wards. However, since management of patients and personnel remained the administrator's primary task, attempts to change the image and the orientation of the clinical administrator were essentially, though not entirely, unsuccessful.

Since clinical administrators tend to be given full autonomy in the way they run their wards, both in regard to patients and in regard to staff, residents find themselves, as far as their work on the ward is concerned, in different social structures depending on the organizational principles of the chief administrator. A resident's opportunity to make independent decisions may be more limited on some halls than on others.

During the course of their training, residents are afforded the opportunity to be exposed to different types of patients because patients are assigned to wards according to the estimated seriousness of their illness. For this reason, as well as because of the different "styles" of ward administrators, the wards differ in their structure and in the amount and types of decisions residents are free to make on their own. Since the rotation of residents is not based primarily on the principle of matching amount of responsibility with length of experience, it may well happen that a third-year resident is assigned to a ward where the opportunity to exercise initiative is more restricted than that of an incoming resident on another ward.

Everybody's work on the ward is highly observable to most participants. As an assistant administrator, the resident observes the administrator's dealings with patients, with nurses, and with patients' relatives, and therefore has the opportunity to learn the principles of professional behavior through direct contact; in turn, the resident's behavior on the ward is open to observation by most role-partners there. During rounds, administrator, assistant administrator, head nurse, and patient confer with one another; at some hall meetings, all staff and patients are assembled; special staff meetings expose the residents to observation by staff members; and coordination of activities between the administrator and the assistant exposes the resident to the values as well as the scrutiny of the administrator. The administrator, more than anyone else on the ward, is in a position to guide and shape the behavior of the resident who is under his or her direct authority.

By virtue of their work on the ward, assistant administrators have to deal directly or indirectly with a number of other persons in the hospital and outside. Outside the hospital, they have to deal with a patient's relatives. They must also maintain relationships established during admissions procedures with social workers, who are in regular contact with the relatives. It is in this indirect way that the social service maintains its share of social control.

Residents relate to the therapists of their ward patients and may easily suffer under cross-pressures emanating from them and the clinical administrator. Indeed, the therapists are much interested in the clinical management of their therapy patients. Yet, the social organization of therapy at O'Brien prevents therapists from interfering, for it is the rule that therapists have no authority over the daily management of the patients' lives. This rule tends to restrict communication between therapists and administrators, a fact that is often decried by both types of psychiatrists. Yet, the rule holds and tends to be effective regardless of the status position of the therapist relative to the resident administrator.

The patients' psychotherapists are either "contract therapists" or, more frequently, other residents. Staff psychiatrists at O'Brien have served as therapists as well. Contract therapists are appointed by the hospital for the sole purpose of giving psychotherapy to specific patients. They are not part of the organizational life of the hospital and come to O'Brien for the contracted time from the outside. Their communication with the administrative staff of a ward is at a minimum, not only because they are not around but because communication between therapists and administrative staff is not highly valued, notwithstanding periodic protestations by O'Brien's authority holders and practitioners.

If the therapist is a staff member of the hospital, there may be more communication between him or her and the assistant administrator than if the therapist is an outsider; it could be argued that staff psychiatrists, although they have no *de jure* authority over the residents on their patients' wards, have *de facto* authority based on seniority in the profession and on their higher position in the organization. They can scrutinize and judge (even though not make decisions about) the assistant resident's ward behavior with the patient. However, because of its lack of organizational legitimacy, the professional and organizational authority of the senior therapists at O'Brien can be used only indirectly—for example, in influencing a resident's career when informal discussions or formal evaluations take place at the Residents' Education Committee.

If the therapist of the ward patient is another resident, it stands to reason that communication between equals is more frequent than between superordinates and subordinates. However, in this case also communication lacks structural legitimacy. The resident therapist has no authority to scrutinize the behavior of the other resident, the patient's assistant administrator on the ward.

The policy at O'Brien of depriving the therapist of authority over ward affairs protects the ward system, and hence the resident on the ward, from interference. This is a built-in safety valve against stressful demands on the assistant administrator. The person who is structurally in a position to know much about what happens on a ward through the confidential reports of patients in psychotherapy has no authority to scrutinize and hence to shape the behavior of the residents on the ward.

The assistant administrator, then, does not have to field interference from the patient's therapist in regard to general management, prescriptions of drugs, or other types of therapy (occupational, recreational, and so on). In turn, however, the assistant administrator is not permitted to interfere in any way with the psychotherapy of any of his or her ward patients. This is because of the high value O'Brien assigns to psychotherapy; nobody, either from a patient's ward or from a high position in the hospital, has a right to interfere in the patient's psychotherapy. If a patient is to be restricted in his or her movements, an escort to the psychotherapist's office must be provided. The assistant administrator who questions the adequacy of a patient's therapeutic relationship will communicate this to the administrator and not to the other resident who happens to be the therapist. This solves the problem of evading conflicting relationships among peers. Even in wards where a resident is given some independence, contradictory demands can be solved by referring the issue to the administrator.

Group Psychotherapy

Residents usually had a "group"—that is, a number of patients with whom they conducted group therapy. These were mostly hospital patients, but some discharged patients continued to participate.

In order to carry out this activity residents did not have to confer much with other members of the staff. Happenings in group psychotherapy were never reported at any staff conference where the progress of patients was being discussed, nor was a group leader ever called upon to add comments to a discussion about a patient. Hence, there was not much professional reward for this activity. Some psychologists were much interested in group process, and I also showed interest. But we were marginal to the organization. For one whole semester I observed a group and taped the sessions, and the group leader was eager to discuss them with me. Yet, most groups did not have an observer, and this left the residents with no one to talk to after this admittedly very tiring weekly activity (I myself shared this fatigue, especially on winter evenings). It seems to me that the effort required exceeded the rewards, as well as the importance the staff attached to this exercise. The senior staff, asked to rank the residents' learning situations in order of importance, gave it ninth or tenth rank in the successive interviews; they ranked supervision of group psychotherapy somewhat higher but went down in their judgment on this to as low as eleventh in the last year of the research. Under these circumstances, it is not surprising that residents ranked the activity sixth to ninth in usefulness, with its supervision usually a rank or so lower (and once, also in year 3 of the research, as low as eleventh out of the thirteen). This ranking increased, however, to fourth and fifth in the last year of the research.

There was only one senior staff member, very devoted to his patients and colleagues and also well regarded generally, who thought highly of group psychotherapy. He was the only one who ever conducted supervision of group psychotherapy with residents in a regular weekly session. However, he complained that residents did not attend regularly, that they walked in and out of the supervisory session as they pleased, and that frequently there was only one resident around at a time.

It can be said that there was no "glamour" attached to this practice. Since social workers had been trained to work with groups and considered themselves experts, they were often heard to say that "residents don't know what they are doing." The chief of social service once expressed the notion that social workers should sit in on the residents' group sessions. Needless to say, this never came to pass. To be sure, there was enough tension between residents and the social service in relation to admissions and to some extent in relation to workups; residents were not enthusiastic about an activity in which they would be made to feel that they were competing with social workers. The following entry in my field notes during the first year of the research seems to express the boundary that psychiatrists want to maintain between these two types of professionals: "I talked to Dr. X [one of the hospital's leaders] about the residents' 'group work.' That was my mistake, for I was immediately corrected with the humorless statement 'Psychiatrists conduct group *therapy;* it is social workers who conduct group *work.*' "

This problem of establishing boundaries between the activities of social workers and psychiatrists did not exist at O'Brien in the highly valued activity of individual psychotherapy.

Psychotherapy: The Supervisor and the Administrator

After the first two or three months of their residency, all residents have patients in psychotherapy. They start out with one patient, and in most cases gradually are assigned one or two additional patients.

Psychotherapy is supervised by senior psychiatrists, some of whom have other assignments in the hospital and some of whom are mainly engaged in private practice outside the hospital or have hospital commitments elsewhere. One psychiatrist on the Residents' Education Committee is in charge of assigning supervisors to resident therapists.

Everybody who was interviewed—supervisors of therapy, clinical administrators, and residents—always gave psychotherapy and its supervision the first two ranks in usefulness out of the thirteen choices they were offered. There was one difference, small though characteristic, between the senior staff and the residents, namely that residents tended to attach more importance to therapy itself, while seniors tended to find supervision the more important training device. They rated supervision of psychotherapy first in two out of three interviews; the residents, in contrast, ranked psychotherapy first in seven out of eight interviews.

Residents have no clinical administrative duties in regard to their therapy patients. They usually welcome this split between their administrative and therapeutic duties because, they say, if they have no authority for the management of the patients' lives on the ward, the patients can feel freer to examine feelings that might otherwise have to be considered in an extratherapeutic light.[5]

The split between therapeutic and administrative treatment of patients will be analyzed in detail in the next chapter. Here it must be noted that the split does not mean that the psychotherapeutic relationship is completely insulated from the clinical management of patients on the ward. The therapist may feel that the course of therapy is affected by a change in a patient's privileges or by a change of wards. Even though they lack authority in the matter, therapists can convey their opinions to administrators. Also, the "ward"—that is, the nursing staff, the administrator, and the assistant—is responsible for getting the patient to the therapist's office, usually in the centrally located administration building. If there is accidental or willful negligence on the ward in this respect, a patient, especially one who has no ground privileges, may get to the hour late or occasionally not show up at all. Usually the ward staff, on the insistence of the administrator, faithfully helps carry out a patient's therapeutic program, which is based on certain shared and valued instrumental rules, such as the following:

Therapy should be scheduled regularly, at fixed hours and days.

Therapy should take place, whenever possible, in the therapist's office.

The usual duration of psychotherapeutic session is 50 minutes.

The psychotherapist should not visit his or her patient on the ward except for well-specified reasons, and then only with the acquiescence (and preferably upon the invitation) of the patient's administrator.

For patients who have no ground privileges, therapists are responsible for seeing to it that they do not leave the office without an escort (to be provided by the ward).

These rules are said to facilitate the therapeutic process, which is highly valued by all concerned. They are a link between the ward staff and the therapist, for all have to cooperate to carry them out. The rules are flexible, of course, and occasional changes require communication between the administrator and the therapist. Such rules contribute to the functional integration of the two aspects of treatment, clinical administration and psychotherapy.

Yet, precisely because of the integration, conflicts between administrator and therapist can and do occur. For example, in case of a patient's physical illness, or if a patient is restricted from leaving the hall, the administrator may ask the therapist to see the patient on the ward instead of in the office. Such requests are not always accepted automatically by the therapist, who may feel that the unusual physical setting prescribed by the administrator is an interference in the course of therapy. Changes in regular procedures are usually initiated by the administrator, who has the authority to control all aspects of a patient's life, although therapists may inform administrators of their opinions if they feel that a change in procedure is indicated. However, although therapists are permitted to express their opinions, there is no incentive for them to do so.

The manner in which disagreements are settled will be discussed in chapter 4. Let it be said in anticipation that in cases of unresolvable disagreements, another role-partner enters the scene: the therapist resident's supervisor of therapy. Although in the interviews residents usually did not volunteer to state that their supervisor would intervene for them, when probed specifically about this they said that the supervisor "could" or "did occasionally" take up some matter with the administrator of a patient whose psychotherapy he or she supervised. Similarly, supervisors all said that if need be they would intervene with administrators for residents whose work they supervised but that they preferred to have the residents handle the situation themselves. The feelings of supervisors in this respect cover quite a range in intensity. One supervisor said, "I would fight, fight and argue it out." Most supervisors are not so bellicose. A more representative answer is that of the supervisor who said, "I would try to get the resident to deal with it . . . but I would be perfectly willing to intervene if I felt very strongly." Supervisors are supportive of their residents and most of the time are ready to stand by as their "allies," as in the following report by a supervisor:

I had to talk to the ward administrator about a problem regarding [my supervisee]. During his absence, while he was sick, a patient of his was transferred to [the disturbed ward] and the therapist had not been informed, nor had he been given the opportunity to discuss the matter with the patient. He then had to go and see the patient on [the disturbed ward] and have an interview with him in the physician's office there. [The resident] felt very uncomfortable about this. I had to talk to the administrator in order to obtain permission for the patient to be escorted to Dr. X's office so that he could see the patient in more comfort.

Just as therapists are interested in administrative decisions concerning their patients, administrators are concerned about the course of therapy. Psychotherapy takes place behind closed doors and is not observable to anyone. Only what the two partners in the relationship, the patient and the therapist, volunteer to bring to the attention of others will be known. This tends to insulate the therapist from interference by other role-partners. A patient's behavior on the ward may arouse the curiosity of the administrator about the effect of therapy, but he or she will have a hard time getting information to satisfy this curiosity. The patient is not likely to talk about the therapy, which is considered a privileged, confidential setting. The resident therapist may volunteer some information to the administrator or the assistant administrator but usually keeps communications about therapy at a minimum. There tends to be, in this respect, a discrepancy between the administrator's expectations and the therapist's behavior.

That there is a conflict here is shown by answers to certain questions in the interviews. Administrators, when asked what they would like to be informed about regarding the psychotherapy of patients on their hall, tend to mention a large number of details pertaining to the therapeutic process. They want to know more than resident therapists usually feel they must communicate. Asked about what things regarding psychotherapy they communicate with a patient's administrator, residents usually name concrete extreme situations, such as a patient who is in danger of doing harm to self or others. Residents believe, and in this respect are supported by their supervisors, that the material brought by the patient to the psychotherapist is to be treated with highest confidentiality except in such extreme situations, and then, the residents usually explain, "I would inform the patient that I would have to talk to the administrator," or, "I would not do it without taking it up with the patient." Supervisors also were asked what they would like their residents to communicate to the administrators of their patients in regard to the course of therapy, and their answers were similar to those of the residents. The norm of confidentiality legitimizes the insulation from observability and knowledgeability which governs the therapeutic situation, and the therapist is, of course, interested in maintaining this insulation.

This situation makes for some difficulties for administrators who would like to be more fully informed. "Lack of communication" is the most frequent complaint. One administrator, asked what was the most difficult thing about clinical administration, responded: "Maintaining communication with the therapists, that's what I would say is the number one, number one problem."

Although resident therapists are insulated from observation by administrators and the staff generally as far as psychotherapy is concerned, they are under the indirect scrutiny of supervisors of therapy. Yet, unlike the administrators, whose interest in the therapy is guided by curiosity about the patients, supervisors are interested primarily in residents, wanting to help them acquire the ability to sit back reflectively, to listen patiently, to feel that there is no need to rush in with an interpretation. Supervisors want residents to acquire the inner freedom even to make mistakes. Their interest in residents is defined by the dual aim of furthering the residents' therapy and their future growth, while the administrators' interest stems from the task of controlling patients. Supervisors have little occasion to be diverted from their interest in their residents by daily occurrences in the patients' lives for, as one supervisor aptly put it, "there are no channels" for the supervisor to become concerned with administrative decisions.

Academic Exercises and Meetings

There were several academic exercises conducted by high-level psychiatrists, most of them on the O'Brien staff, some from the outside. Some psychiatrists high up in the structure gave lectures, conducted discussions, or gave "group supervision," meaning that residents would bring some of their problems to the meeting. There was also a "continuing case supervision," where a group of residents followed a reported course of psychotherapy over several weeks under the guidance of a high-level therapist. All these meetings were a source of support for the residents, and they were usually well attended, with some ups and downs that will be discussed later in this book.

All-staff meetings were conducted once a week. These meetings were formal, usually with a resident reporting a case. Otherwise residents did not take much part in the discussions. Everybody in the hospital was invited, and the meetings usually included nurses and occupational and recreational therapists concerned about a particular case. The inclusiveness of these meetings was a source of complaint on the part of some residents, who felt that the meetings should be held for the medical staff only. Yet, the policy of inclusiveness was not changed.

Contradictory Norms

It should be clear by now that there are cross-pressures on the resident that are endemic to the social structure. Some conflicts stem from the differences between the demands of a bureaucratic organization and those inherent in the definition of the therapeutic relationship.[6]

For example, supervisors may teach residents the importance of the therapeutic hour for the patient and insist that the resident let nothing interfere in the relationship with the patient during this hour. Yet, organizational requirements state that the resident on rotation be available for the admission of new patients. Some psychiatrists who occupy authoritative positions in the hierarchy of the hospital feel that a schedule with a patient can be changed. They believe that this is one of many reality situations that a patient has to face; that such a situation may even help elicit material from a patient that will afford the opportunity to "work it through"—that it is, in the vernacular of the profession, "grist to the therapeutic mill." However, one supervisor has this to say about such an incident:

> The rules of the hospital are that the admission doctor has to go as soon as the call comes that a patient has arrived—for him to dash over to Admissions and see the patient. His patient [in therapy] tells him that she feels alone, isolated and pushed out, and brings a dream in this regard, then a buzzer rings . . . that means he has to get up and go. . . . I took the opportunity to discuss with the resident this question about devotion and dedication to a patient, that is, when you are with a patient not to be disturbed for any reason whatsoever unless the building burns down.

In addition to such conflicts between the values governing psychotherapy and the functional requirements of the organization, there is a conflict in outlook between the residents' senior role-partners: the supervisor of therapy and the patients' clinical administrator. A resident who has three patients potentially faces three such conflicts. One example of this difference in outlook is the fact reported earlier, that the social structure of the ward is based on a short time perspective, while the social structure of psychotherapy is based on a long time perspective. A resident's report of one incident illustrates this: "[The administrator] got rather anxious about [the patient] and was talking about getting a consultant. . . . My supervisor sided with me. . . . *One ought to take a fairly long-term view of this and not get too perturbed at any one period when things are a bit more upset than some other time*" (emphasis supplied).

Supervisors of therapy and administrators, then, use different criteria. One supervisor explained that one of the most difficult of things for residents to learn is to be patient: "They want to do something that won't delay. They learned in medical school to think in terms of emergencies." Yet on the ward there *are* emergencies, as this supervisor recognized, as an afterthought: "It's true, you do have a death problem." And a clinical administrator knows this first-hand: "As an administrator, one sort of feels responsible for what the patients do. . . . In the hospital there's no question about it that the patient acts out and I am on the spot." Another administrator had this to say: "Somehow one gets the impression that the therapist has all the time in the world and that the insight is a painful, long-drawn-out process—and, of course, it is—but somehow or other the days at so many bucks a day keep rolling on, and we have to account to the relatives for what we are doing and what is being done with the patient." That such different perspectives are not personality attributes but role expectations is shown by the fact that this administrator practices psychotherapy himself, and he himself agrees that therapy is a "long-drawn-out process." It is in his *role* as clinical administrator that he must be more present-oriented than the psychotherapist.

Residents know from their previous training that acting quickly in matters of illness is important. In psychotherapy, this has to be unlearned, yet in clinical administration it has to be remembered.

Closely related to the difference in time perspective is the fact, as the foregoing quotes also show, that on the ward psychiatrists are interested primarily in the immediate consequences of behavior while psychotherapy focuses on internal dispositions. More will be said about this in the next chapter.

Thus residents are exposed to different values—the "psychothera-peutic" values, which place highest importance on the therapeutic relationship with the patient, envisaged as a continuous one, some-times lasting several years, and the values underlying the organization as an ongoing concern, which hold that the job has to be done, that everything is limited in time and place, that resources are scarce, and that disruptions should be minimized.

Hence, following Merton, we can say that a basic source of potential disturbance in the residents' role performances is the struc-tural circumstances that they have role-partners differently located in the social structure.[7] The administrator and the supervisor tend to have different values and moral expectations, and these may also differ from the values and expectations held by residents. Such cross-pressures are not necessarily dysfunctional either for the resi-dents' articulation of their roles or for the group of participants in this interaction. This becomes immediately clear if one imagines what would happen if a resident had to deal with only one role-partner instead of two: if the supervisor happened to be also the administrator of the therapy patient, the resident would be deprived of protection when feeling critical of the patient's clinical management.

Cross-pressures may be functional, as when they bring to the awareness of all role-partners the value premises guiding their actions. By rallying the support of the supervisor when in disagreement with the patient's administrator, a resident

> redirects the conflict so that it is now one between members of the role-set rather than, as was at first the case, between [one role-partner and the resident himself]. It is the members of the role-set who are now in a position in which *they* are being required to articulate their role expectations. At the very least, this serves to make evident that it is not willful misfeasance on the part of the status-occupant which keeps him from conforming to all the contradictory expectations imposed upon him. In some instances, the replacing of pluralistic ignorance by common knowledge serves to make for a redefinition of what can properly be expected of the status-occupant. In other cases, the process serves simply to allow him to go his own way, while the members of his role-set are engaged in their conflict.[8]

Thus, at the same time as the cross-pressures make themselves felt, their structure itself provides a mechanism for their alleviation. Conflict with one role-partner leads to alliance with another.[9] The conflict can be displaced to take place between two psychiatrists of senior status rather than in the asymmetrical relationship between resident and staff psychiatrist.

The attention that is here paid to cross-pressures facing a resident therapist and to potential conflicts with a patient's administrator may give the erroneous impression that the resident therapist is constantly engaged in a cold war with the patient's administrator. Since the resident usually has three patients in therapy, such a cold war would have to be conducted on three fronts. It should be stressed that such a condition of war does not exist; rather, the normal state of affairs is one of peace occasionally interrupted by an "incident." How, then, one is led to ask, is a peaceful state of affairs possible if it has just been demonstrated that the relationship is pregnant with conflict?

To be sure, the resident would not have the steadiness of mind required to work effectively and to learn were there no social mechanisms available that tend to reduce the burden of differing expectations. One such mechanism, for example, is the fact that not all role-partners show equal interest in the resident's behavior.[10] The interest of the administrator is focused primarily on the patient, while the interest of the supervisor is mainly in the therapist. Another stress-reducing mechanism is provided by the fact that not all role-partners are equally in a position to know about the behavior of the therapist. Finally, another stress-mitigating mechanism lies in the fact that not all role-partners are equally influential in shaping a resident's behavior.[11] The power of a resident's two role-partners differs sharply.

The aim of the relationship of the supervisor with the resident therapist is to guide the latter's psychotherapeutic relationship. To this end, the supervisor has no means of coercion; without being in a position to make practical decisions, the supervisor's role remains only advisory. Supervisors rarely tell residents precisely what to do, endeavoring to bring about a change primarily in their outlook and feelings and only secondarily in the details of behavior. Supervisors can hardly exercise negative sanctions other than expression of disapproval.

Administrators, in contrast, cannot advise residents on how to conduct therapy. Even if an administrator doubts that the patient is deriving benefit from therapy, there is no way of interfering authoritatively. Yet the administrator can voice concern, can *recommend* that the number of therapeutic hours be reduced, or, in extreme cases, can *recommend* a change of therapist. Such instances are rare and cannot take place without consultation, yet even a few instances serve as reminders that clinical administration is an important, though usually indirect, source of social control.

There is a check against the misuse of such control. In the relationship between the resident therapist and a patient's administrator regarding a patient, there is a stress-reducing mechanism consisting of a peculiar combination of two of the mechanisms already mentioned: namely, the distribution of authority over and knowledge about the behavior of the resident therapist. If the latter can actually conduct psychotherapy with considerable freedom, this is due in part to the fact that the person who has more authority to initiate action, the administrator, has less access to knowledge about the details of the therapeutic hour.

So far, the relations between the ward system and the therapy system have been discussed from two perspectives in turn, that of the resident as an assistant administrator and that of the resident as a psychotherapist. However, the two tasks of administration and therapy are not divided up among the residents, but each resident is a member of and plays a role in both systems. This means that residents have two significant role-partners: the clinical administrator in charge of the ward to which they are assigned and a supervisor of psychotherapy for each patient they treat. The difference between these two relationships remains to be stressed.

Clinical Administration and Psychotherapy:
Two Different Perspectives

In regard to a given patient, the clinical administrator and the supervisor of therapy have structurally different interests. Consequently, their interests in the resident differ as well. The administrator is interested in the behavior of the assistant on the hall in regard to its immediate *external consequences;* the supervisor is less interested in immediate consequences for the patient's behavior than in how the clues obtained from the resident's reports may be used as a basis for judging the resident's inner disposition for the therapeutic role.

During their training at O'Brien, residents are exposed to two different value systems, each referring to a different set of tasks in the treatment of patients. Difficult as it is for residents to learn the technique of psychotherapy, they must at the same time learn to make decisions about the patients' everyday behavior—for example, discharges, visits, and various types of "privileges." Residents must learn to take the social context into account so as not to disrupt the social life of the ward, with its many patients and caretakers. On the ward, the resident learns *not* to limit attention to the patient's psychological state, which is precisely the reverse of what is to be learned in psychotherapy. On the ward the resident must suspend to some extent the newly acquired knowledge of depth psychology and refrain from doing much interpreting of psychodynamics, so as to arrive at a "balanced" picture. In this situation, a psychiatrist faces a problem similar to that of parents who are good psychologists but can use their psychological knowledge in guiding their children's daily lives only at great risk. This contradiction between the psychotherapeutic and the milieu approach to psychiatric practice has been recognized by some supervisors of psychotherapy at O'Brien, who say that the residents are "wearing two hats."

The performance of this dual role is facilitated at O'Brien by the arrangement that residents do not treat any patients in psychotherapy who are living on their own wards. This makes it easier for residents to help manage the ward patients, since they are not encumbered by knowledge and interpretations of the patients' unconscious motives. And in their relations with their psychotherapy patients, they will be freer to listen if they know that they have no responsibility for managing the patients' lives. Having to deal with different patients in these two activities enables residents to learn two aspects of psychiatric treatment, milieu therapy and psychotherapy, without as much conflict as would otherwise arise from the different demands of these two treatment situations.

This division of tasks is the most important aspect of the social structure of psychiatric treatment at O'Brien. While it is of benefit to residents in their training, the main purpose of the split between these two types of psychiatric treatment is the benefit that can be derived for patients. In this arrangement, a patient deals with two types of psychiatrists, the psychiatrists in charge of the ward on which the patient lives (the clinical administrator and the resident assistant) and the psychotherapist whom the patient usually sees three times a week for 50 minutes at an appointed time. The dynamics of this structural arrangement will be discussed in the next chapter.

3
The Therapeutic Triad

A basic contradiction in psychiatric hospital practice, as was noted in chapter 1, derives from the fact that the hospital has the mandate both to control the behavior of its patients and to treat them.[1] As the mental hospital defines the mandate it has received from the public, and more specifically from patients' relatives, patients are entrusted to its care so that they will be prevented from violating basic taboos—killing or hurting themselves or others, engaging in sexually disapproved behavior, setting fires, etc.—and so that they can learn not to violate such taboos in the future. That is, the mental hospital has as a goal to control the behavior of its patients in such a way that their relatives and the community remain undisturbed, that the hospital can go about its business as the hospital defines it, and that all patients will be protected physically.

Whatever other responses the use of authority, and if need be coercion, calls forth, such as a sense of security and protection, for example, it always mobilizes some measure of hostility and distrust in those over whom it is exercised.[2] This tends to impair the basic ingredient of the therapist-patient relationship, which is trust, and the basic aim, which is to help patients redefine their interpersonal relationships so that they can be relied upon not to violate social taboos.

Mutual trust is an important element of any professional-client relationship. Talcott Parsons has stated this well in an address to a group of lawyers:

In situations of strain, there seems to be required scope for a certain permissiveness for expression of attitudes and sentiments which, in ordinary

35

circumstances, would not be acceptable. If this permissiveness is to operate effectively, it must be associated with relief from anxiety. In order to be capable psychologically of "getting things off his chest," a person must be assured that, within certain limits, otherwise ordinary or possible sanctions will not operate. In general, this implies a protected situation. The confidential character of the lawyer's relation to his client provides just such a situation.[3]

If such leeway in social sanctions is needed in any professional-client relationship, it is much more important in the encounter between psychotherapist and patient, especially in psychoanalytically oriented psychiatry. Patients are expected to reveal fantasies and wishes, illicit or not. To do this, they must be able to expect a large measure of immunity. In this way they will learn to integrate unconscious fantasies into the realm of rational thinking, so that the latter will inform their social behavior.

The psychoanalytically oriented technique of psychiatric treatment is especially well suited to grant patients the measure of immunity of which Parsons speaks because it is based on what psychotherapists call a "therapeutic alliance" between psychiatrist and patient; that is, on a relationship of mutual trust. Yet, the question remains how such "alliance" can be brought about and maintained under conditions of control and restrictions imposed by the hospital.

The double aspect of psychiatric practice—the control of patients' behavior and their psychotherapy—has given rise in some hospitals, including O'Brien, to a social arrangement in which both aspects are dealt with through a division of labor among the staff. Such division may take place informally. In some mental hospitals, such as OBrien, psychiatric residents who are in charge of a service usually do not conduct psychotherapy with patients on their own service. In some other hospitals, experimenting with modern ideas of participation, the patients themselves are in charge of controlling one another, and the psychiatrist plays the role of a benevolent supervisor and "guide." In this case, the psychiatrist delegates the use of authority to patients' peers, thus remaining free to play a supportive role.

At O'Brien, the separation between ward psychiatry and psychotherapy has been made explicit.[4] The split of the administrative and therapeutic tasks has brought about an intricate social structure, which is the source of the stability of the system at the same time that it brings in its wake a new set of ambiguities for both patients and practitioners. It provides emotional support to patients, granting them some permissiveness and leeway for learning, at the same time that it is suited for maintaining control over their everyday behavior.

Yet, it also generates stresses in the relationships among the psychiatrists themselves.

The fact that a patient has two psychiatrists, one in charge of guiding everyday life in the hospital and another in charge of individual psychotherapy, means that the patient is part of a triadic relationship in which he or she is subordinate to two role partners who relate in different ways. An examination of the complex relationships that are part of such a triadic arrangement will make it possible to specify some of the functions it serves for patients, as well as some of the stresses and conflicts it has brought in its wake.

Control and Support

Merton's theory of role-set[5] provides a useful point of departure for analyzing the social structure of therapy at O'Brien. This theory analyzes the structural circumstance that a status occupant relates to several role-partners, some or all of whom may differ in their expectations owing to their own differing positions in the structure. At O'Brien, the psychotherapist and the clinical administrator are two role-partners who relate differently to the patient. The psychotherapist requires the patient to reveal fantasies, wishes, and feelings irrespective of their legitimacy in social life; the administrator, in contrast, tries to help the patient learn to conform to the social requirements of interpersonal relations in everyday life.

The distinction between these two types of expectations is similar to that made by Merton between *attitudes* and *behavior*,[6] if *attitude* is defined not only as "readiness to act" but also as encompassing all internal dispositions, including feelings, fantasies, and wishes as well as attitudes toward norms, which are the object of interpretation and manipulation by the psychotherapist. The split in the treatment of patients at O'Brien results in providing two different social settings, one in which patients' behavior and its immediate consequences are the main focus of scrutiny, and another in which patients are expected to reveal their attitudes in regard to self and others. In the ward, the main emphasis is on *behavioral* conformity; in the psychotherapeutic relationship, the main concern is to explore *attitudes*, whether or not they conform to behavioral expectations.[7]

In society generally, people would find it even more difficult than they ordinarily do to live up to all expectations facing them, since these are often incompatible or even contradictory, if they were not able to conform in different ways in their various relationships. The fact that they can withhold their attitudinal conformity in some

situations permits them to face their multiple and varied obligations.[8] Were they to invest their attitudinal commitment in all of
their conforming behavior, they would find it hard to maintain any
degree of stability. Occasions for withholding such attitudinal commitment exist in patterned social situations. A "zone of indiffer-
ence"[9] in regard to attitudes exists in many social relationships and
makes it possible to conform without involving inner feelings of
either attitudinal commitment or antagonism.

The point is not merely that a person can "put on an act" for the
benefit of an authority holder. Rather, selection between these types
of conformity is often socially prescribed. Some status holders may
expect that a person show mainly attitudinal conformity, as expressed in the phrase: "It's not that I mind the way he acts, it's his
attitude I object to." Others demand behavioral conformity only, as
when they criticize someone's deeper involvement: "Why doesn't he
just do his job; who cares what he thinks?" These different expectations are by no means just happenstance but flow from the structural
positions occupied by particular role-partners.

Differences in types of expected conformity make it possible for
the status occupant to maintain reasonable stability in the face of
contradictory expectations. This provides some degree of freedom in
dealing with others. The ability to defer expression of attitudes and
to adapt behavior to demands is expected, as when someone is
positively valued for "being able to get along with people." To be
sure, the person who exaggerates this ability is accused of being "just
an operator." In other words, the differentiated behavior of the
status occupant in relation to the members of the role-set is itself an
expectation, conformity to which invites approval and overconformity to which, here as elsewhere, invites negative sanction.[10]

At O'Brien a similar structural mechanism is made available to
patients, who are expected to reveal their inner dispositions to the
psychotherapist but to be guided on the ward by expectations for
behavioral conformity emanating from ward psychiatrists and nurses.
Here also overconformity calls forth sanctions, as when a patient is
said to "show signs of social recovery only" or is said to pretend
improvement in order to be discharged. But if used with measure,
behavioral conformity is rewarded with an increase in privileges, such
as more freedom of movement or transfer to a less disturbed ward.

Although rewards may be withheld from the overconformer, patients' ability to differentiate between their internal dispositions and
their actual conduct is considered a sign of health. Indeed, the
distinction made here between attitudes and behavior has its psychological parallel in the distinction psychiatrists make when they say

that patients have to learn not to "act out" their fantasies, and that they must learn the difference between thoughts and reality. A patient who says he must die because of an illicit wish to kill, must be helped to realize that this wish is distinct from behavior and is inconsequential if not acted upon. To be sure, it is believed that the inner conflicts such inhibited wishes create will have to be "worked through," but to this end alone hospitalization would not be needed. It has taken place because the boundary between inner dispositions and reality appeared to have broken down. The hospital is said to provide an environment in which patients will be led not to "act upon their impulses," where they will be confronted with the "limitations that reality puts upon their fantasies" until such a time as they are able to "keep them under control."

In sociological terms, the two social settings are intended to help patients learn to differentiate between social situations that require primarily the involvement of their internal dispositions and those in which they are expected to focus on behavior and its immediate consequences. The split between the ward situation and the therapeutic hour helps impress this distinction: in the therapeutic hour, the *wish to kill* for example, can be expressed without sanctions; in the ward setting, such expression is considered a danger signal. Hence patients are permitted, and often encouraged, to express their antisocial thoughts (if they have them) in one setting (although, of course, not to act on them). In the other setting, the mere verbalization of these thoughts would be considered asocial behavior and would have consequences in the patients' management.[11]

When we apply the distinction between attitudes and behavior to the theory of role-set, which points to the relationship between a status occupant and his or her various role-partners, patients in this hospital can be seen as relating both to a ward psychiatrist and to a psychotherapist (leaving out, for the purpose of this analysis, the other role-partners on the ward, such as the assistant administrator, nurses, aides, and fellow patients). The therapist may try to encourage patients freely to acknowledge their feelings of anger, which so far seem to have remained unconscious. The psychiatrist on the ward, however, is likely to be more interested in seeing patients suppress or deny their anger, lest they act out their hostile feelings against the staff or their fellow patients. Sometimes these differing expectations are a source of strain, as when administrators interpret a patient's "acting out" as a result of psychotherapy.

Yet the provision of two role-partners helps alleviate the burden of contradictory expectations in that it provides more leeway for patients' articulation of their role—that is, for learning to distinguish between conflicting feelings and between different spheres of activity, and to assess the special meaning of their various relationships—than if they were to get contradictory messages from a single role-partner. If the same psychiatrist were in charge of managing a patient's life on the ward *and* conducting psychotherapy with him or her, the patient would get contradictory messages from *the same person;* this would constitute *sociological ambivalence* in the core sense of this term as Merton and Elinor Barber defined it, in that antithetical behavior would be expected from the *same* role-partner.[12] (This would be the sociological parallel of psychological ambivalence as first conceptualized by Bleuler and later by Freud.)

In this type of ambivalent relationship people hardly have any leverage for articulating their role. Such learning is seriously blocked under conditions of sociological ambivalence, where a person will not be rewarded for living up to *either* of the antithetical expectations. A patient would be expected to reveal socially inappropriate feelings to the same psychiatrist who supervises the patient's social conduct and who is also empowered to constrain that patient's freedom. It is useful, as Alfred H. Stanton puts it, that "the demand for full disclosure of thoughts and fantasies which is implicit in much intensive psychotherapy [be] made by a different person than the administrator, whose control of the patient is greater than that of anyone else in his life except his parents when he was a very young child."[13]

To put this in another way, if expectations are incompatible, having to face them in relation to different role-partners may be considerably less burdensome than having to comply with them in relation to the same person. This is the case because where contradictory expectations emanate from more than one role-partner, there are mechanisms available that reduce the burden of having to comply with all of them. In specifying selected social mechanisms that reduce the conflict imposed by different expectations facing a status occupant, Merton mentions the structural circumstance that various role-partners may have different *interests* in the status occupant's behavior—that is, they may be involved in different ways; that different role-partners are not equally powerful in *controlling* that behavior; and that these role-partners are not equally in a position to *observe* that behavior.[14]

To these mechanisms must be added one that derives from the distinction between attitudes and behavior. Alleviation of the burden of having to conform to conflicting expectations can be obtained from the structural circumstance that a person is not expected always to involve internal dispositions in order to conform to the demands of various role-partners.

For these mechanisms to operate well there must be a "division of labor" between the role-partners in regard to their use of authority, their observation of behavior, and the interest they have in internal dispositions. This is indeed the case in the network of relationships described here: the role-partner who is mainly interested in patients' internal dispositions, the psychotherapist, does not observe their daily behavior and does not have the power to control it. The other role-partner, who observes their behavior more directly and has power of control—that is, the administrator—is not expected to be interested mainly in their unexpressed internal dispositions.

A system of social control that would put both the attitudes and the behavior of patients under scrutiny by the same person, who has power to control their lives on the basis of knowledge of their innermost dispositions, would be a totalitarian institution in the most dramatic sense: the person who is in a position to observe the subordinate's behavior would have access to the revelation of inner dispositions as well, and also have the power and authority to sanction both.

Such an authority holder would be in a similar structural position as the "domineering mother" whom psychiatrists are wont to call "schizophrenegenic." Elsewhere I have contrasted the position of the modern American middle-class mother with the mother in the traditional Eastern European Jewish family.[15] In that type of family there seems to be an allocation of different types of authority between the parental figures: they tend to expect different types of conformity of the children and to differ markedly in their socially patterned interest as well as in the extent to which they observe the children's behavior. Father is primarily concerned with their attitudes. He is in charge of their religious education and watches over the type of behavior that seems to manifest inner dispositions for becoming "a good Jew." Mother is concerned with the children's daily behavior in terms of its immediate consequences. She must supervise them for their own well-being and for the smooth functioning of the household. In addition—and this is perhaps more important than the socially patterned "division of interest" between the parents—the person who is mostly concerned with attitudes (that is, with that aspect of the personality that lends itself more readily to what Arnold Green has called "personality absorption"[16]) does not observe the everyday details of the children's behavior, and the person who has greater access to these daily details does not focus as much on attitudes.

The cultural expectations of the modern middle-class mother are such that she is pressured into becoming overinvolved in her children's lives. She focuses on their inner dispositions for their personality development, while at the same time she must supervise all of her children's activities. The combined socially induced interest the modern mother has in both behavioral and attitudinal conformity of her children may well lead her to become the kind of domineering mother so deplored by modern psychiatrists.

The most important consequence of her interest in both types of conformity is not merely her domination, but the fact that her expectations are directed at both the immediate consequences of behavior and inner dispositions. These expectations are based on different and not always compatible time perspectives. Expectations of attitudinal conformity presuppose a long time perspective and a willingness to overlook concrete details of the present. Expectations of behavioral conformity, in contrast, are directed toward the immediate present. For example, should a child who breaks an appliance while experimenting with its mechanics be scolded for the damage or commended for showing "initiative" and "scientific interest"? Chances are that mother will expect both initiative and care and put the child into what Gregory Bateson and others have called "the double bind."17

There is more than a simple distribution of authority between paternal figures. There is a distribution of types of authority, of types of socially patterned interest in the children, and of the extent of observability of the children's behavior. Neither parent, of course, is indifferent to the primary interest of the other. The system of complementary role allocation in the family, as in all groups, requires a degree of consensus among all authority holders. Yet, in this type of family leeway is afforded the child to conform in a somewhat different manner to the expectations of each parent; the child is able to gain distance from or organize these expectations—that is, to articulate its other role.

In a psychoanalytically oriented hospital, where treatment is directed at long-range changes in the personality and where patients are at the same time held in confinement and observed closely, patients would find themselves in a structural position similar to that of the child who is made to suffer from personality absorption and is subjected to expectations of "the double bind." Since patients assumedly have a low threshold of tolerance for such situations, which possibly have brought them into the hospital in the first place, a type of treatment that would put both their inner dispositions and their everyday behavior under the control of the same person would constitute a type of subordination so encompassing that they would hardly be able to articulate their roles. In psychiatric terms, it would nourish patients' fantasies of persecution and omnipotence, and they would have the choice between hitting out diffusely and withdrawing into apathetic stupor.

Such a system of control is, of course, purely imaginary, because it would be likely to founder on the hard rock of patients' resistance. Patients would conceal their inner dispositions to the best of their abilities, either deliberately or because repression had done its job. Some evidence of this comes from a patient in another psychoanalytically oriented hospital where the split has not been put into effect: "In the morning I tell my psychotherapist the dream I've had during the night, and then he turns around and tells the nurse to keep me in the hall, and not even to let me go to occupational therapy, where I wanted to finish a job I had started. So that taught me, I won't tell him things like this any more."[18] If such reactions are called forth in patients, psychotherapy can hardly be conducted, at least not according to the psychoanalytic technique based on therapeutic alliance.

Considered from the perspective of social control, the organizational device of splitting psychotherapy from psychiatric management is an ingenious social invention. By making possible a differentiation between attitudes and behavior, the organization has devised a structural form for the control of both while still leaving leeway for patients to articulate their roles. This organizational device brings about a patterned distribution of various types of interest in the patient—the interest in attitudes and the interest in behavior—and allows differential allocation of time and space for observation and the use of authority.

However, this social arrangement is more than a form of social control that leaves the individual some leeway for role articulation. So far in this chapter, the problem of adaptation to various role-partners has been discussed only from the point of view of the differences in their expectations and in the manner of coping with them. This perspective, if taken one-sidedly, would be based on the assumption that conformity consists only in coping with the system. However, the system also holds out rewards. Role-partners not only hold out expectations for one another that are more or less likely to be met; they give something in return. Indeed, social relationships are maintained by reciprocity. Although the relationship may be asymmetrical in that one partner may obtain greater rewards than the other or may have more power than the other to secure compliance to expectations, no matter how small the return for one of the partners, there has to be that little something that makes it possible to share at least in some minimal way the definition of the relationship.[19]

When we apply the theory of reciprocity to the theory of role-set, we are led to ask what patients get in return for their conformity to the expectations of each of their role-partners. It turns out that the ingenious invention of supplying patients with two main role-partners rather than only one is more than a mechanism of social control. Patients can fruitfully use this leverage for role articulation because from one of their role-partners they receive emotional *support* and from the other they derive protection and *guidelines* for assessment of the reality situation to which they are expected to learn to adapt. This corresponds to the Parsons- Bales model of dual leadership.[20] A patient is given both an *instrumental* and an *expressive* leader, the first to set forth the demands of the reality situation, the second to provide emotional support.

The psychiatric view, expressed in psychoanalytic terminology, holds that the availability of two psychiatrists who play different roles vis-à-vis patients makes it possible for them to "split their transference." This view is given sociological meaning by being grounded in a paradigm derived from the theory of role-set and the theory of leadership. In psychoanalytic theory, split transference means that a patient can divide antithetical feelings between two "objects," one who arouses hate, the other love, and in this way can avoid psychological ambivalence. Sociological theory now adds that the provision of two role-partners, one who supplies support, the other guidelines, avoids a condition of sociological ambivalence, in which contradictory expectations emanate from one person.

The dynamics of this triadic relationship are such that patients tend to derive important advantages from being able to relate to two psychiatrists; the one, in return for the patients' willingness to reveal their internal dispositions, will give them support and will withhold sanctions; the other, in return for behavioral conformity, will give them guidelines and will not ask for revelations concerning their inner life.

This arrangement is, of course, ideal-typical in that its effectiveness depends on the noninterference of disturbing factors. Further analysis of the triadic relationship will reveal, however, that countervailing forces are at work within the arrangement itself. In order for them to be neutralized, the arrangement needs the support of an unequivocal normative system.

Before exploring the normative system, it will be necessary first to specify the structural elements within the triadic relationship that help or hinder the balance of this arrangement. The Parsons- Bales theory of leadership having been integrated with Merton's theory of role-set, this combined conceptualization can now be taken one step further in a direction suggested by Georg Simmel in his theory of the triad.[21] Simmel points out that the properties of the triad do not derive merely from the fact that each partner relates to two others but also from the fact that any of the three combinations of two partners faces a third. This directs our attention to the fact that the role partner who gives support and the one who provides guidelines must be in some relation with each other if they are to treat the same patient.

Relations between Authority Holders

The relations between the two psychiatrists can best be explored according to the Simmel-related model of the "natural triad" developed by Morris Freilich on the basis of the kinship structure of patrilineal families, such as the Tikopia.[22] There, a growing young man has a supportive maternal uncle who counteracts the tension created by his father's exercise of authority. Freilich relates this triadic relationship of father, son, and maternal uncle to the Parsons–Bales dichotomy of instrumental and expressive leadership and calls attention to the fact that such triads exist in all sorts of social organizations in which a "high-status friend" like an uncle and a "high-status authority" like a father both relate to a "low-status subordinate" like a son. The fact that the image of the friendly uncle calls to mind such idiomatic expression as "he is the avuncular type," or "he is everybody's uncle," testifies to the broad application of Freilich's model.

The advantage of conceiving of a patient and his or her two role-partners as forming such a triad, in which the clinical administrator is the high-status authority and the psychotherapist the high-status friend of the patient, is that it directs attention not only to the relation between the patient and each of two role-partners, as has been done so far, but also to the relationship that must be upheld between the supportive and the instrumental leader. This brings us back to one of the most important points Merton makes in his theory of role-set. He deduces from the fact that a person in a single role relates to several role-partners the structural circumstance that these role-partners have to enter into relation with each other by virtue of their common involvement with the same status occupant. For example, a teacher and the parent of one of the pupils will relate to each other for no other reason than that both are involved with the same child.

Similarly, in the hospital setting described here, two psychiatrists relate to each other by virtue of having a common patient. In order to analyze the relation between such supportive and instrumental leadership in their common involvement with the same subordinate, five propositions from Freilich's theory of the "natural triad" will be examined.

1. The high-status friend helps relieve the tension created by the high-status authority.
2. The high-status friend and the high-status authority provide benefits for each other.
3. The high-status friend is a check on the power of the high-status authority.
4. Conflict is endemic in the relationship between high-status friend and high-status authority.
5. In order to maintain the relationship, the high-status friend and the high-status authority must avoid each other to some extent.

[1] *The psychotherapist helps relieve the tension* and antagonism created in the patient by the clinical administrator by helping the patient to re-evaluate the control imposed by the administrator. The psychotherapist helps strip the patient's hostile feelings of their distorting emotional content, as when countering complaints about life on the ward with the phrase: "There is really nothing I can do about ward policy; but let us explore the feelings you have about it."

The psychotherapist's refusal to alter the reality situation helps patients realize what the limitations are on changing the system. It encourages them to turn attention toward themselves and at the same time invites them to withdraw their antagonistic affect from the "high-status authority." A resident expressed this bluntly: "Frustration encountered by the patient in dealing with the administrator is taken care of in the therapeutic session." In this way, the psychotherapist helps cushion the system of ward psychiatry.

[2] The patient's high-status *role-partners benefit from each other.* Not only does the administrator derive advantage from the tension-relieving activity of the psychotherapist, but also the latter gains assurance from not having to worry about the immediate consequences of supportive and permissive intervention. In the words of one supervisor of therapy, the administrator "relieves the [psychotherapist] of a certain burden." The psychotherapist feels that it is a good thing that "the other fellow" will take care of safety precautions, as when this same supervisor explains: "I am thinking of a very sick, severely schizophrenic boy who is homicidal and suicidal. . . . I feel that it is very helpful for [the psychotherapist] to have an

administrator who is in continuous contact with the behavior of the patient." Because of the benefits that the psychotherapist and the clinical administrator derive from each other, they are interested in maintaining a balanced relationship.

[3] As the patient's high-status friend, *the psychotherapist can exercise some subtle control over the administrator* even without having authority to interfere in ward policy. The psychotherapist can act as a conveyor of information between the patient and the hospital system, feeding into the system the information that comes from the patient about the management of the ward by letting the word go to the "right people" (the staff lunchroom being the preferred setting for this type of communication), and hence helping to protect the system from ignorance about an administrator's management of the ward. One hospital psychiatrist who holds a top position had this to say: "Dr. X comes to me to tell me what he hears from his therapy patient about the ward. Of course, he puts it in general terms, trying not to focus attention on his patient. He says, 'From what I hear, all is not going well there.' "

The psychotherapist does not actually have to pass on the precise information he receives. The mere knowledge on the part of the administrator that the psychotherapist can potentially do so serves as a deterrent and is therefore a means of social control.

[4] *Conflicts are endemic* in the very mechanisms that assure the stability of the triad. For example, administrators who feel that a psychotherapist has pulled too strongly on the lever of indirect control will conclude that the information channel has been misused for interference with their authority.

Another source of antagonism is the fact that both role-partners derive benefit from each other. The mutuality of expectations makes it possible for each to try to get more than is considered legitimate. That is, the very notion of reciprocity implies the danger of some asymmetry judged by the partners to be illegitimate, in that one of the partners may try to obtain a larger share of the benefit than entitled to. (The partner may also give *more* benefit than expected, thereby obligating the other beyond the measure required by the definition of the relationship.)[23]

Indeed, psychotherapists often complain that some administrators' decisions about patients are too restrictive to be therapeutic, or not restrictive enough in view of their own permissive stance; and administrators often feel that some patients' misbehavior on the ward is the result of a psychotherapist's permissiveness and hence that "psychotherapy is not going well." The first complaint means that the administrator is said to create more tension than the psychotherapist wants to deal with or less safety than the therapist thinks he or she must be able to count on; the second implies that the administrator is relied upon too much to provide safety for a patient, which the psychotherapist can too easily ignore.

Since both high-status role-partners claim competence in the same field, each claims the right to judge the other's performance. Yet since they are interested in maintaining a balanced relationship from which they both can derive benefits, they will try to withhold negative judgment of each other as much as they feel is possible.

[5] *The two high-status role-partners must avoid each other.* If they become too antagonistic, the psychotherapist can hardly remain a tension reliever, since the antagonism raises rather than lowers the tension level of the patient and, through the patient, often that of the whole ward.[24]

Nor should the therapist be too friendly with the administrator, for a patient would sense this and would feel that the high-status friend could not be relied on because of his or her other seeming alliance with authority. This would threaten the therapeutic alliance which both high-status partners are interested in maintaining.

In order to remain the patient's high-status friend, the psychotherapist must be in some conflict with the administrator, but not too much. There are structural sources that press for or permit avoidance, both in order to prevent conflicts from coming to a head, and in order to prevent intensive interactions of any kind. Interaction brings in its wake a strengthening of sentiments, either positive or negative,[25] each of which threatens the smooth functioning of the triad. In other words, if in order to "cool out" the patient the therapist wants to remain a high-status friend, he or she must be able to remain "cool" in relation to the administrator.

There are various ways of resolving conflicts, some more disruptive of the balance of the triad than others. For example, if the administrator feels that the psychotherapist has interfered with his or her authority or if a therapist is annoyed by some action of the patient's administrator, the aggrieved party can resort to a diagnostic device, by which the patient is said to have "manipulated the psychiatrists." This means that equilibrium between the psychiatrists is being attained by displacing the conflict between themselves with a conflict between each of them and the patient.[26] The view of one clinical administrator expresses a widely held opinion at O'Brien: "There are patients who are very manipulative and they immediately try to find ways to pit the administrator and the psychotherapist against each other. Now, this causes trouble."

A patient is said to have "manipulated his or her psychiatrists" when a conflict between them has occurred as a result of the patient's attempt to obtain the help of one psychiatrist to score gains with the other, as when the patient asks the administrator to help obtain a change in therapist, or asks the therapist to help the patient get discharged. It is no wonder that psychiatrists at O'Brien call such "manipulation" catastrophic, for it threatens the therapeutic triad both directly, through the patient's intention to remove one high-status role-partner, and through the psychiatrists' attempt at solution, which the incident calls forth. This is because the "solution" consists of an alliance by the two psychiatrists in their common accusation of "manipulation." While this alliance makes it easier for any one of them to conduct the conflict with the patient, it inhibits the psychotherapist's ability to support the patient and hence also the ability to cushion the system. This manner of displacing the conflict can take place only through interaction between the two high-status role-partners and tends to strengthen the bond between them through their realization of their common interest in not being "manipulated." It means at best a temporary weakening of the therapeutic triad and at worst, if the therapeutic alliance cannot be restored, the triad's dissolution. It is no wonder that an assessment of having been manipulated gets everybody concerned up in arms.

It should be noted in passing that the use of the mechanism by which a conflict is diverted neither contradicts nor confirms the correctness of the diagnosis itself. Correct or not, the diagnosis helps bring about a temporary alliance between partners who previously had some reason for mutual antagonism. A patient's possible "manipulation" of the two role-partners is part of the dynamics of any triad in which one member manages to become *tertius gaudens*—that is, the third party of a relationship who has benefited from conflict between the two other partners.[27]

We recognize here the operation of a mechanism described by Merton by which the occupant of a status who is subjected to conflicting expectations "acts to make these contradictions manifest" and thereby attempts to "redirect the conflict so that it is one between members of the role-set, rather than, as was at first the case, between them and the occupant of the status."[28] The patient who is said to "manipulate" his or her psychiatrists makes use of this mechanism, having managed to force them to confront each other. Thus a subtle interplay takes place in the triadic relationship in which conflicts arise, are displaced, and are used more or less profitably to establish temporary alliances by which a balance is threatened at the same time as it is obtained.

There are other ways than by displacement of the conflict to introduce a corrective into the working of the triad. If an administrator feels that a patient's misbehavior is the result of a psychotherapist's manner of treatment, he or she can withdraw from the triad through a legitimate procedure—that is, by transferring the patient to another ward that is said to provide more adequate physical and mental security for that patient. In this way the problem can be passed on to a colleague on another ward, who will now become the new high-status authority.

This is not to say, of course, that transfers of patients usually take place for reasons of maintaining equilibrium among the staff. From the point of view of the clinical management of patients as it is defined in the hospital, a patient who is "acting out" for whatever reasons is required to be provided with stronger "security." The point here is merely that whatever the administrator's motives, by having a patient transferred out of the ward the administrator removes himself or herself from this therapeutic triad.

The psychotherapist does not have similar organizational means for withdrawing from the triad. The main means available for introducing a corrective remains the indirect one provided by informal channels of communication. This is because the psychotherapist lacks the power of decision for changing the patient's program and also because the psychotherapeutic relationship is considered "sacred" in the normative system of the hospital in that it is defined as enduring and highly personal.

Both the administrator's withdrawal from the triad and the psychotherapist's indirect control can take place without any interaction between the patient's two high-status role-partners. There are, of course, other informal and formal ways of dealing with conflict through interaction. Informally, the two psychiatrists can stop each other in the hallway or talk over lunch. In this way, they make an attempt to be "nice" about something they in some measure feel antagonistic about. This informal handling of the relationship precludes the sustained interaction that would strengthen positive or negative sentiments and thereby threaten the triad.

In situations of extreme antagonism between the two high-status rolepartners, a formal institutionalized procedure of consultation can be used. This is done only when the conflict cannot be solved within the triadic relationship itself. It is a measure of last resort not because it threatens the triad but because the conflict is so strong already that the dissolution of the triad is being envisaged. Consultation, which is a means for bringing such a change about, puts the relationship of all members of the triad into the field of visibility— that is, of social control within the hierarchy of the hospital. This situation both high-status role-partners are interested in avoiding.

One reason consultantship is usually needed to change a patient's psychotherapist is that in the value system of O'Brien the dyadic psychotherapeutic relationship is considered so important that it cannot easily be broken without being subject to social control emanating from a larger network than that of the involved triad. This raises the question of the extent to which the working of the "therapeutic triad" depends not only on its internal mechanisms, which have been explored so far, but on the normative structure of the organization.

The Normative Structure of Avoidance and Conflict

In order for the two role-partners to avoid each other to some extent within this limited setting, they must have an interest in doing so. Moreover, such an interest must be reinforced through the hospital's policy and through its value system.

The patient's two high-status partners have an interest in limiting contact with each other because this enables them better to perform their respective roles of "friend" and "authority," and thereby to benefit from each other's services. Yet, their interest in mutual avoidance is "skewed": each high-status role-partner is interested in preventing the other from influencing his or her own jurisdictional field but does not equally desire to be excluded from the other's jurisdictional field.

It is this unilateral interest in obtaining information "from the *other* guy" that accounts for a commonplace phrase in the hospital that "therapy goes best when there is good communication between therapist and administrator." That this notion is questioned by some other hospital psychiatrists, who call it an "empty cliché," explaining that they are "dubious of it on purely clinical grounds," is evidence of the coexistence of norms and counternorms. Indeed, there are forces at work within the hospital that press for both junction and disjunction between these two psychiatrists.

Interaction between the two psychiatrists is minimized by some purely physical arrangements that assure geographical separation and limit the time available for mutual briefing. Psychotherapists see patients in their offices, which usually are located in the central administration building, where patients go from their wards either by themselves or with an escort. This reduces the chance of casual meetings between a patient's administrator and the psychotherapist. Moreover, interaction between them is limited by the sheer pressure of work and the large number of psychiatrists who are active in this hospital. An administrator in charge of a ward of about twenty patients, of whom, say, ten are in psychotherapy would have to confer with as many as ten psychotherapists. For this, the pressure of work does not leave enough time.

Of course, if contacts between these two role-partners were highly valued in the hospital, the physical arrangements could be changed. For example, psychotherapists could be required to see their patients on the wards, where brief encounters with the.ward psychiatrists would be possible. In fact, the norm is that the realm of psychotherapy be separated from ward life.

This directs our attention to the normative system. There are, first, inherently contradictory norms governing the relations between the two types of psychiatrists. Second, the practitioners face contradictory expectations from their various role-partners. Third, there is an unequal distribution of valued resources in the hospital's status and authority system.

Avoidance between the two high-status role-partners is formally provided through the policy of the training center, according to which ward management is not to be the psychotherapist's concern and, conversely, psychotherapy is to be insulated from observability. However, to what extent psychotherapy must also be insulated from knowledge by the psychiatrist who supervises the patient's management on the ward is not clearly defined.

As has been noted, the split between psychotherapy and ward management is based on the principle of freeing patients to reveal their inner dispositions without concern for any decisions that might be made about them regarding the regulation of daily life on the ward. Against this norm, however, there exists the norm that the provision of two psychiatrists for the same patient makes it possible for a second professional opinion to be "available," reached independently to some extent, and on the basis of important data.[29] This implies (1) that there must be some contact between the psychotherapist and the administrator, in order to combine the two judgments, but (2) that the contact should not be so frequent as to impair "independence of judgment."

To be sure, it would be excessive to prevent all contact between the two psychiatrists. This would make for the coexistence of two different systems within the same hospital, with resulting lack of integration and polarization of perspectives and interests. Moreover, evaluation of patients' progress or readiness for discharge could never be arrived at through collective reasoning, which is the normative basis of work for any professional collectivity.

In spite of this need for communication, it is generally understood, although never clearly stated, that psychotherapists will refrain from giving details about the concrete content of a patient's hourly revelations. This is why it is possible for much of the psychotherapy at O'Brien to be conducted by "contract therapists," whose relations with the hospital staff are minimal. These outside psychotherapists usually do not partake of the hospital's organizational life; they do not participate in regular meetings, neither in the regular morning conferences, where reports about all the wards are exchanged, nor in the periodic staff meetings, where cases are being presented for discussion. They attend staff meetings only when their own patients are being evaluated, which may happen at intervals of several months. Their professional time, outside of the hours they are contracted for by the hospital, is their own, and hence they neither are present physically nor have the time for much interaction with the permanent hospital staff. If the patients' well-being in the hospital were thought of as requiring much communication between psychotherapists and clinical administrators, psychotherapy would not be conducted by outside psychiatrists.

As to residents, although they are at the hospital continuously, this is not solely by virtue of the psychotherapy they are conducting with patients but also by virtue of their total involvement in a learning situation. Yet, the mere fact of their availability and the fact of their lower professional and organizational status put them under more pressure to interact with their patients' clinical administrators than is the case with contract therapists. The problems this creates and the ways in which they are handled will be discussed in the next chapter.

The norms of avoidance and communication are difficult to deal with because of the ambiguous notion of confidentiality. Confidentiality is usually understood as having to be maintained against laymen, not between professionals who have a common interest in task performance. However, in the psychotherapeutic relationship, the patient is led to believe—whether deliberately told or not—that communications in therapy are confidential within the hospital, since this is one firm component of the "therapeutic alliance." It is unclear to everybody, not only to patients, how much information is or should be passed on between a psychotherapist and the ward administrator about their common patient, as is revealed by the following answer by a supervisor of therapy to a query on the issue: "Dr. A decided to keep strictly to the rule that he would keep everything confidential, that he wouldn't even tell the administrator. Dr. B was the administrator. When he heard this, he blew his top. How could he be administrator if A refused to tell him? I agreed with A, but didn't really know. . . ."

This little report is instructive on several counts. It seems that the administrator felt he had a right to "blow his top" at the therapist's insistence to live up to the contract with the patient. Also, the supervisor claims he "didn't really know" the rules of the game. And above all, it seems that the psychotherapist had to make an individual decision "to keep strictly to the rule." There seems to be some uncertainty, to say the least, about a rule that, if adhered to, arouses legitimately felt indignation.

In order to obtain some clarification on the subject, a senior psychiatrist who is a protagonist of the split between the two types of psychiatry was asked what he thought a therapist should communicate to an administrator. He said:

> Quite a lot. . . . I would like to have him ideally, I think it would be awfully nice if the psychotherapist gave the administrator practically an hour-by-hour account . . . of how things went, broadly. . . . That may be too much. . . . The therapist has to, I believe, constrain himself to the right to tell the administrator anything that amounts to serious danger of life and death. . . . [Beyond that an administrator] probably should not be told, if the patient doesn't want it.

In listing the whole range of possibilities, between informing an administrator hour by hour or only "broadly" or only in matters of "life and death," and otherwise letting the matter rest at the discretion of the patient, this psychiatrist is the spokesman for a whole variety of unclarified opinions among the staff. The confusion is not just a "weird phenomenon," nor is it due to ignorance or to personal whim. It results from contradictions embedded in the social structure.

Indeed, what both of the above responses reveal is that the norms are confused and contradictory and that the psychotherapist has to meet both the administrator's and the patient's expectations, although these are not always compatible.

Perhaps in extreme situations of "life and death" there would be no ambiguity about the need for communication. But many if not most issues are not so clearly definable. What if the therapist's woman patient has a sexual relationship? Here the administrator, who has to face responsibilities toward the family, may feel that these should be given priority rather than the patient's and the therapist's expectations of confidentiality.

There are also problems inherent in "doing a good job." It is commonly believed that decisions as well as treatment should be based on knowledge, and that the more knowledge is available, the better one can arrive at a sound judgment. As a generality, this view can hardly be disputed. But the question arises whether an administrator should consult with a therapist about the advisability of prescribing drugs or of transferring a patient to another ward. Or, conversely, whether a therapist should inform an administrator that the patient has this day revealed serious material concerning Oedipal fantasies which would make a planned weekend leave inadvisable.

Each type of psychiatrist wants to obtain such pertinent information from the other, but each resists living up to the other's expectations. This is because such close cooperation between them would tend to restrict the administrator's autonomous authority and weaken the psychotherapist's therapeutic alliance.

Such matters are discussed usually *a posteriori* as individual "cases," when at some point one role-partner feels the need for information from the other, but they are hardly dealt with as issues that need normative guidance. There is a patterned and legitimate way of avoiding the need to define guidelines for behavior—namely, the use of the phrase, "it depends on the patient." The leeway for individual decisions that this phrase implies is, of course, part of the medical and professional ethic, according to which every practitioner follows his or her own best judgment. As a result of contradictory norms and expectations, however, there is confusion about the type of information a psychotherapist should convey to an administrator and in return how much information and consultation a psychotherapist can expect from an administrator. Such confusion threatens the balance of the therapeutic triad in that it harms the psychotherapist's therapeutic alliance with the patient at the same time that it blocks the administrator's instrumental wisdom.

These conditions lead to a questioning among the staff of the usefulness of the system of separation between the two spheres. Consequently, while the staunchest protagonists of the system— almost all the psychiatrists who occupy top rank in the hospital— continue to explain the clinical soundness of the split, a quiet (and sometimes not so quiet) battle goes on in the middle ranks, with expressions of dissatisfaction ranging from joking and shrugging of shoulders to raging controversies and open display of anger.

An argument that comes primarily from the contract therapists is that a psychotherapist cannot do good work with a patient without being consulted or even informed when major measures are taken, such as severe restrictions, a transfer to another ward, or the prescription of drugs. They, as well as some of the residents' supervisors of therapy, often invoke the professional norm that physicians have to be in authority over their patients. Another complaint, this one stemming primarily from administrators, is that psychotherapists have too little concern for the patients' behavior on the ward and that administrators have a right to know whether this behavior is a result of what goes on in therapy, although not all are so insistent as the one who said in an interview that he wanted to know "everything, from the coarse to the refined."

Administrators want to know more than psychotherapists are willing to reveal. And psychotherapists want to have more say about patients than administrators are willing to grant them. Underlying the administrators' wish to know is the conviction that psychotherapy is the *real* thing, where the important matters concerning the patients' health are being revealed. Underlying the psychotherapists' claim for more say is also the conviction that the psychotherapist *really* knows what is important for the patients' health. Hence, underlying the conflict is a deeply entrenched consensus about the high value of psychotherapy for the health of patients. We have the paradoxical situation where a serious conflict results from the common adherence to strongly held values.[30]

This is, of course, no paradox if we realize that a differentiated opportunity structure prevails at O'Brien. Some people have more access than others to a highly valued resource for the production of health: the revelation of the patients' inner dispositions. The situation is similar structurally to that prevailing in American society, where much conflict can be accounted for by the fact that the value of success tends to be shared by all, but access to the means for obtaining it is denied to many.[31] Were this value not shared, the society would be much more stable; those who prefer not to seek success would be satisfied with the limited opportunities for obtaining it, and such limitations would hence not give rise to conflict. It is for this reason that those who glorify subcultures that allegedly do not share the American Dream are unwittingly advocating a stratified society in which all are neatly kept in place by their own inclinations so that the differentiated opportunity structure can remain stable.[32]

Similarly, if in the hospital the values underlying the choice of treatment technique were legitimately divided between psychotherapy and milieu therapy, there would be more stability. But such a system would be mobility-blocked not only for staff but for patients as well. For them, it would mean that some would be given a high-status friend and others deprived of this privilege, and that the two types of patient would each have "their own" type of psychiatrist.

At the same time that it presses for conflict in the hospital system, the common value of psychotherapy is an integrative factor. Upon it depends the functioning of the natural triad, for it motivates the ward psychiatrist to support the patients' psychotherapy and makes it possible for the psychotherapist to exercise some measure of indirect control over the administrator. If it were not for this common value, there might be more "peace" in the hospital, but the whole hospital would be split into two noncomplementary systems, making it impossible for the psychotherapist to be an effective high-status friend, as defined in the therapeutic triad. The psychotherapist would be in the marginal role of a chaplain in a prison or in the military. The impact of such a completely split system on its patients, many of whom suffer from "split personality," can only be conjectured.

On the wards the commonly adhered-to psychoanalytic principle serves as a check against restrictiveness. Although decisions there are to be made on the basis of the reality situation, the staff, under the leadership of the ward psychiatrist and with the active participation of one or two residents, explore the "real meaning" of the patients' behavior. This introduces a measure of permissiveness. It also serves as a "cooling-out" process for an often legitimately angered and fearful staff, at the same time offering support through the affirmation of solidarity based on a common and highly valued perspective, that of depth psychology.

Yet, the high value placed on psychotherapy creates some problems in that everyone wants to have some share in it. The word "therapy" is imbued with magical attributes. The closer anyone comes to doing "therapy," the more important the role for the presentation of self. Hence, the person in charge of the gym is a "recreational therapist," the one in charge of crafts is an "occupational therapist." And the nurses see themselves as being part of the team to the extent that they understand the "deeper" implications of behavior and are prepared to sit and talk with patients.[33]

At O'Brien, all concerned tend to have a share in the pie of the unconscious. Looked at from the point of view of the goal of the organization, the production of health, psychiatrists who make decisions about matters pertaining to health and illness—the administrators—are largely deprived of access to this highly valued raw material on the ward. And psychotherapists, who dispose of this highly valued resource, do not have access to the decision-making process. Hence, in both these activities, psychiatrists are alienated from important means of production and therefore to some extent from assessment of the product.

It has become fashionable to apply the term "alienation" to all sorts of frustrations and malaise.[34] But here we have a case of alienation that approximates the core meaning of the concept as it was formulated by Marx, for whom alienation is rooted in the unequal distribution of rights and privileges. This at once directs our attention to the status structure of O'Brien.

The Status System

Discussing the importance of the Parsons-Bales model of dual leadership for different types of organizations, Amitai Etzioni raises a point regarding organizations that is similar to Freilich's discussion of the natural triad. Etzioni shows that both types of authority figures, the supportive ("friend") and the instrumental ("authority"), are needed in every type of organization, but he makes the further observation that their relative importance varies according to the organization's goal because power must be allocated so as to establish the superiority of the desired kind of leadership over the other. This can be done by giving one type of leader higher rank or by selecting one kind of leader with higher prestige than the other. Etzioni distinguishes between organizations that produce goods and services and those that produce "growth"—that is, changes in individuals— and makes the important point that the second type, which includes mental hospitals, must, in contrast to the first, give priority to noninstrumental, that is, expressive considerations.[35] If Etzioni's scheme were followed, the "expressive" leader, or the "high-status friend" psychotherapist, would have higher rank or prestige than the administrator.

Being engaged in the highly valued activity of psychotherapy, the psychotherapist at O'Brien would logically command more respect. High status would be commensurate with the importance attached to this activity. But in fact, this would mean polarization between the "haves" and the "have nots": the administrator would be reduced to the role of a foreman. This would run counter to the professional self-image of any medical practitioner. And even in the unlikely event that a psychiatrist would accept such a demeaned position, the inherent responsibility for decision making would be backed up by relatively little authority. The natural triad could not function as defined because the high-status authority would not be enough of an authority to furnish guidelines for the low-status subordinate.

If the psychotherapist's position cannot, as a rule, be vested with hierarchical authority in the hospital, the question must be raised whether authority could rest on high professional prestige. For this to be possible, the psychotherapist would have to be selected among those outside the hospital who have high prestige on the basis of professional seniority and obtained rewards. Although this might create a financial problem, it should not be insurmountable at a private hospital.

But this would not work either as a general pattern, because highly prestigious psychotherapists would not have to accept the limitations on their authority that the hospital system imposes. If, however, they were willing to be psychotherapists at this hospital under such limiting conditions, they would feel too free, given their recognized professional competence, to interfere, subtly or not, in ward policies.

The following exceptional case provides an illustration of the type of problem prestigious practitioners in the community would tend to create if their service were enlisted on a regular basis. A patient who belonged to a prominent family was in therapy with a psychoanalyst of some renown who had already treated the patient before hospitalization. The patient was permitted to see the therapist in his private office outside the hospital. The following story was reported by a member of the social service:

> The patient's mother was just wild. Friday night her son had come home from [his therapist] and said that [the therapist] said he could stay home. On that evening [the assistant administrator of the ward] called and said: Where is the patient? And so the mother said: [The therapist] said he could stay home. So [the assistant administrator] said he didn't care what [the therapist] said, that he [the assistant administrator] insisted that the patient had to come back to the hospital. Whereupon [the mother] got quite upset. . . .
>
> Finally, the patient was allowed to stay home. But if it is true that [the resident] said he didn't care what [the therapist] said, that is very bad. The point is that you just don't say that about an outside person, especially someone of prominence.

That such an incident, which was caused by the fact that a prominent psychotherapist did not hesitate to use his own authority over the patient, endangers the triadic arrangement is confirmed by this social worker's further report: "So I told [the administrator] . . . that perhaps this had been one of the contributing factors [for the family to remove the patient from the hospital]."

Even in the event that prestigious psychiatrists could be persuaded to respect the hospital's authority structure, clinical administrators would be made to feel, as the quoted social worker indeed implied, that they were under the scrutiny of role-partners who had high prestige in the profession and who, in this capacity, helped to control the reputation of its younger and lesser members, like themselves, for the furtherance of their career. That is, the psychotherapist would be too important a role-partner for the administrator to feel at ease in his or her own decision making. The two roles would no longer be complementary, for the administrator would need the psychotherapist more than the administrator was needed by the latter.

It must also be borne in mind that the administrator, with about twenty patients on the ward, could have a number of prestigeful psychotherapists to deal with, at least some of whom would differ among themselves in their judgments of what ward policy should be. If only a few of those highly prestigious colleagues were potential critics with differing ideas about ward management, the administrator could hardly remain sane in the attempt to care for the sanity of patients.

In fact, the more prestigious psychiatrists in the community rarely conduct psychotherapy at O'Brien, although there are notable exceptions. Nor does it happen, except in a rare case, that a psychiatrist who has a high position at O'Brien conducts psychotherapy with a hospital patient. Most psychotherapy is conducted by the residents or by contract therapists who have not yet attained high prestige in the profession.

The residents' roles will be analyzed in the next chapter. Here it is only necessary to note that since they are not yet full-fledged members of the profession, they do not feel strongly that their professional status is violated by being deprived of decision making about patients. But the contract therapists find themselves in contradictory status positions, in which their authority in the hospital is not commensurate with the authority vested in a physician in the community. Being close in professional status to the administrators, and sharing professional status with colleagues outside the hospital, they find that the limitation on their authority within the hospital puts them in a situation of status inconsistency.[36] This gives rise to strong feelings of relative deprivation [37] when they compare their situation with that of regular therapists. Hence, the contract therapists are more frustrated in their status claims than any other status group at O'Brien. Since, however, they remain outsiders, their dissatisfactions are largely ineffective in producing change or disruption.

The fact that those who conduct psychotherapy have no decision-making power over their patients and are likely neither to have top positions in the hospital nor to enjoy top prestige in the profession tends to make the supportive leadership subordinate to the instrumental leadership, a condition which, as Etzioni has suggested, may conceivably limit therapeutic effectiveness. However, in one respect the supportive activity of psychotherapy is given importance in the patients' eyes, and that is through the high value that is placed by all members of O'Brien's staff on psychotherapy as the most important technique for treating mental illness. This high value is put into practice by not allowing anyone, not even the clinical administrators in charge of the patients' total programs, to interfere in any way with psychotherapy, either by preventing patients even occasionally from seeing their psychotherapists or by deciding that psychotherapy should be discontinued. It will be remembered that a change in therapists can be brought about only through a cumbersome procedure which involves the hospital's hierarchy. Not only administrators but the nursing staff as well know that they have to cooperate fully in getting patients to their therapeutic hour. Nobody is permitted to tamper with psychotherapy. It is this "sacred" quality of psychotherapy, although it is not backed up by a system of rank and prestige grading, that gives moral importance to the supportive leadership.

The triadic arrangement that has been described is, of course, an "ideal type." The preceding analysis has proceeded on the "as if" premise of two high-status role partners of a patient who both have a large measure of authority. At this stage of the analysis it becomes important to take account of the crucial feature of a teaching hospital: much of the practice is conducted by residents—that is, by people who are psychiatrists in their relations with patients but are advanced students in their relations with the senior staff of the hospital. The relatively low status of residents in the hospital requires that the triadic arrangements in which they operate be supported by outside "pillars." The lack of self-sufficiency of a therapeutic triad led by residents introduces a complexity into the picture which makes the maintenance of balance a subtle interplay of alliances, conflicts, and ambivalent relationships. This will become clear in the next chapter.

4
The Treatment Set

In neither their role as assistants to clinical administrators on wards nor in their role as psychotherapists with patients from other wards are residents strong enough, professionally or in their organizational position, to assure the working of the mechanisms that keep the therapeutic triad in balance. Senior staff members enter the scene. The resulting complexity will become clear in an analysis of the residents' role-sets.

In each of the two roles, residents are part of a network of multiple relationships. On the ward and under the authority of the ward's clinical administrator, a resident relates to the therapists of the ward patients. And in the capacity of therapist of patients from other wards, under the supervision of senior therapists, the same resident relates to his or her therapy patients' ward administrators and assistant administrators. This fact is an important element for the integration of the two activity systems. The multiple relationships residents maintain with both systems in their dual roles makes them members of several triadic treatment sets in which conflicts, avoidances, and alliances are endemic.

Figure 1 illustrates the network that is being formed for one resident (R1) by virtue of helping to administer one ward patient (P1) and treating one therapy patient (P2). For purposes of clarity, the following discussion will generally proceed as if each resident had only one patient in each of the two activity systems, but it is to be remembered that on their wards they may have as many as ten patients who are in therapy with their own psychotherapists, and they may have up to three patients in therapy from as many as three other wards.

62

Since patients (P1 and P2 in figure 1) are being treated both on the ward and in psychotherapy, for each of them four psychiatrists interact with one another in different combinations and with different degrees of mutual interest. Some of these relationships, of course, are less salient than others, depending upon the different degrees of interest vested in various status positions. Because of the low status of the resident on the ward in relation to the administrator and because of the high value attached to therapy, it is in the capacity of therapist more than in the capacity of assistant administrator that the resident mobilizes the interest of the role-partners from the other system. An administrator (A1 and A2) is much more interested in the ward patients' resident therapist than the therapist's supervisor (S1 and S2) is in a patient's assistant administrator. That is, in figure 1, A1 and A2 are much more interested in the therapeutic activities of R3 and R1 respectively than S1 and S2 are in the ward activities of R2 and R1. As a low-status assistant administrator, the resident does not invite the scrutiny of a high-status role-partner from the other activity system to the same extent as in the capacity of therapist.

As a therapist, the resident is "in charge" of a patient in a different way than on the ward. Although the course of therapy is being scrutinized by a supervisor, the details of the resident's behavior are not. Psychotherapy is not subject to detailed guidance. In the dyadic relationship with the patient, the resident has sole responsibility and is insulated from observability. But it is precisely the resident's low status and limited competence in this highly valued and highly individualized activity that invites the concern of the therapy

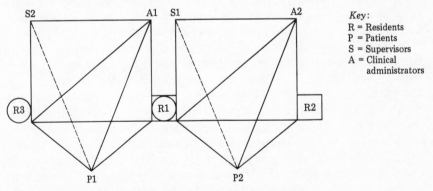

Key:
R = Residents
P = Patients
S = Supervisors
A = Clinical
    administrators

Figure 1. Social relations between the two activity systems

The resident R1, who has the administrator A1 and the supervisor S1 as a training set, relates to resident R3, who treats one of R1's ward patients P1 in psychotherapy, and to resident R2, who is an assistant administrator for R1's therapy patient P2.

patient's ward administrator. In contrast, as an assistant administrator the resident will hardly attract the concern of the supervisor of therapy because whatever authority and responsibility are delegated on a particular ward, it is the administrator who remains chiefly responsible. The resident's low status explains both the interest his or her therapeutic activity evokes in the therapy patient's administrator, and the lack of interest his or her administrative performance evokes in the supervisors of therapy of the ward patients.

Since the administrator is ultimately responsible for the patient's management, it is the administrator rather than the assistant who is likely to be questioned about important decisions regarding a patient on the ward. In therapy with individual patients, in contrast, it is the resident who is the focus of much interest on the part of the administrative team, since this highly valued activity of psychotherapy is conducted independently and behind closed doors. This leads to the paradoxical situation that the low status of the resident administrator *deflects* the attention of the role-partners in the other system to the administrator, whereas the low status of the resident therapist, combined as it is with high value and lack of visibility, *invites* attention from the role-partners in the other system.

But the withdrawal of interest from one of the resident's tasks and the focusing of interest on the other have one similar consequence. As the status superior on the ward sometimes enters the scene because of the relatively inconsequential role of the assistant, so the supervisor of therapy occasionally enters the scene because the supervisee has to be protected in a consequential activity. For the fact that the resident therapist is the object of much interest on the part of the therapy patient's administrator and assistant administrator puts the resident therapist in a vulnerable position, especially since he or she has to deal with two or three such teams, one for each therapy patient. As a therapist, the resident is under pressure (though not under authority) from the higher-status clinical administrator, who, moreover, is allied in interest in the fate of the ward patient with one of the resident therapist's own status equals, the resident on the ward. Under combined pressure from a prestigious status superior and a less prestigious status equal, both of whom have authority on the ward over a therapy patient, the resident therapist could hardly carry on the individualized and autonomous activity of psychotherapy if it were not for the support of the supervisor of therapy. In order to explore the ambiguities and conflicts that arise for residents in this complex network, it is useful to consider once more the triadic relationship in which residents are involved.

The resident's low status position and the differences in the principles governing the hierarchy in the two activity systems—the

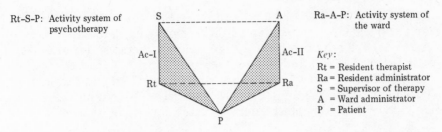

Rt-S-P: Activity system of
      psychotherapy

Ra-A-P: Activity system of
      the ward

Key:
Rt = Resident therapist
Ra = Resident administrator
S = Supervisor of therapy
A = Ward administrator
P = Patient

Figure 2. The two activity systems

one being patterned after the medical, the other after the bureaucratic model—have implications for the dynamics that govern the
mechanisms at work in the therapeutic triad. Only some mechanisms
that are expected to operate in the natural triad tend to be at work
between the resident therapist and the resident administrator—that
is, on the Rt- Ra axis (figure 2). These concern the cushioning of the
impact of the administrative system by the resident therapist and the
benefits the two junior psychiatrists bestow on each other. Some
other mechanisms, notably the check on administrative power, conflict, and its resolution, tend to operate on the higher echelon
between the resident therapist's supervisor and the therapy patient's
administrator—that is, on the S-A axis in figure 2—rather than
directly between the residents in the two activity systems. The
therapeutic triad has been transformed into a therapeutic pentad,
and some of the mechanisms of the natural triad have been displaced
upward from triad T-I to triad T-IV in figure 3.

Just as in geometry the properties of a polygon can best be
explored by examining those of its component triangles, in social
relations any set consisting of more than three role-partners can be
examined in terms of its component triads. The juxtaposition of two
activity systems, Ac-I and Ac-II (figure 2), that are separated in time
and space gives rise to crisscrossing and integrative relations between
these systems through the operation of triads T-I, T-II, T-III, and

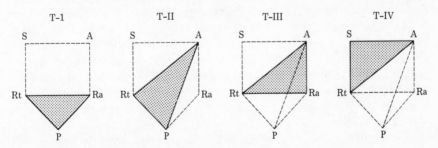

Figure 3. Triadic relationships in the treatment set (see key for figure 2)

T-IV (figure 3). The first of these represents the relations between the two residents and their common patient (triad T-I, figure 3). T-II represents the relations between the resident therapist and the ward administrator in relation to *their* common patient. T-III is the triadic constellation of the two residents and the ward administrator, and T-IV depicts the relations between the patient's administrator, the patient's resident therapist, and the latter's supervisor of therapy.

The Low-Status Therapeutic Triad

The lower triad in figure 3, the therapeutic triad proper, in which the resident therapist and the resident administrator relate to each other by virtue of their common interest in their patient, is not self-sufficient. The patient's high-status role-partners having residency status, the triad lacks the measure of autonomy of the ideal type of therapeutic triad discussed in the previous chapter. The mechanisms that are supposed to be at work in the natural triad, and that were shown to function fairly well (that is, with only very occasional need for external interference) between the high-status role-partners of full professional status, operate insufficiently in the residents' triad with their common patient. This is because the degree to which these mechanisms operate tends to be directly associated with the measure of independence vested in the status position of the triad's leaders.

In triad T-I, only some of the mechanisms are at work: the resident therapist, acting as a high-status friend for the patient, helps cushion the system of the ward; and the resident therapist and the resident administrator who acts as the patient's high-status authority, derive benefits from each other in their respective roles. The principle of avoidance between them also operates; as a matter of fact, it operates so strongly that interaction between them is minimal. Yet, we remember that some interaction between the patient's high-status role-partners is required to assure the functioning of the triad. This, however, tends to take place on higher-status levels, between the resident and the clinical administrator (Rt-A), and sometimes between the latter and the supervisor of therapy (A-S). The main reason for this is the structural position of the resident therapist.

An examination of the first two mechanisms, the relief of the tension created on the ward and the mutual benefits derived between the two systems, will show that the resident therapist is in a better position to put these mechanisms to work than is the status equal in the other system.

The resident therapist does help the patient come to terms with life on the ward. Here is how one supervisor describes this: "The therapist has said to the patient that he is sorry, but he can't do anything about [administrative policy]. 'How about seeing what *we* can do?' And if the patient has a good therapeutic alliance, he will be able to cope with that." And we remember the resident who explained that "frustration encountered by the patient in dealing with the administrator is taken care of in the therapeutic session."

That is, just as in the ideal type of the therapeutic triad described in the previous chapter, the therapist helps "cool out" the patient and hence helps relieve the tension the patient experiences or threatens to act out on the ward. The quoted resident who recognizes this also senses that the ward system is not the only one to benefit from the division of labor between the two types of psychiatrists, explaining that "it helps more in preserving the therapeutic alliance between the therapist and the patient." Another resident concurs that it permits him to "stay in the . . . more positive transference of the patient rather than having to write orders the patient doesn't like."

Hence, residents in the two systems help relieve each other so they can concentrate with patients on one task at a time. The resident therapist who explores the patient's inner dispositions needs to pay little attention to the reality situation on the ward; conversely, the resident who "administers" the patient's reality situation does not have to delve into underlying motivations. One resident explains how he, in his two roles, benefits from this division of labor: "[In administration] all we talk about is what the patient wants, which is the important thing she has to learn. [In psychotherapy] I don't have to get into arguments about what the patient wants. . . . I can take up some of the anger that she has with the administrator, and work in this area with her."

All residents acknowledge the fact that the split between the two activity systems makes things easier for them in psychotherapy, because it puts them "in a better situation to discuss things with [the patient]," or "it takes some of the strain off the therapist with patients who tend to act out." One resident explains how a good administrator can help a therapist: "I think the most tricky things are handled by an administrator. . . . If he is doing a really beautiful job of it, the therapy will just unfold."

Yet it is usually not the assistant administrator who is credited with such benefits but rather the system as a whole or the administrator, as the above responses indicate. Supervisors of therapy also tend to refer to the administrator when they mention the advantages that accrue to the resident therapist. As one supervisor said, "I think it relieves the young resident of a certain burden." Similarly, it is the administrator who is held responsible for the patients' management.

All resident therapists were asked: "If you are concerned about some administrative decision concerning a patient whom you have in psychotherapy, what do you do?" The answer is, most of the time, "Talk to the administrator." If they say that they talk to the assistant, it is usually a means of paying lip service to the hierarchy, as in the following answer by a resident who was known to be smooth in social relations: "More frequently the assistant administrator. I talk to the administrator too, but I don't like to bypass [the assistant administrator], it tends to create less cooperation."

That this alleged willingness to talk to the assistant administrator was only obeisance to routine expectations was confirmed later in the interview when the same resident was asked what he does if, in his capacity as therapist, he disagrees with the management of his therapy patient. He simply replied, "Go talk to the administrator." Another resident explains: "If the administrator runs the hall, I prefer to deal with him directly. If the resident is managing the patient, you work with the resident in order not to make it seem that you bypass him. Of course, it would be easier to talk to the resident, but it is not the most effective way." One resident was quite blunt: "Where the residents communicate with each other, the split is not as effective."

It will be remembered that in the ideal-type of therapeutic triad the fact that the two psychiatrists provide benefits for each other may become a source of conflict, as when in one system it is felt that insufficient benefits are being derived from the other.

It is mainly the attempt of each to maximize benefits for his or her own situation that brings about a dialogue between the two psychiatrists, even when, or rather because, they have conflicting concerns. In the ideal-type of therapeutic triad, this dialogue takes place between status equals. And we would expect that where residents are in charge of patients, the dialogue would be even easier because they have much in common in their shared low-status positions in the organization.

Yet, it will be remembered that residents, in their roles as therapists, tend to bypass their own status equals on their patients' wards if they have some concern about their patients' management. Conversely, if on the ward a patient's behavior calls attention to the course of therapy, it is the administrator, rather than the assistant, who will seek out the resident therapist.

This should not be surprising if it is realized that the resident administrator cannot claim enough authority or competence to voice a judgment about the conduct of psychotherapy. Moreover, even with more information a resident administrator's position on the ward is not strong enough to implement policy. One resident explains this: "The assistant administrator is not so interested in the therapist. . . . Where the resident is not directly responsible for the patient, he doesn't seek out information because he can't use it."

Yet, it is not only that resident administrators cannot take action on the ward on the basis of knowledge obtained from therapists; their position is also not strong enough to reciprocate to their therapist colleagues for having obliged with information. That is, in talking to the assistant administrator, the therapist is eager to get something in return, as if to say, "What can *you* do for my patient on the ward?" Exchange between the residents in regard to their common patient is stymied because one of the partners cannot give as much as the other. To have a meaningful exchange of ideas there must be an exchange of benefits.[1] This can take place much more easily between the resident therapist and the ward administrator. This is an administrator's account of such an exchange: "There were instances where I had reservations about what [the resident therapist] was doing in the hour, and he had reservations about what I was doing administratively; we talked about it and got things worked out."

The fact that negotiations between therapists and administrators are a matter of exchange, where each wants to get something from the other, is most evident in cases where a conflict has developed to a point that involves another high-status role-partner in the pentad. One supervisor describes how he entered into interactions with an administrator: "Sometimes I felt that it was important to communicate something to the administrator, very occasionally. . . . When an administrator nabs me and says, 'Now, how do you think this is going?' then I might say: 'I think that it is going pretty well but I have wondered a little bit about the wisdom of keeping the patient on the hall.' "

Since therapists and their supervisors do not have power of decision making, they like to keep their knowledge of a patient as currency to be used in exchange for exercising influence on the administrator. To compensate for the authority vested in the administrator, they like to wait to be approached rather than taking the initiative themselves, thus putting the initiator in the respondent's debt. "The establishment of exchange relations involves making investments that constitute commitments to the other party."[2] An outside therapist described his negotiations with an administrator in the following words: "The patient signed out. This brought the administrator to me. . . . Now he came and asked *me.*"

Residents don't have enough status to play this game successfully. The resident therapist cannot hope to force a hand that has little to give. The resident administrator is in a weak position in relation to the resident therapist because of the weakness of the authority position (therapeutic triad T-I in figure 3). Triad T-I is out of balance because the resident administrator tends to be less effective as a high-status authority with his or her ward patient than the resident therapist is as the same patient's high-status friend. This fact calls for specification of some structural properties of the two activity systems.

Dual Leadership in the Triad

The dynamics involved in the relation between the two residents who independently treat the same patient provide the opportunity to examine once more Etzioni's theory of dual leadership.[3] It will be remembered from chapter 3 that Etzioni believes that both types of authority figures, the supportive and the instrumental, are needed in every type of organization. In this respect his theory is similar to that of Freilich concerning the natural triad, derived from the model of the Tikopian kinship system, according to which a low-status subordinate has a high-status friend, like an uncle, and a high-status authority, like a father.[4] But Etzioni adds the further point that for such dual leadership to be effective, the relative importance of these high-status role-partners must vary according to the organization's goal, so that the superiority of the desired kind of leadership is established. Thus, says Etzioni, in organizations that produce goods and services, the instrumental leader must be stronger than the supportive leader. In contrast, in organizations that produce "growth"—that is, personality change—priority must be given to the supportive leader. Such priority can be established by giving higher rank or more prestige to the leader who is more important for implementing the organization's goal.

In the analysis of the ideal-type of natural triad in the previous chapter, it was shown that if Etzioni's model were put into effect at O'Brien, it would so weaken the status of the instrumental leader as to destroy the balance of the therapeutic triad. This would happen precisely because the goal of the organization is personality growth, not in spite of that fact. For it is this goal that makes psychotherapy such a highly valued activity. If the status of the status occupant who puts this value into practice were enhanced through high rank or other prestige symbols, he or she would gain such clearcut superiority over the instrumental leader that the latter would be deprived of meaningful rewards and in addition would hardly be regarded by patients as a high-status authority. Yet, without such high-status authority the principle of dual leadership would be significantly weakened.

The reasoning suggesting that Etzioni's model of status inequality between the patient's high-status role-partners cannot work by assigning higher prestige or rank to the supportive leader gains support from the foregoing analysis of triad T-I (figure 3). Although at first sight the shared status of residency puts the patient's high-status role-partners on an equal footing, the small measure of authority vested in the resident administrator deprives the latter of the compensating resource for matching the strength of the resident therapist in the highly valued activity of psychotherapy. Hence, this triad does correspond to the Etzioni model, in which superiority is given to the supportive leader. But it is in a state of imbalance which can be rectified only through the introduction of another high-status role-partner, who redresses the balance with decision-making power. This is why the patient's ward administrator has to be on the scene.

It could be objected that the foregoing analysis does not apply to those resident administrators to whom more authority has been delegated by their status superiors. In this case, it would be argued, the assistant administrator would enter the scene and negotiate with the resident therapist concerning issues of interest to both in regard to their common patient.

To be sure, in this case the resident administrator would be somewhat more active in conferring with a status equal who gives therapy to the ward patient. Yet, further analysis will show that no matter how much authority is delegated to the resident on the ward, he or she would still not be strong enough in triad T-I (figure 3) to maintain the triadic balance.

There is another reason for a felt need for authoritative watchfulness of the therapist-patient relationship. Not only does an administrator have structured interest in the course of therapy, but the triad involving the two psychiatrists and their common patient is vulnerable because the patient-therapist relationship is potentially so much stronger and more positive than the patient's relationship with the administrator. The privacy, regularity, and social isolation of the therapist-patient relationship are likely to increase sentiments between these two members of the triad.[5] The therapeutic alliance, which is the normative and consensual definition of this dyadic relationship, is ever in danger of turning into a coalition,[6] which would threaten to destroy the therapeutic triad. Therefore, the high-status authority must be powerful enough to prevent such a coalition.

The alliance between therapist and patient represents the only coalition that is always potentially present in this triadic arrangement. The resident explains: "If I know that a patient doesn't want me to communicate with the administrator, I don't. Some patients like me to, some don't. Sometimes they say that if the therapist communicates with the administrator, they can be understood better. In those cases you communicate more."

Applying Caplow's reasoning about the possibilities for forming coalitions in a triad in which two members are strong and one is weak to Freilich's theory of the natural triad, the following coalitions are possible in the resident's therapeutic triad: (1) The superior members form a coalition with each other and thereby maintain and strengthen their own superiority over the patient. (2) One of the two superior members enters a coalition with the weaker member. That is, either the resident administrator or the resident therapist forms an alliance with the patient. This solution Caplow calls "revolutionary" in that it would upset the organizational power structure.[7]

The first solution is indeed conservative, as Caplow calls it, because an alliance between those who have authority over the patient maintains the power structure. Yet, it does so at the risk of subverting the value system and therefore can be used only rarely. It will be remembered that there are instances of such alliances when a patient is said to have "manipulated his psychiatrists." Indeed, the solution to such alleged "manipulation"—that is, alliance between the two psychiatrists against the patient—weakens if it does not destroy the therapeutic alliance between therapist and patient, who is made to feel that the high-status friend can no longer be trusted. Without therapeutic alliance, however, there can be no psychotherapy, and this we know to be the highest shared value at O'Brien. Therefore, a coalition between a patient's two psychiatrists is rare and, if it happens, of short duration. Conservative as it is, it violates the common value of therapeutic alliance between therapist and patient.

Solution 2, in which the weak member of the triad forms an alliance with one of its stronger members, is indeed subversive of the system. Of the two possibilities, the one in which the patient becomes an ally of the resident administrator is the least likely. It could happen only if the assistant administrator had something to offer the patient, such as privileges and freedom from restrictions. This, however, would fail to provide the patient with the safety on which the therapist relies for the supportive activity (irrespective of the fact that the assistant administrator would also deviate from the hospital's definition of how commitment to the community and patients' families should be discharged). Simply stated, the resident administrator would get into trouble. Trouble would also arise if a resident administrator were to establish a coalition with the patient by engaging in a clear-cut "supportive" relationship, because he or she would thus destroy the division of labor of the natural triad.

Such a coalition would violate the normative injunction that patients not be encouraged to reveal their inner dispositions to anybody but their therapists lest the therapeutic relationship be "diluted," in O'Brien's vernacular. It is believed that patients are less likely to open themselves up to their therapists if other role-partners encourage them to do so. One resident told how things can be made difficult for the therapist if therapy is "sabotaged" in this way "and you can't help it." He explained upon being probed: "I know one resident who had a patient on the ward and [gave him] one- or two-hour interviews a week, and got involved with the patient, and was very proud because now all the patient had to do was go to the therapist once for the final interpretation, and I have seen him blow up these episodes." We recognize behind the norm that the assistant administrator not get too "involved with the patient" a means of protecting the relationship between patient and psychotherapist— that is, a desire not to threaten the balance of the therapeutic triad, in which only one of the two authority holders is supposed to elicit and support expressive behavior.

Coalition between the therapist and the patient is more likely to occur because the therapist has the resource for it, thanks to the therapeutic alliance between them. This is contrary to Caplow's prediction that such a coalition is unlikely because the stronger partner does not "need" alliance with the weaker one.[8] In examining the sources of potential coalitions in the triad, it is not sufficient to rely on the variable of the role-partners' "strength" in general. "Strength" is too easily construed as deriving from a position of power. Other variables—for example, "trust" as a structural element of a relationship—may determine the formation of temporary alliances. Although it would seem that the resident therapist does not really need coalition with a patient for the sake of strengthening authority, it should be remembered that the therapist often is interested in weakening the administrative system. He or she may well want to use a patient as leverage in a struggle with an administrator. There are times when professional loyalty to the patient creates antagonism to the administrative system. Conversely, the patient may want to enlist the therapist's help and may actually succeed in winning his or her support against the administrator.

The therapeutic alliance between therapist and patient is in constant danger of becoming a coalition against the administrative system. It is the ward administrator who is most interested in preventing this. All agree that the therapeutic alliance should be a means of helping patients bring some order into their fantasies and attitudes so that these can be mobilized effectively for strengthening instrumental behavior. But if the therapeutic alliance turns into a coalition that threatens the effectiveness of the instrumental leadership, sanctions will be used against the patient, such as the accusation of "manipulating the psychiatrists," or against the therapist, by accusing him or her of "countertransference" (that is, of letting personal feelings determine the relationship with the patient).

The administrator is the third party who, as Caplow points out, "monitors relationships on behalf of the larger social system, maintaining a link between social norms and private relationships." A coalition between therapist and patient, which is endemic in the therapeutic alliance, would not only impinge upon the interests vested in the administrative system but would also threaten the effectiveness of the therapeutic triad by weakening the authority of the instrumental leader. All partners have an interest in preventing this from happening. Hence, sanctions must be available against such a coalition, but these could not be applied by residents, even if all authority over ward patients were delegated to them. This is because the assistant administrator's possible authority over ward patients would not extend to a status equal. A resident has no access to effective sanctions against another resident and is therefore too weak to break or offset the coalition. Although administrators have no direct authority over the resident therapists either, they have enough influence in the system because of their higher organizational and professional status.

Further, the available sanctions are dangerous tools that are best kept out of the hands of residents. By the accusation of "manipulation," the therapist-patient coalition is broken, but it is replaced by a coalition between the patient's high-status role-partners. Yet, we have seen that such a coalition (solution 1) is subversive of the value system in that it threatens the therapeutic alliance and hence could be as destructive as the coalition between therapist and patient, which it is intended to break up. It is no wonder that all psychiatrists in the hospital get very upset if they come to believe that a patient has "manipulated his psychiatrists." In simple parlance, a resident is not strong enough as an authority holder on the ward, not only because of insufficient experience to deal autonomously with very sick patients but also because of insufficient experience and lack of sufficient stature to help prevent a coalition against him- or herself between the psychotherapist and the patient.

Hence, it is useful that the coalition between the patient's psychiatrists be short-lived. This points to another reason for the limitation of the resident administrator's power: if the coalition is between the resident therapist and the administrator, it is likely to be transitional because of the status difference between them. A coalition between two residents, who have much in common in their student status, would be more difficult to dissolve.

It now turns out that in addition to the mechanisms that were shown to be at work in the natural triad, there is an additional one that Freilich fails to mention. For not only does the high-status friend check the power of the high-status authority; conversely, it now turns out, the high-status authority must check the autonomy of the high-status friend. This is why Etzioni's model, in which more power would be assigned to the latter, is likely not to be effective. Contrary to Etzioni's hypothesis, the instrumental leader must have enough authority or status to have leverage against a possible coalition between the subordinate and the expressive leader.

A resident does not have enough authority or status to provide such leadership. Moreover, it turns out that residents on a ward find themselves in a position of structural ambivalence in relation to the resident therapists.

Structural Ambivalence, Avoidance, and Coalition

Not only is the resident administrator too weak to be a full-fledged partner for the resident therapist, but he or she is also interested in withdrawing from the relationship. This is because of the cross-pressures the resident administrator faces in relation to both the status superior on the ward and the status equal in the therapeutic triad. The fact that the resident administrator is involved in both triad T-I and triad T-III (figure 3) calls attention to an important property of the pentad, which consists in making one status occupant a member of two different triads. This is a convenient conceptualization in searching for structural sources of sociological ambivalence. Indeed, further analysis will show that such an interstitial position is likely to become associated with contradictory expectations stemming from the *same* role-partners in the various triadic sets.

In examining the structural sources of instability in multiple relationships, Merton makes the point, as I read him, not merely that a status occupant has several role-partners whose expectations may be incompatible or contradictory, but that the relations between these role-partners exist by virtue of their common interest in *several* others.[9] That is, the same role-partners relate to one another in different constellations, which may call forth different and incompatible expectations. A neighbor who is my friend is also the father of a youngster who fights with my child, and his brother is my student. My relation with my neighbor is chummy in the first instance, hostile in the second, and professionally friendly in the third. [10]

The role of schoolteacher provides a convenient example. By virtue of relating to pupils, the teacher also relates to the principal of the school. They may disagree about what is best for pupils, and the conflict that develops gains strength from two sources: the tension generated by the principal's exercise of authority, and the teacher's knowledge that other teachers expect solidarity with them in their common defense of their interests against the status superior. But consider the hypothetical case of a pupil's parent, to whom both the principal and this teacher relate because of their common interest in the pupil, who tries to influence the conduct of the school's and the classroom's affairs. This time, solidarity is likely to develop between teacher and principal because of their common antagonism to a parent who threatens their academic freedom.

There are, of course, other possibilities: In their antagonism to each other, teacher or principal may welcome an alliance with the parent for the purpose of gaining strength in the conflict with the other. Or the teacher, caught in the cross-pressure between expected solidarity with and expected antagonism toward the principal, may decide to sever the relationship and find another job. Whatever the outcome, the relationship is determined not only by the constellation of principal, teacher, and parent but also by the way in which this constellation impinges on another one.

The teacher who is expected by colleagues not to be too friendly with the principal lest this interfere with the solidarity expected to prevail among peers is expected by the principal, and by peers as well, to show solidarity with the status superior in defending the faculty's autonomy against what is considered to be an intruder from the "outside." It is this overlap of relationships between role-partners in different constellations that creates conditions of sociological ambivalence, where contradictory norms or expectations face the status occupants.

In order to apply this reasoning to the triads involving residents in their therapeutic network, it is useful to turn once more to Freilich's theory of the natural triad. Freilich points out, on the basis of Fritz Heider's theory of sentimental congruence, [11] that for the triad to remain in balance either all relationships must be positive or each negative relation must be balanced by another negative one or two negative relations must be balanced by a third, positive one. [12] For example, if there are negative feelings between father and son, the existence of positive feelings between uncle and nephew creates negative sentiments between father and uncle; in turn, negative feelings between father and uncle create a positive bond between

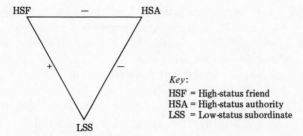

Key:
HSF = High-status friend
HSA = High-status authority
LSS = Low-status subordinate

Figure 4. Positive and negative sentiments in the natural triad

uncle and nephew. That is, in the natural triad, since the high-status friend supports the low-status subordinate whom the high-status authority disciplines, negative feelings can be expected to arise between the two high-status leaders (figure 4). This, it will be remembered from chapter 3, is indeed the case: the psychotherapist and the administrator tend to develop conflicts between themselves by virtue of their common but different relations with their patient. In the case discussed here, negative feelings can be expected to develop between Rt and Ra in triad T-I (figure 5).

However, this relationship between the two residents has other components that derive from the relationship of administrator, assistant administrator, and resident therapist. The properties of this triad can be inferred from the others. We already know that in T-I, negative feelings are likely to exist between the resident therapist (Rt) and the assistant administrator (Ra) as a result of their common but different relations with the patient (P). We must now add that negative feelings are likely to arise as well between the resident therapist and the patient's administrator (T-II), also because of their common and different relations with the same patient. If these two minus signs are transposed onto T-III, it can be predicted that the two negative relationships—that is, the one between the resident therapist and the administrator, and the one between the resident

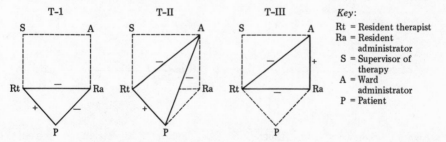

Key:
Rt = Resident therapist
Ra = Resident administrator
S = Supervisor of therapy
A = Ward administrator
P = Patient

Figure 5. Positive and negative sentiments in three triads

therapist and the resident administrator—will be balanced by positive sentiments between the administrator and the resident administrator. This stands to reason, since the administrator and the assistant share concerns about how their common ward patient is doing in therapy; hence solidarity is likely to develop between them in their common concern about the patient's therapist.

However, there are also negative sentiments between the resident administrator and the administrator, because of the administrator's exercise of authority. Remembering that the resident therapist also has reason to develop negative sentiments in regard to the administrator (T-II, figure 5), we can expect that the two residents will develop positive sentiments toward each other in their common antagonism to the ward administrator. This is, of course, the familiar situation where two status inferiors to the same superordinate develop solidarity with each other (figure 6).

If now the sentiments in T-III in figure 5 are compared with the sentiments in T—III in figure 6, it turns out that there are both negative and positive relations developing between the two residents; similarly contradictory feelings will develop between the two administrative psychiatrists of unequal status. The resident administrator is under cross-pressure to develop solidarity with the resident therapist against the common authority holder, or solidarity with the latter against the patient's therapist (figure 7). The resident in the role of administrator is even more torn than the resident in the role of therapist, because for the assistant administrator both relations in the triad are ambivalent (figure 7).

Cross-pressures, it is well known, lead to temporary or permanent withdrawal.[13] Caught between contradictory expectations emanating from two role-partners in triad T-III, the resident administra-

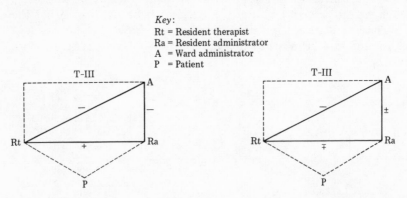

Key:
Rt = Resident therapist
Ra = Resident administrator
A = Ward administrator
P = Patient

Figure 6. Solidarity and conflict in the treatment set

Figure 7. Ambivalent relationships in the treatment set

tor tends to welcome the opportunity to "pass the buck"—indeed, a common maneuver in organizational life—and let the status superior deal with the resident therapist.

It now turns out that it is to the residents' advantage not to have full authority delegated to them by the ward administrators. Not only because of the structural ambivalence arising from their triadic relationships with status superior, status equal, and patient, but generally because they all share interests relating to their common status in the hospital, residents would be caught in a conflict of loyalties between their status equals and the administrators with whom they have common interests in regard to the ward patients. This explains one supervisor's bewilderment about his inability "to do business with residents." He claims that "residents are acting out," that dealing with administrators directly is much more gratifying, and that it is "hard to communicate with residents." With limited authority delegated to them, residents can claim the right to remain detached concerning the issues that arise between administrative and psychotherapeutic psychiatry.

One administrator at the hospital, who had been in his position for a little over a year, could not understand why the resident administrator resisted communicating with his colleague, the resident therapist, in regard to their common patient: "I like to delegate responsibility to my residents. For example, when I have a question concerning a patient's therapy, I tell the resident to get in touch with the therapist. *But this doesn't always work because for some reason, and I don't understand it, the resident doesn't do it, and I have to do it myself*" (emphasis added). This is how a resident, who said "it's hard to communicate with other residents about their patients," described this mutual avoidance: "There were two patients on my hall who had residents as therapists. . . . We had very little contact. We were in a lot of meetings together, we were friends, but we didn't make it a point to talk about these patients."

The ambivalence in the residents' relationships with their role-partners helps explain, at least in part, some surprising findings in the interviews with residents. To the question whether they had "too little, too much, or just enough" responsibility on the ward, it was expected that residents would tend to reply, "too little." This expectation stemmed from the fact that some senior staff had expressed concern about the residents' limited authority on the wards, which, it was felt, deprived them of deserved recognition. Moreover, the residents' low status on the ward is visible to patients and nurses, who periodically challenge their competence and authority. In spite of this, in the interview residents said that they had "just about enough" responsibility.

The authority structure on the ward, which sharply limits the authority of the assistant administrator, helps assure that interaction between the patient's high-status role-partners in the therapeutic triad will be restricted. Since they occupy similarly subordinate status positions in the organization, residents would be easily tempted to exchange much information with each other and to be "chummy" to an extent that would threaten the therapist's therapeutic alliance with the patient. But since the assistant administrator acts toward the ward patient only as an intermediary between the patient and the head of the ward, he or she is entitled to "pass the buck" to the administrator, and in turn the resident therapist is entitled to bypass his agemate and address the administrator directly. Hence, the residents' withdrawal from their ambivalent relationship is legitimized by their low status in the authority structure.

When issues become so important that communication about a patient is felt to be essential, it tends to take place at a higher level in the hierarchy.

The Resident Therapist and His Status Superiors

The triadic relationship between the resident therapist, the patient's administrator, and the assistant administrator (triad T-III) cannot operate effectively as an interactive system because none of its members is interested in including the resident administrator as an active negotiator. We already know that the resident administrator is likely not to be much interested in negotiating with the resident therapist, as a result of the ambivalence in their relationship concerning particular patients. This ambivalence is mutual, of course. The resident therapist also is not strongly motivated to deal with the resident administrator. The resident who said he "didn't make it a point to talk about [his ward] patients" with his friends the therapists added, when he was asked, "How do you feel about this in your capacity as therapist?": "I wouldn't make it a point to say too much. In one case, we talked a lot about the case without really saying anything, there was really no communication. [Smiling]: This was hard work." The ambivalence between them reinforces a tendency not to deal much with each other in regard to their common patient because one of them does not have sufficient resources in authority and power to reciprocate the other partner's resources in knowledge about the patient's inner dispositions.

The third partner in this triad, the administrator of the ward, is not much interested either in having the resident administrator be an active member of the triad because the administrator must keep a watchful eye on the therapist's relation with the patient lest the therapeutic alliance turn into a coalition that threatens the therapeutic triad. For these reasons, the effective therapeutic triad is that between the clinical administrator, the ward patient, and the resident therapist—that is, triad T-II (figure 5).

However, this triad is out of balance because the power relations between the patient's two role-partners are too asymmetrical. Low status and lack of professional experience would lead the resident therapist to give in to the requests of the patient's administrator, without, however, having sufficient status to press requests in turn. Lack of reciprocity between a patient's two psychiatrists introduces a threat to the balance of the triad. In spite of this, the balance can be maintained because the resident therapist can rely on support from the supervisor of therapy. The following report shows both a resident's vulnerability in relation to the patient's administrator and the importance of the supervisor's support.

> I was seeing a patient [in psychotherapy] who for weeks had refused to come. There was a telephone ring and it was the administrator, who said that [the patient's] husband wanted her very much to sign a voluntary. The administrator was there with the husband, and wanted to come in. . . . So I told [the patient] I would see her later on in the afternoon. With that, they walked in. . . .
>
> I got quite angry and quite depressed. . . . I took it up both with my supervisor and the administrator. The positive thing that happened is that I got pretty clear in my mind that nothing from that point on ever would interrupt us.

In all the issues that arise, the supervisor encourages the supervisee to face the patient's administrator squarely. Supervisors of therapy were asked in the interview: "If you are concerned about some administrative decision concerning the patient of a resident whom you supervise, what do you do?" They all said that they prodded the residents: "I suggest that the resident ask some questions [of the administrator], 'Why don't you go and talk with Dr. So-and-so and find out?' " Or, "I tell the resident to tell the administrator that I am concerned; I think that would be the first step." Another one concurs: "What I do is, I suggest that the resident ask some questions. . . . I say, 'Why don't you go to [the administrator] and find out?' "

It will be remembered that one of the functions performed by the high-status friend in the natural triad is that of checking the power of the high-status authority. In the therapeutic triad that involves residents, this could not be done by the resident therapist if it were not for the backing, in the form of encouragement or even prodding, of the supervisor, who in the last resort will step on the scene. One supervisor reports: "If I hadn't backed him [the resident] up, I don't know what would have happened. I am not sure that a resident would be allowed that much independence of action without the backing of a supervisor. He would have to have an awful lot of nerve, which [smiling] would disqualify him as a psychiatrist to start with."

The supervisor is a potential check on the administrator's power not only over the patient but over the resident as well. When asked, "What happens if an administrator asks you to reveal things you don't want to talk about?" a resident did not hesitate to say: "If you have a supervisor, you have a senior person behind you, and you can easily resist what the administrator wants you to say."

Although, as will be remembered, the patient's administrator has no authority over the resident therapist—that is, cannot exercise *legitimate* power—he or she could use power on the basis of clinical authority over the therapy patient and on the basis of professional and hierarchical status in the system if not checked by a colleague of at least equal prestige who sides with the resident.

Yet, in this triad (T-II, figure 5) the administrator is also in an ambiguous situation, being unable to interfere directly in the therapy in spite of being in charge of the patients' program because of the norms that make psychotherapy a privileged activity and because of the medical-ethical injunction that physicians are in charge of their patients. Only the resident's own supervisor can make recommendations in regard to therapy. If need be, an administrator will address the supervisor to gain influence over the resident or to gain some information.

The patient's immediate treatment set, then, consists of the resident therapist, the ward administrator, and the therapist's supervisor (triad T-IV, figure 8). It is in the triad between the resident and the two high-status role partners that most little dramas are played. They can rightfully be called dramas because the actors are governed by fate in the form of social organization, which builds considerable

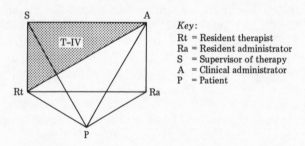

Key:
Rt = Resident therapist
Ra = Resident administrator
S = Supervisor of therapy
A = Clinical administrator
P = Patient

Figure 8. The treatment set in the hierarchy of the pentad

lack of control into all three status positions. The supervisor is an outsider or a top-level hospital psychiatrist who knows that she or he has no say in regard to the management of the resident's patient. The supervisor's main task is to guide the resident and not be too much concerned about the patient's life in the hospital. Administrators, although the sole decision makers concerning patients' management, cannot tamper with patients' psychotherapy; that is, although they must make decisions about medication or about occupational therapy or group therapy, they cannot decide that a patient should discontinue psychotherapy or change the therapist. Moreover, they are deprived of much knowledge about the patient's internal dispositions that would be valuable for making decisions. The resident therapists, by contrast, have the most valuable of all resources—knowledge of their patients' fantasies and inner conflicts. Yet, they cannot use this resource to initiate changes in a patient's status.

This lack of legitimate power or access to resources for shaping the conditions of patients' lives induces all participants in the treatment set to use informal means for mutual influence. Supervisors especially are reluctant to approach administrators directly. One supervisor said that he talked to the administrator "on one occasion." But, he explained, he made use of a prerogative stemming from another relationship: "because I am also supervising him as a student." This administrator, who happened to be a candidate at the Psychoanalytic Institute, by chance had the same supervisor at the institute as one of his patient's resident therapists in the hospital, and the supervisor used this channel to intervene for his resident therapist's patient. This specific instance of handling an issue may be unusual because it is based on a rare coincidence of multiple role playing. Yet, the complex network of professionals in a community surrounding a university-affiliated hospital involves the type of crisscrossing of multiple role relationships that makes it possible to use the influence available in one type of relationship to settle conflicts occurring in another.

In the triad consisting of the resident and the two high-status role-partners, in which the one gives the resident support and the other tries to influence the resident through organizational authority, all three actors have an interest in settling issues informally. This means that all, including the supervisor, have an interest in keeping the supervisor in the background. If the supervisor enters the scene directly, all three actors tend to lose in the bargain. The supervisor has a hard time winning against the administrator if for no other reason than that the hospital must support the authority vested in the administrator. The following report from a supervisor illustrates this:

The person I supervised and I myself, we together had the feeling that certain changes in administrative policy were important. First the resident discussed it with the administrator; and if the administrator didn't feel that it was appropriate, we would sit back and wait for a while, and if then we felt strongly that really there was a need for a change, we requested a consultation with another senior person [from outside the hospital], and I can give you chapter and verse of cases in which the consultant who came in agreed with my version and made it very clear, and nevertheless the administrator refused to implement the recommendation. . . . I spoke, we had a conference, and then I told the consultant that I thought that he was more respected than I am, could he speak to [the psychiatrist-in-chief]. He said to me: "I'm afraid I can't do a thing but I will try." And indeed, it was true, he couldn't.

But an administrator's victory over a supervisor and resident therapist may make matters more difficult, by risking their withdrawal of cooperation in the future. This is what is implied in the manner in which another supervisor concluded a story about a hassle he had: "I didn't win them over, but they could not make a move as long as the therapist says no." Moreover, an administrator has to watch out, after "winning" a case, not to get involved in similar incidents repeatedly, for this would call forth some sanctions from higher authority. And resident therapists also lose credit when issues concerning their professional practice with a patient are being dealt with for them by the two status superiors. Being unable to handle issues casts a shadow on one's professional growth. Once a supervisor and a patient's administrator come into conflict with each other, the resident is left out of the interaction. As one supervisor said, "[the resident] would have surrendered, but because I backed him up, it became my battle against theirs."

When issues reach this point, the therapeutic triad is likely to be paralyzed. The mechanisms that regulate the relations between the patient's psychiatrists can hardly operate any longer. Being, very antagonistic to the administrator, the therapist can hardly help relieve the patient's tension on the ward. And since such antagonism has become manifest through the supervisor's active interference, the therapist is no longer an effective check on the administrator's power. He or she has spent the available currency, so to speak. The check on the administrator's power is effective only as long as it can be held in reserve or used unobtrusively. At the same time, the therapist has lost in the patient's administrator a role-partner from whom benefits can be derived. During the five years of the research, there were no more than five cases that were fought on higher levels, and in each of these the therapeutic triad was dissolved through some maneuver that removed the resident therapist from the field.

When a conflict reaches the top axis of the therapeutic pentad, it has come to a head. Each one of the resident's status superiors can then appeal to status occupants outside the treatment set—by asking for consultation either with some hospital psychiatrist from the top of the hierarchy or with a high-status professional from the community. But all members of the treatment set are interested in avoiding a situation where they have to accept such interference. It would seem that the forces that make for avoidance are stronger than the forces that make for cooperation. When all goes well, there is little incentive for interaction among the residents, and between the residents and their role-partners in the treatment set. Normative injunctions, the balance of the therapeutic triad, and the ambivalence created in the various relationships all seem to press for avoidance. These pressures are stronger than those that encourage interdependence and solidarity within the treatment set.

This raises the question of the source of socially patterned support for a resident's activities and learning at O'Brien.

5

The Training Set

As an agency of socialization, the teaching hospital has two distinct yet related tasks: it has to socialize patients into becoming useful members of the community, and it has to socialize residents into becoming useful members of the profession.

Since residents learn to be psychiatrists by *being* psychiatrists, their learning must be organized around the patients' treatment. Hence, there are parallel elements in the social structure of socialization for both patients and residents. Just as patients have two psychiatrists, one on the ward and one for psychotherapy, residents partake of the two activity systems, and in each of these they receive guidance from specialized status superiors.

The fact that both patients and residents take part in the two activity systems provides structural similarities in regard to the distribution of authority over the "socializees," the differential access to observation of their behavior, and the differential interest status superiors have in their attitudinal involvement. There are, however, important differences in the manner in which the high-status role-partners of patients and residents relate to one another. This should not be surprising, since the socialization of these different status occupants differs in at least one important aspect: patients are expected to change mainly in regard to the integration of their total personality. Residents—and this is the distinctive aspect of *professional* socialization—are expected to develop their functional skills (even if these involve deep psychological commitments for the control of their internal dispositions). While the split between psychotherapy and ward management helps patients differentiate internal dispositions from reality for the purpose of their better integration,

86

for residents the split serves to delimit and define two types of skills.

In respect to their two main tasks, which are the two major skills residents are trained in, their most important role-partners are the clinical administrator of the ward on which they serve and the supervisor of therapy. Residents relate to them in a manner reminiscent of the patients' relationships. Like the patients, each resident relates to two significant authority holders: the clinical administrator, who focuses mainly on the details of ward life and its patients and is concerned with the manner in which the resident handles them; and the supervisor of therapy, who focuses on the details of a patient's internal personality dynamics and is concerned with the manner in which the resident's own attitudes help strengthen predispositions for coping with the patient's attitudes.

These role-partners are here called *significant* because they have direct responsibility for the residents' training and interact with them more frequently, more regularly, and in a more sustained fashion than any other role-partners. They must be distinguished from other role-partners among the upper-status psychiatrists of the hospital who, under the leadership of the psychiatrist-in-chief and the director of residency training, are involved with residents because they play a part in planning residency programs or conducting academic exercises. They know the residents, participate in postadmission interviews and in periodic evaluation, and judge performance according to their expectations of appropriate professional conduct. Hence, they are part of the residents' training set, but they are not expected to interact with them daily or weekly on an individual basis. However, these high-status role-partners also take some residents in supervision of psychotherapy, and in their capacity as supervisors some of them become *significant* role-partners of some individual residents.

The significant role-partners must also be distinguished from the treatment set, described in the previous chapter. This, it will be remembered, consists of those role-partners who are interested in residents because of their involvement with the residents' *patients*. By virtue of treating a patient in psychotherapy, a resident is involved with this patient's clinical administrator and assistant administrator. Conversely, as an assistant administrator, the resident is involved with the ward patient's psychotherapists. These relationships are focused on the treatment of patients, not the training of residents.

The Training Set

Most of the residents' time and their physical and emotional energy is invested in work that puts them under the guidance of their significant role-partners, the supervisor of therapy and the clinical administrator. This is because O'Brien concentrates its training, as well as its treatment of patients, mainly on psychotherapy and milieu therapy.

As has been noted, supervisors of therapy are selected from among some prestigious practitioners outside the hospital and those high-status psychiatrists within the hospital who usually do not do clinical administration. Below them in rank are the clinical administrators, all of whom belong to the staff (although they may and usually do have some private patients on the outside), and who can best be described as occupying a middle status position in the hospital.

Although clinical administrators are sometimes referred to as "preceptors," residents continue to call them "my administrator," because the more salient part of this role is to "administer"—that is, to deal with ward patients and personnel. The administrator's role is more akin to that of manager than to that of teacher. Administrators are involved with residents by virtue of their responsibility for the ward, which must be their primary concern, and only secondarily by virtue of their interest in the resident's professional progress. The administrators have authority over the residents on their wards, according to the principle of bureaucratic organization, although they differ in regard to the amount of authority they delegate to their assistants.

Everybody on the ward is highly observable to most participants. The resident observes the administrator in many of his or her dealings with patients, nurses, and patients' relatives and therefore has the opportunity to learn the principles of professional behavior through direct contact. In turn, much of the resident's behavior on the ward is open to observation by most of the role-partners there. During rounds, the administrator, resident, head nurse, and patient confer with one another. Staff meetings on the wards and hall meetings with patients usually include all psychiatric and nursing staff. Rounds, meetings, and the coordination of activities between the administrator and the assistant expose residents to the values as well as to the scrutiny of the administrators, who more than anyone else on the wards are in a position to guide and shape the residents' behavior.

In contrast to ward administrators, supervisors of therapy do not give residents instructions about how to behave with their patients. They may make recommendations and suggestions but mainly they help the residents develop the style that will best establish and improve rapport with patients.

The resident's relation with the supervisor is dyadic; that is, in contrast to the relation with the ward administration it is insulated from observability by staff and patients. The supervisor never sees the resident conduct psychotherapy. Guidance proceeds on the basis of the resident's own reports. The relationship is considered a private one, so much so that residents report in the interviews that they are not likely to speak to others about the content of their supervisory sessions.[1] This need for privacy is, as Merton has noted, "the individual counterpart to the functional requirement of social structure" that insulation from observability be provided.[2] Not only is such exemption from knowledge by others patterned after the therapist's own relationship with patients, it is similar to professional relationships generally, when during conferences with a client the professional's interest is focused on the client only, assuring the latter the measure of immunity this relationship requires. The supervisor is interested mainly in the resident and is concerned with the resident's patient only by virtue of his or her involvement with the resident as a therapist. The supervisor's conduct in relation to the resident is governed by an etiquette derived from the ethic of colleagueship in the medical and academic professions, in which a teacher's demeanor with an advanced student is one of support of and respect for a junior colleague. As one supervisor explained: "As an older person, I would like to help the other person be able to do the kind of work that I think is worthwhile, that I like." This concern for a junior colleague leads to a protective attitude, which the same supervisor expresses when she says, "The most difficult thing for residents is not to become too quickly discouraged. . . . I reassure them and back them up."

The distinction between the administrator as authority holder and the supervisor as supportive teacher refers to their structural positions, not to personal manners or character. It is useful to remember that *social roles*, not persons, are being analyzed here. Individual supervisors give some residents "a hard time," and some administrators are gentle, kind, polite, and supportive; in some measure they all are, and many take pride in teaching the residents many skills. Moreover, administrators also obey the ethic of the medical profession in relating to young psychiatrists. The point here is that the structural requirements of the organization put different demands on people occupying different positions. The exercise of authority on the ward is a property of the social structure, not of the persons running the wards. This was explained by one administrator, who was widely considered one of the best psychiatrists, well liked by both staff and patients, and who adopted a democratic style in running his ward. He explained, "With our administrator-resident system, we can't really let the resident take over."

The essential point concerning the distinction between these two high-status role-partners is that the two activity systems differ according to the demands put on the residents' involvement with internal dispositions. It will be remembered from chapter 3 that behavioral and attitudinal conformity are different trends of adaptation and that social systems differ in the extent to which authority holders expect more of one or of the other type. The administrator's interest in the resident is governed mainly by instrumental considerations and concern with the immediate consequences of the resident's actions. Consequently, the interest is mainly in the details of the resident's *behavior*. The supervisor of therapy, in contrast, is interested in having the resident "understand a patient's message," as one supervisor put it. "Understanding," we know from Weber, Mead, and Piaget,[3] consists of the ability to put oneself, in imagination, in the position of the other person, by "taking the attitude of the other player in the game" (Mead). What the residents have to learn, said one supervisor, is "to have a capacity for empathy." In daily social interaction, this is more or less successfully achieved because interacting persons, especially if they are members of a similar culture, tend to share the norms and premises that govern communication. But it is not so easily achieved with patients who have been hospitalized precisely because their ability to "understand" and "be understood" has broken down within their own culture. It therefore takes a special ability to detach one's mind from learned communication patterns in order to understand what has been called "autistic" language, verbal or nonverbal, and to make sure to be understood in turn. This interchange tends to help re-establish a normative basis, which sickness has disrupted. It is the detachment from hitherto internalized dispositions in regard to patterns of communication that the supervisor is supposed to help bring about in the supervisee.

Hence, supervisors are more interested in the residents' *attitudes* as these affect behavior with therapy patients. The supervisors supply the support the residents need to become free of anxieties so that strongly embedded dispositions or internal conflicts will not interfere with their relationships with their patients. For example, one supervisor, commenting on a supervisee, said: "The most difficult thing for [this resident] has been to be free with the patient and not be encumbered by his own thinking or speculations, or obsessive tendencies . . . and to give the patient a reasonable amount of warmth without feeling that he is seducing the patient."

The difference between the demands made in their two activities was expressed by the residents in answer to an open-ended question about their preferences. "I guess I consider psychotherapy . . . a more intricate relationship which is more intense," one resident said. Another explained that administration "is more superficial; it is more reality-oriented." Another resident was more specific: "I think one can do administration on the basis of one's general skills with people. . . . Psychotherapy takes much more training, thought, sensitivity, and patience."

In general, where demands are made on one's internal dispositions, there is a different exercise of authority over that person and different access to observation of his or her behavior than where behavioral conformity is required. It would seem that in social systems generally, attitudinal conformity is brought about with much less exercise of direct authority and much less direct observation of behavior than behavioral conformity. The latter tends to be enforced through the direct exercise of authority and through the detailed observation of behavior. To be sure, there are always *some* authority and *some* observation involved, even where internal dispositions are being relied on, and there is also some relaxation of authority and observation, even where close behavioral adherence to prescriptions is required. The point here is merely one of relative emphasis and serves to highlight the structural circumstance that attitudinal and behavioral conformity depend on different properties.[4] Indeed, it should not be surprising that where the immediate consequences of behavior are at stake, these gain salience over internal commitments, and more direct social control is required; and this is accomplished through observation and the exercise of authority over details of behavior. However, such explicit social control leaves less room for the exercise of "thought, sensitivity, and patience," in the words of the quoted resident. Hence, where these qualities have primacy, it is a person's own internal dispositions rather than externally derived authority based on observation that must control behavior.

In roles in which behavior cannot be so easily observed, as in the case of the physician in private practice[5] or, even more, the psychiatrist during the therapeutic hour, which precludes even the presence of a nurse, or the priest within the confessional, the demands on attitudinal conformity—that is, on *inner* acceptance of the values and norms of the particular social system—will be greater, and the demands for living up to specified behavior will be less exacting. This applies also to residents who are in training for psychotherapy. One supervisor explained:

I think it isn't so important *what one does* as long as one knows why one does it and as long as it is being done for a constructive therapeutic purpose. . . . It isn't *what you do*, in my opinion, that is essential, it is whether you know why you do it. . . . I wonder whether it is their skills especially that improve [in residency] . . . ; there is a kind of permeation of psychodynamic principles [emphasis added].

In contrast, people who operate "in the glare of the spotlight"—as politicians, for example—are compensated for having to take into account in their pronouncements the widely differing publics to which they must address themselves[6] by the fact that their attitudinal commitments are under less scrutiny.[7] This is also true for residents in clinical administration, in which people in widely different social positions have to be dealt with. The fact that there is little need for strong internal involvement compensates for this difficult task. Indeed, one of the things residents consider "most difficult" in clinical administration is "dealing with a large number of different people," but many find clinical administration easier than psychotherapy because their inner dispositions are less deeply involved. They say, "It takes less energy to control the situation," it is "less emotionally loaded for the doctor," or "it gives you the less traumatic and more tolerable way of getting some sophistication, you're less involved."

On the ward, residents could hardly bear the burden of involving their inner dispositions in all their relationships, visible as the residents there are to the patients, the nursing staff, and the administrator. They have to take account of widely differing expectations—for example, being careful not to interfere with the authority of a nurse or aide when dealing with a patient—and they are able to handle the situation more easily by not having their attitudes strongly scrutinized. In contrast to their relationship with the supervisor of therapy, where their attitudes are being scrutinized, the burden of this involvement is alleviated by the absence of exercise of authority and by insulation from observation by any other role-partners.[8]

Hence, the difference in the residents' involvement in the two activity systems, and correlatively the difference in the type of interest of the two significant role-partners, is accompanied by a differentiated structure of authority and by differential observability of behavior. As in the relationships between the patient and the two psychiatrists, there is a subtle distribution of mechanisms of control between the two significant role-partners: authority and observation are exercised over behavioral adaptation, while attitudinal involvement remains relatively free of direct interference from authority and observability. The administrator, who exercises authority over the resident at the same time as observing behavior, does not have much access to the revelation of the resident's inner dispositions. The supervisor, in contrast, who *is* concerned with the resident's inner dispositions, does not exercise power of command or observe the resident's behavior with the patient. The supervisor monitors rather than controls.

The analytical procedure that was pursued in an earlier chapter leads to the question of what benefits residents derive from adapting their behavior to the demands of the two activity systems. It turns out that they derive advantages similar to those enjoyed by patients. On the ward, residents learn to orient themselves toward reality and to the control of complex situations involving both unpredictable behavior and the environment: "what to do with a patient when he goes psychotic," "learning how to handle psychotic patients from a practical point of view," "dealing with [that patient's] family and his finances and all this junk," "to know ... the world of mental illness and families and communities and how people get into things the way they do," and "giving the patient antibiotics, you still have to know about feeding the patient and giving sleep medication, and all sorts of less attractive things." One resident was able to formulate concretely the advantage derived from the administrator: "I've seen a skilled administrator read the patient's behavior and requests very efficiently and sort of pinpoint some of the patient's trouble spots in life and maladaptations in life, and be able to concretely point these out to the patient."

Residents usually appreciate learning to exercise their judgment about reality situations. It is important, one of them volunteered, "for a psychiatrist to know ... what is healthy and what is unhealthy behavior before he gets very involved with fantasies and projections and identifications and the whole spectrum of intrapsychic problems," thus echoing one of his peers, who said that clinical administration "is very valuable because in psychotherapy you can get lost in unconscious fantasies and just forget that realities exist."

While residents receive guidance in reality orientation concerning problems of management and social environment from administrators, they gain support for overcoming their anxieties and general insecurities from supervisors. In the words of one supervisor: "There is anxiety, 'have they got everything and what will their supervisor say?' I say, 'you don't have to find out everything as long as you have given yourself the opportunity ... and can justify for yourself why you don't know.' "

This division of labor between the clinical administrator and the supervisor of therapy reminds us once more of the Parsons-Bales theory of dual leadership and Freilich's theory of the natural triad which were used in the analysis of the therapeutic triad: both an instrumental leader in the person of a high-status authority and an expressive leader in the person of a high-status friend are involved in the socialization of a patient. However, the similarity between residents and patients in patterns of socialization ends here. For whereas the patients' high-status role-partners are much interested in each other's work and perform reciprocal services at the same time that they engage in avoidance, conflict, and restricted interaction, the residents' significant role-partners do not have to relate to each other in spite of the fact that both are interested in the same resident.

The reason for this separation is that these two role-partners are in charge of two different and unrelated activities. An administrator is not much interested in the development of the resident's therapeutic skills, nor does the supervisor of therapy care whether the resident therapist learns to manage the daily lives of patients. Since the resident's psychotherapy patients are not on the administrator's ward, the administrator has no reason to be concerned about the treatment of patients for whom he or she is not responsible; similarly, since the resident therapist does not have a hand in managing the daily life of the therapy patients, supervisors have no interest in this part of a resident's activity.

Hence, the resident's nuclear role-set is unlike the patient's in that it is not a natural triad, in Freilich's conceptualization. Rather, the resident's relations with the two high-status role-partners are parallel in the strict sense of the term: the two have no reason ever to meet. Figure 9 illustrates these relationships.

The demands emanating from the two high-status role-partners concern different types of involvement and activities, and these are segregated in time and space. This helps residents handle whatever dilemma they may experience when they have to apply different criteria for behavior in the two activity systems. One resident explained: "I use different criteria as a therapist than as an administrator. For example, regarding sexual acting out, as a therapist, I

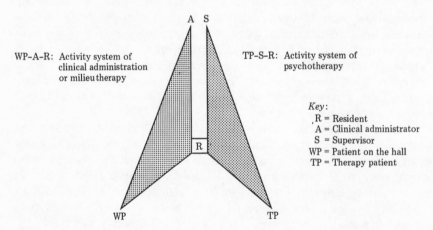

WP-A-R: Activity system of clinical administration or milieu therapy

TP-S-R: Activity system of psychotherapy

Key:
 R = Resident
 A = Clinical administrator
 S = Supervisor
WP = Patient on the hall
TP = Therapy patient

Figure 9. The two activity systems of psychotherapy and ward psychiatry

might not communicate this to the administrator. . . . A therapist must keep it confidential. If you discover a patient smoking on the hall, you are more strict." The contradictory expectations facing residents in these two activity systems do, of course, create some conflict, as this same resident observes when he adds: "I feel a bit disturbed as an administrator and I begin to have doubts how strict I should be." Yet, the fact that the administrator on the ward and the supervisor of therapy are interested in different patients and in different types of tasks alleviates the conflict. Moreover, the fact that on the ward the administrator has the final authority helps relieve the resident of guilt.

It is useful for the resident to relate to different authority holders in the two systems. If the same psychiatrist were in charge of supervising both a resident's psychotherapy and his or her work on the ward, the resident would be put in a situation of *structural ambivalence* by being subject to contradictory demands.

It now becomes understandable why hospital psychiatrists of high rank who supervise residents in their psychotherapy do not engage in ward administration. At one time at O'Brien, a number of high-status psychiatrists did administer some wards and also acted as supervisors. But they gradually withdrew from clinical administration until no overlap remained. Even during the time when staff psychiatrists played this dual role, only once was it performed in relation to the same resident. This occasion affords a telling example of the dysfunctional aspect of such an arrangement. A resident who had a remarkably good relationship with her supervisor became an assistant administrator on the ward which the same supervisor administered. The ambivalence that developed from the circumstance that the same person was both a high-status friend and a high-status authority led to rupture of the relationship. If the two roles are divided, there is no functional necessity for either of the role-partners to be informed of the resident's behavior in the other system.

Given the complete separation between the two high-status role-partners, the mechanisms that Freilich identifies as operating in the natural triad must be re-examined. In his analysis, it will be remembered, these mechanisms derive from the fact that the two high-status role-partners relate to each other. In the natural triad, as exemplified by the relation between the patient and the two psychiatrists, the two high-status role-partners derive benefits from each other; the high-status friend helps relieve the tension created by the high-status authority and also helps check the latter's power over the status occupant. Conflict is endemic in the relationship between these two authority holders at the same time that interaction between them, whether antagonistic or friendly, must be limited.

It could be said that the first two mechanisms—relief of tension and provision of mutual benefit—operate to some extent even though the two authority holders do not interact. In some sense administrator and supervisor each help to relieve the tension created in the other activity system by providing the opportunity for a different type of involvement. Such tension relief, if it occurs, would be due simply to a change in pace. This is not much more than saying that variation in one's involvement in work is less tiring than repetition, and residents indeed acknowledge this. Asked whether it is difficult to be trained in the two areas of psychiatry at the same time, one resident said: "I think it provides a very useful balance for one's own stability to be able to do both things. . . . I find it restful." Another replied: "Administration alone after a while would get very dull, and therapy alone . . . would be too tiring."

In providing a change of pace, each of the two role-partners may help make the resident more fit for the other task, and in this indirect way they may each help relieve some tension generated in the other system. This resembles the type of relief that vacation provides from work, or work provides from too much vacation. Yet, although changes in routine are welcome, the benefits bestowed by each of the two systems do not directly help modify the one or the other, as is the case in the therapeutic triad. There, it will be remembered, the therapist helps take the edge off the hostility a patient experiences on the ward in regard to the administrator; and the administrator, by providing the necessary safety precautions, helps relieve the therapist of worries that would interfere with the therapeutic alliance with the patient.

Whatever each of the resident's activity systems gains from the change of pace is due to their co-existence, not to their interdependence. And it is for this reason that the supervisor cannot check the administrator's power over the resident and that supervisor and administrator have no occasion either to enter into conflict or to cooperate with each other. Hence there is no need for the operation of mechanisms of avoidance between the significant high-status role-partners, nor can the resident manipulate these two role-partners to any advantage, nor will they in turn attempt to shape his or her behavior through some temporary alliance between them.

Residents lack a high-status friend on the ward, and they lack a taskmaster in conducting psychotherapy. Although some administrators may attempt to give support, and some supervisors may be more direct than others when counseling their residents, the extent to which this happens depends on the individual inclinations of these high-status role-partners; it is not rooted in the social structure.

As far as the residents' exposure to contradictory expectations is concerned, the ward situation is more critical than psychotherapy. The resident, moreover, discusses only one patient with a supervisor. The role-set that is involved in a patient's psychotherapy is therefore simple compared to the complex role-set on the ward. There residents deal with many patients as well as with personnel, and their manner of dealing is observable by role-partners occupying different status positions in the ward structure. In this more difficult situation, residents do not have high-status friends to help them cope with their tasks. They tend to be left to their own resources. One manner of dealing with the contradictory nature of their position on the ward will be discussed in the next chapter.

6
Structural Ambivalence and Patterned Mechanisms of Defense

Psychotherapy and clinical administration differ in the manner in which they allow residents to articulate their dual roles as practitioners and students of psychiatry. It turns out that a resident's student status is more difficult to deal with on the ward than in psychotherapy.

It will be recalled that one source of structural ambivalence for residents is the fact that they are practicing psychiatry while they are learning to become psychiatrists. Patients expect residents to behave like full-fledged professionals; yet, they also use the residents' student status in dealing with their own fears and insecurities by challenging the residents' competence and authority. Whether this is an expression of their fear of not being taken care of properly or of a desire to get back at authority, patients on the wards were heard to say such things as: "You're a nice person to talk to, but you have no authority here anyway, you are no help to me." Similarly, in psychotherapy patients often challenge their resident therapists: "You're only a resident, but I don't mind helping you out in your training."

Before turning to specification of the structural properties that help and those that tend to hinder residents in dealing with their contradictory status, it is important to explore the broader meaning of the patients' challenge. This challenge is not merely personal; it is a questioning of the legitimacy of the resident's status as a psychia-

Special note: Part of this chapter appeared previously under the title "Evasiveness as a Response to Structural Ambivalence" in *Social Science and Medicine* 1 (1967): 203–18, and is reprinted by permission of Pergamon Press, Ltd.

trist. The issue is not a matter of individual ability but of the *right* to treat.

Hence the ambivalence is twice compounded: not only is residency status-ambivalent in that it exposes the status occupant to the contradictory expectations of student and practitioner behavior; in addition, the values underlying the legitimacy of treatment are themselves ambiguous.

Learning through Doing: A Moral Dilemma

Practicing medicine as a means of learning it is a source of ambiguities in *all* teaching hospitals.[1] It poses a moral dilemma for the medical staff generally and creates a role conflict in the younger recruits to the profession. The moral dilemma inherent in a situation where patients are treated by those who are not yet quite able to do so raises in all involved the question of whether patients are being used for the staff's purposes and whether caring for patients is of only secondary importance to those whose main purpose is to teach and learn.[2] Mental hospitals that are affiliated with a university are not immune to this dilemma, which is ever-present in all teaching hospitals. "If it weren't that we have to learn," said one resident in a general teaching hospital, "these patients wouldn't have to go through so many tests; they wouldn't have to give their history three times and wouldn't go through admission procedures three times; first the medical student sees them, then the intern, and then one of us residents. But then, we *are* here to learn."[3]

One means of alleviating social guilt of this kind is by instilling in all house staff the view that "we give patients the best quality of care," "we have the newest treatment techniques available," "at least we don't miss anything when we examine and test them so thoroughly," and "we have a tradition of excellence."[4] Such pride easily becomes a spur for further excellence. It works as a self-fulfilling prophecy in that it is a "public definition of a situation [which] becomes an integral part of [that] situation and thus affects subsequent development."[5]

At O'Brien the senior staff is firmly convinced—and repeatedly transmits this conviction after first stating it to young recruits in orientation speeches at the beginning of residency—that learning and teaching make for better rather than for worse care of patients. Thus a supervisor asserts that "one of the advantages that residents have over the older psychiatrists ... is that they have special interest in learning and so it becomes especially important for them to do well; and I think enthusiasm of youth can sometimes make up for the scope of experience an older person might have." Implicit in this statement is not only that learning makes for better treatment but also that excellence in treatment provides the best learning situation. There is a general commitment to the high value of this conviction. This provides the consensual basis upon which disagreements about treatment and teaching programs are discussed, often fervently, by the director of training and the members of the Residency Education Committee with staff members who feel that they are primarily responsible for the care of patients.

Teaching hospitals also share the academic tradition that learning is an ongoing process throughout life and that one learns from those whom one serves. Everett Hughes tells how Robert Park admonished young instructors in sociology at the University of Chicago: "You will find that each time you leave a classroom, you have learned from your students. If one day you feel you have not learned from them, then it's time for you to stop teaching."[6] A similar opinion was expressed by a second-year resident when he was asked, "How do you feel if your patient says to you, 'I know you are here to learn'?" The resident said, "I would agree with him, he is right, I am only a resident, and every patient I see I learn from, and I *never* want to stop the ability to learn new things."

At the general hospitals where the residents used to be medical students and interns, they learned the importance of giving service through learning and learning through giving service. Some first-year residents at O'Brien, while perhaps not quite sure that their services are valuable at this early stage of their psychiatric career, nevertheless consider combined learning and service a normative expectation. Asked whether he considers his work in the hospital an opportunity to learn or to give service, a second-year resident says: "I would hope that it would be both," and a first-year resident states: "I would say that I look for both." He explains that the ability to give service is part of his self-image as a practitioner: "I would hate to state that I am looking only for the education, I would consider myself a poor physician if I would be looking only for that."

In order to find out whether in the course of their three-year training program residents change their perceptions of what their work in the hospital means to them, they were asked in the interview: "Do you think of psychotherapy as primarily an opportunity to learn psychiatry or primarily as service?" The same question was asked in regard to their work on the ward.

If we distinguish between respondents who said that the psychotherapy they conduct with patients is primarily a part of learning or service and those who say that it is "both," we see that the older residents are more likely than the younger ones to believe that their psychotherapeutic practice serves both learning and service purposes (table 1). At the beginning of residency, respondents are more likely than later to consider psychotherapy primarily an opportunity to learn psychiatry. As the years go by, they decreasingly conceive of conducting psychotherapy as an opportunity to learn and increasingly answer that service and training loom equally large in their conception of their role.

A resident's view that work is primarily an opportunity to learn psychiatry is likely to express some lack of self-confidence, perhaps accompanied by some feeling of guilt about the ability to live up to expectations for the excellence in service that is the mark of a self-respecting professional. Even some older residents, as table 1 shows, express such views, as in the following statement by a third-year resident who was at the training center for his second year: "I look at it primarily as an opportunity to learn psychiatry . . . because at my level of training, if they had somebody else who was really trained, they probably would do better. But on the other hand, I think I have a certain loyalty to my patients." This response betrays both a sense of insecurity about the ability to give service and some need to reassure the interviewer or himself that he is not using patients for his own benefit. The issue, as is implicit in the way the question was asked, is conflictual. If residents see their activities as consisting primarily of "learning," the implication is that they are not fully competent practitioners or that they are using patients for their own advantage. If, however, they feel that they are mainly giving "service," there is the implication that the training center falls

Table 1. Differences in self-perception as "learners" or "servers" in the practice of psychotherapy,* by year of residency

Respondent considers activity:	Year of residency			
	Start of 1st year	*Start of 2d year*	*Start of 3d year*	*End of 3d year*
Primarily learning	39%	25%	29%	17%
Primarily service	15%	25%	18%	14%
Both	46%	50%	53%	69%
N answering	26	44	45	35
No answer	3	5	1	3

*In answer to the question "Do you look upon your psychotherapy with patients primarily as an opportunity to help patients or primarily as an opportunity to learn psychiatry?"

short of its promise, and thus their opinion is critical of the organization. The answer that "both" learning and service are part of their residency experience not only expresses a shared value but also helps deny the dilemma involved in the issue. Thus one third-year resident who flatly answered "both" when queried added: "I'm sorry to be evasive." Another resident clearly shows in his lengthy answer how ambiguous the issue is for him: "Both. They have to be both. This is what you are here for. Also the fascinating business of finding out why they are doing what they are doing, and applying principles of psychotherapy that you know about and seeing what will happen and the whole aspect of learning about psychotherapy, but primarily you are also here to help somebody."

Many residents tend to be unsure of themselves when answering this question, not only because of the moral problems inherent in this issue for all practitioners in teaching hospitals but also because they face a special problem in their dual roles: as students, they believe that they are not, and they know they are not expected to be, fully able to give the best of service; yet, as practitioners in the hospital, the ability to give "primarily service" is the test of both professional competence and growth.

The changes in the residents' perception of their role on the wards are not linear (table 2). Unlike their reported experience in psychotherapy, their view of this work does not progress steadily away from "learning" and toward "learning and serving." The contradictions inherent in residents' learning situations are not only of a moral nature; some contradictions stem from the residents' structural positions in their various activities. It will turn out that the ambiguities

Table 2. Differences in self-perception as "learners" or "servers" in clinical administration,* by year of residency

Respondent considers activity:	Year of residency			
	Start of 1st year	*Start of 2d year*	*Start of 3d year*	*End of 3d year*
Primarily learning	61%	36%	59%	39%
Primarily service	14%	26%	15%	23%
Both	25%	38%	26%	28%
N answering	28	47	41	31
No answer	1	2	5	7

*In answer to the question "Do you look upon your work on the ward primarily as an opportunity to help patients or primarily as an opportunity to learn psychiatry?"

residents encounter in their work on the wards are much more complex in nature than those facing them in psychotherapy.

Learning through Treating: A Contradiction in Status

In "learning through doing," trainees play a double role. Insofar as they are learning, they are students; insofar as they are doing, they act as professionals. Moreover, professional activity is not a mere exercise; they actually enact the role of the professionals they are preparing to become. Hence, they are engaged not only in "learning through doing" but also in "learning through being": the young physician is a psychiatrist to the patients while being an advanced student of psychiatry to the senior staff of the hospital.

We recognize here what Merton has identified as a structural source of instability: the fact that a status occupant has role-partners who are variously located in the social structure and consequently tends to be faced with different or even conflicting expectations.[7] Patients expect young psychiatrists to behave with the assured professional stance that inspires trust. In contrast, the senior staff, who also act as teachers, expect residents to show the humility appropriate in students. In order better to understand this dual role, it is useful to examine the structural circumstances that heighten, and those that lessen, the burden of contradictory expectations.

One way of doing this is to ask how residents propose to deal with concrete situations in which their double role is put to a test and to compare these situations in regard to the structural opportunities they offer for coping with this burden. One such structural opportunity consists in a previously described mechanism at work within the role-set deriving from the circumstance that status occupants are not equally visible to all their role-partners when they carry out the behavior associated with their status.[8] By comparing an activity system that provides insulation from simultaneous observation by several role-partners with one that does not provide this insulation, it will be possible to illustrate both the role-conflict and the attempts to resolve it.

In both activity systems, psychotherapy and ward management, residents are in the roles of both students and practitioners, and in each they have patients and senior psychiatrists as their main role-partners. That is, in both activity systems residents want to live up to the expectations governing their relationships with patients and to those governing their relationships with status superiors. Yet, in psychotherapy they face their two role-partners separately; on the ward, they face them together. In the first situation, interaction with one role-partner is strictly insulated from observation by the other; in the second, no such rigid insulation exists.

In the first situation—that is, under conditions of insulation from observability—the ambiguity of the role can be dealt with more easily: when with the patient, a resident acts as a psychotherapist and when with the supervisor as a student who reports about activities and accepts recommendations. On the ward such separation is much more difficult, if it is possible at all. Whereas the psychotherapeutic relationship is removed from the reality of everyday life, a resident administrator deals with patients within the social context of the whole ward and therefore exposes his or her behavior to the scrutiny of ward personnel, nurses and aides, and the status superior, the clinical administrator. The administrator's judgment bears both on the resident's ability to be a good student and subordinate and on his or her ability to be an authoritative psychiatrist with the ward patients. Thus contradictory expectations emanate from the *same* role-partner. Since the relationship between the clinical administrator and the resident is not limited to that of the dyad, as in the supervisor-psychotherapist relationship, the status superior on the ward cannot limit judgment to bear mainly on the resident's performance as a student, nor can he or she relate to the resident only as a junior colleague. This ambiguity, which is not understood by those involved in the system, finds expression in personal complaints such as the following from a second-year resident: "I don't understand Dr. X [the administrator]. At times he treats me like a flunky, yet he consults me and even sometimes accepts my opinion." Clearly, this is the situation that Merton and Elinor Barber have identified as sociological ambivalence[9]—that is, one in which a status occupant faces incompatible normative expectations of attitudes and behavior emanating from the same role-partner.

Residents also face contradictory expectations from patients over whom they themselves exercise authority. However, this authority is continuously being undercut by the structure of the ward. The following exchange, which was recorded in field notes, illustrates this point:

> *First resident:* The patients say I'm wet behind the ears; they tell the administrator that I am too young to treat them.
> *Q:* In your presence?
> *A:* Of course.
> *Q:* And how does the administrator react?
> *A:* He backs me up by saying, "Dr. G is your doctor."
> *Q:* Do the patients accept this?
> *A:* Until the next rounds.

Second resident: My administrator backs me up very strongly. He makes a point of it.

Q: Do patients make remarks of the same kind on your hall?

A: They do, but the psychiatrist in charge is always on my side.

Q: Have the patients learned?

A: They always try this sort of thing, and they have to be told over and over again.

It seems that the ambiguity is not relieved if administrators make public statements about having delegated authority to residents. Despite differences among authority holders in the extent to which they delegate authority, the social structure perpetuates the ambivalence.

Social Mechanisms of Defense

Although the ambiguity inherent in the role of the practicing student seems manifest, it is never articulated by the staff. Residents' individual complaints are perceived as referring to happenstances in the personal sphere.

The maintenance of such pluralistic ignorance should not be surprising.[10] Merton has called attention to the fact that one consequence of sociological ambivalence is that those involved in the system resist recognition of the problems it presents.[11] He is referring to the resistance of scientists to face the issue of priority of discoveries as a legitimate problem because they are under the dual expectation of making their findings the property of the collectivity and showing their colleagues that they themselves have made a contribution to the field. In the case I am presenting here, in a completely different social situation, a similar phenomenon appears: the problem of status anxiety, which has its source in a structure characterized by sociological ambivalence, is ignored or denied.

The pluralistic ignorance of socially patterned contradictions is maintained through consensual denial by most actors in the system, or at least among the medical staff. But it is an uneasy harmony; the residents' status ambiguity readily becomes the Achilles heel for an attack by the underdog. Nurses may make use of this vulnerability in the system to allay their own status anxieties, and patients, as has been noted, often emphasize or even exaggerate the residents' lack of authority either for fear of not getting helped or to score a point against the staff. Thus the breakdown of the uneasy harmony must be defended against repeatedly. The mechanism of defense—in this case, denial—becomes patterned. Thus a mechanism that has usually been thought of as serving the defense of the ego becomes socially institutionalized to serve the defense of the social structure. In helping suppress awareness of issues, this mechanism serves not only the personality structure but the social structure as well.

In the interviews conducted for systematic data collection, the patient's observation quoted earlier was used to present residents with a hypothetical situation. They were asked: "If a patient on your ward were to say to you, 'You're a nice person to talk to, but you have no authority here anyway; you are no help to me,' how would you handle it?" The following is a noteworthy response: "At first I felt quite attacked by it, but I feel less so now. At first it was because I guess I agreed with the patient, and now perhaps I don't agree with the patient so much; and maybe that is not a fact as such, and sometimes I want to say, 'So what if I don't have the authority?' " We note that "at first" this resident recognized his lack of authority, but then was prepared to deny its importance.

Patterned ways of dealing with ambivalence differ according to the social context. When patients are not present, as at staff meetings, one way of establishing consensus through denial is the use of humor.[12] For example, a resident reporting to the staff about his patient called forth general laughter when he said: "Her brother came to the ward. He once was my Sunday-school teacher. He said I had grown up." Through humor, the ambiguity is brought to the surface at the same time that it is collectively denied. But humor is a risky weapon. Because of its implicit or explicit aggressive content,[13] it has to be used sparingly by persons of low status in the presence of their status superiors,[14] and its use is not considered legitimate in the presence of patients in a hospital that prides itself on its patient orientation.[15]

When faced with the ambivalence of their status and authority position in the presence of patients, residents typically deal with it by evasion, redefining the issue in terms of the patients' state of mind and thus denying the rational basis of the problem. Patients can easily be demoted from the status of rational role-partners, not only because they are defined as "sick," but also because the mere fact of their making manifest what is normatively being denied is evidence of their "not playing the game." By breaking through the consensual denial of the staff, patients place themselves outside the system. They are the ones, therefore, who "must have a problem with authority." Thus recognition of the problem is avoided by projecting it onto a challenging patient.

Evading the issue in this manner becomes a typical way of coping with ambivalence, as in the following responses to the question concerning a patient's hypothetical challenge of a resident's authority: "I think you have to explore with the patient some reason why he may feel that way." "It would depend entirely upon the patient. For an average, I think I would say, 'That's interesting that you feel that way,' and so forth, and 'Why do you feel that way?' "

These means of denying the problem are readily available in the technique of psychiatric treatment prevalent in a psychoanalytically oriented hospital like O'Brien. In psychoanalysis and psychoanalytically oriented therapy, the purpose is to make patients aware of their inner problems by encouraging them to explore, with the help of the therapist, their feelings, reactions, and associations. The focus of therapy is the patient, not any issue that the patient may happen to bring up. This was well expressed by a staff member of high position in the hospital when asked whether he agreed that a "patient who comes late to an appointment shows resistance against the therapist." He answered: "The lateness is not the issue. But when he is late, he must have feelings about it, and those have to be explored." In psychoanalytic treatment and in psychotherapy, it is believed that issues can be, and most of the time *must* be, ignored. Thus the therapeutic orientation of the hospital provides a legitimate means to resist acknowledging an issue that has its source in the hospital's own structure.

Comparison between the Two Activity Systems

In interpreting evasiveness as a defense against the threat of status ambiguity, caution must be exercised not to confuse such defense with the actual technique of treatment. Residents are taught by their supervisors of therapy to concentrate their attention on their patients and not on themselves. The purpose of psychiatric supervision is to help residents free themselves from their own anxieties, the better to focus on patients. One supervisor of therapy expressed this clearly when asked how he would want a resident to respond if a patient were to ask him whether he has supervision: "This is grist for the therapeutic mill. . . . [The way to handle it is to find out] what does the patient want?" The technique taught in psychotherapy is to ignore concrete issues and to concentrate instead on the motives that underlie them. Thus one must distinguish between a technique that consists in taking distance from an issue that concerns the self and evasiveness that is used as a structurally induced mechanism of defense against having to deal with an ambiguous issue.

Although the technique of taking distance is taught in psychotherapy, it is not the technique explicitly advocated in ward psychiatry. In the ward, patients are to be faced with reality situations because this is where they lead their daily lives, in the company of other patients. Hence their treatment there has to take into account the total ward situation. One would therefore expect that, when faced by patients with the ambiguity of being both a student and a psychiatrist, residents would less readily ignore issues involving details of daily living on the ward than in psychotherapy, where refusal to deal with concrete issues is a legitimate technique. If, however, we should find that evasiveness is used more often in regard to ambiguity arising on the ward, there is *a fortiori* reason to believe that in this situation it is a response to the sociological ambivalence prevailing in that particular structure.

In order to ascertain the residents' reactions to the ambiguity they face as student therapists, their professional competence, which serves to legitimize their authority, was subjected to a challenge in the interview. They were asked: "If your patient in psychotherapy were to ask you whether you have supervision, what would you say?" A comparison between answers to this question and answers to the question challenging the residents' authority on the ward ("You're a nice person to talk to, but you have no authority in this place and you're no help to me") will make it possible to address the following problems:

[1] If evasiveness is a learned and legitimate technique of treatment, it should occur more frequently in response to the question arising in psychotherapy, since this is the activity system in which it is to be applied; if, however, evasiveness is primarily a manner of coping with role ambivalence, it should occur less frequently in relation to psychotherapy, where the residents' behavior is insulated from observability. In this case we would expect this response to occur more frequently in regard to the challenge of authority on the ward than in regard to the challenge of competence in psychotherapy.

[2] If and insofar as evasiveness is a learned technique, it must be acquired gradually over the years of residency, and its occurrence should increase in frequency over those years. In contrast, if and insofar as evasiveness is a manner of coping with ambivalence, there should be no time trend in its frequency associated with stages of training.

Answers to the two questions concerning the residents' authority on the ward and their competence in psychotherapy were coded according to whether or not a respondent would address the question directly.[16] There were those who said they would face the issue, as the following: "I would sit down and talk with the patient and explain that there is a certain appropriate amount of authority involved and that I do have the ability to help." Some respondents made the question the patient's problem: "It depends entirely upon what the patient is really saying. . . . My answer depends entirely on . . . what he is really saying to you." Others gave both answers; they made the issue the patient's problem but were also willing to discuss it in straightforward fashion, as in the following example: "It depends upon whether the patient needs to understand all the facts. . . . I would certainly want to be thoroughly honest. . . . I don't think what the patient knows is important. It's why they ask it, and why they are interested in it."

This classification of answers, which clearly refers to the use or nonuse of a psychotherapeutic technique, was expected to reveal higher scores in response to the question concerning supervision in psychotherapy than in response to the question concerning ward authority. However, in each interview series, many more residents said that they would take up the issue of their authority with the therapy patient than would deal with it with the ward patient (figure 10).

It seems that what could be conceived as a "psychotherapeutic technique" was not advocated as frequently for the psychotherapeutic relationship as for the ward situation.[17] This lends support to the hypothesis that evasiveness is more prevalent in the ward system, where the mechanism of insulation from observation is not available for dealing with the structural ambivalence of being a student psychiatrist.

Supporting evidence for the structural importance of visibility as a source of social anxiety comes from a study of professional identity.[18] In an empirical comparative study in a treatment setting for emotionally disturbed children, Arthur and Birnbaum found that the psychiatrists were more concerned than psychologists with how they appeared to patients and staff. In this study, both types of practi-

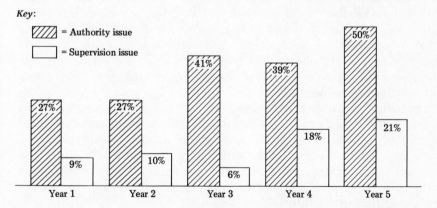

Figure 10. Percent of respondents making an ambiguous issue "the patient's problem" in two activity systems in consecutive years of the research

tioners were asked to recall some unpleasant incidents with patients. The following is one of several typical responses of psychologists: "Sarah and I had . . . managed to begin a fairly direct dialogue . . . yet [she] gradually began slipping back toward her . . . autistic stage. . . . *I grew more frustrated, disheartened, angry and discouraged, and felt myself slipping into feelings of impotence and therapeutic despair*" (emphasis in the original). This report about a difficult therapeutic experience contrasts sharply with the psychiatrists' reports, all of which contained descriptions of how their activities were witnessed by others, as in the following: "[The youngster] refused to come to the office. *The waiting room was filled with parents and kids.* The secretaries at the desk were uneasy and were warning me that he wasn't going to move. . . . *I was concerned as I felt that the secretaries at the desk and other residents passing in the waiting room were watching me*" (emphasis in the original).

The authors explain these differences in reported experiences in terms of differences between two types of practitioners in professional training and professional identity. Yet in their descriptions of task performances the authors note that the psychologists "had considerable investment in *individual diagnostic testing* as well as *individual psychotherapy* with child patients," while the psychiatrists "carried considerable administrative responsibility for *patient management* and also for *coordination* of family treatment" (emphasis added). The division of labor between psychiatrists and psychologists in this study seems to be similar to the division of labor between the ward system and the psychotherapy system at O'Brien.

Moreover, the authors do not seem to attach importance to the fact that the psychiatrists in their study were residents; this datum appears only indirectly, when *en passant* there occurs the phrase "regardless of their level of training." Yet, this is a most important piece of information because it reveals that in addition to having their authority challenged in full visibility of others, these psychiatrists found themselves in the dual role of practitioners and advanced students. In addition, the ambiguity resulting from being an authority holder while still in training would seem to be sharpened for these subjects because of added responsibility: we learn that "regardless of their level of training and experience, all members of the psychiatric staff functioned as leaders of the orthopsychiatric teams with which they were involved in the diagnosis and/or treatment of child patients." These psychiatrists not only were practicing while they were in training, they even occupied leadership positions.

It would seem that the data obtained in this research can be fruitfully analyzed in terms of structurally induced differences in self-image. To be sure, there may well be some differences in professional identity also, and to test this one would have to use controls by comparing psychologists and psychiatrists both in insulated dyadic systems and in systems that offer observability by people variously placed in the structure.

In the present research, the subjects are their own controls because the *same* status occupants find themselves at different times in both of these structural situations. If evasiveness as a hypothetical response to patients were the result of a learned technique, as it might well be in psychoanalytically oriented psychotherapy, we should find an increase in this response with length of training.

In order to compare responses regarding the two activity systems at different stages of residency, evasiveness scores were obtained by constructing an evasiveness index both for the answers to the question referring to the ward and for those to the question referring to psychotherapy. This index was based on a two-dimensional code. The previous categorization of answers as to *whether or not* a respondent would address him- or herself directly to the question provided the first dimension. If the respondent did, the score was 1; it was 3 if the issue was referred back to the patient, and 2 if both answers were given. The second dimension was obtained by coding the answers a second time according to the way in which respondents intended to clarify their position, if at all. A respondent who scored 1 on this second dimension gave an answer such as the following: "I'd say I would agree with this. Dr. So-and-so is in charge." A score of 2 was given to a response, as in the next example, that acknowledged position in the hierarchy while belittling its importance: "Well, I usually tell the patient that the person in authority is not always the most talkative. In other words, there are things that can be done with people just talking, or something like that." If the hierarchy was not referred to at all, or if status superiors were described as persons whom the resident "consults with" or "discusses with," a score of 3 was assigned on this dimension: "Well, probably what I would tell him is that . . . there are other people we do consult with concerning major plans and decisions in the hospital."

The evasiveness index was obtained by cross-tabulating the residents' scores on these two dimensions (table 3). This was done because the two dimensions essentially express the same characteristic so that they can be combined into a single dimension for analysis. Such index construction has the practical advantage of reducing the number of categories from nine to five, as table 3 shows, and the theoretical advantage of putting the variables "evasiveness" and "nonevasiveness" at the two ends of a continuum rather than making them dichotomous or trichotomous.[19]

Table 3. Construction of evasiveness index

		Score obtained on dimension I		
		1	*2*	*3*
Score obtained on dimension II	*1*	1	2	3
	2	2	3	4
	3	3	4	5

Dimension I:
1. Handles patient's statement at face value
2. Handles patient's statement at face value *and* treats it as the patient's problem
3. Treats it as the patient's problem

Dimension II
1. Clarifies or acknowledges hierarchy
2. Minimizes hierarchy
3. No reference to hierarchy or denial of hierarchy

Table 4 compares the mean evasiveness score for each year of residency in regard to the questions concerning authority on the ward and competence in psychotherapy. It turns out that for each stage of residency, "evasiveness" is significantly higher when authority on the ward is hypothetically challenged than when competence in psychotherapy is questioned.

As table 4 also shows, evasiveness in regard to the psychotherapy situation, though possibly serving defensive purposes also, seems to be increasingly acquired at successive stages of residency. If there is reason to believe that what has been called "evasiveness" is a learned technique in psychotherapy, an increase in its use should take place *for each cohort* as it moves through its stages of training. Table 5 shows that the same cohorts show a linear trend in their responses concerning the hypothetical challenge to their therapeutic competence. All four cohorts that were interviewed at the start of their first and their second year increased in evasiveness during that period; and of the four cohorts that were interviewed at the beginning of the second and the beginning of the third year, three increased their

Table 4. Mean evasiveness scores for two activity systems, by stage in residency training

Stage of training	Psychotherapy	*N*	Ward	*N*
Start of 1st year	1.86	28	3.73	26
Start of 2d year	2.46	48	3.87	47
Start of 3d year	2.86	44	3.70	40
End of 3d year	2.85	34	3.78	23

Table 5. Mean evasiveness scores in regard to supervision of therapy, by cohort and year of residency

Cohort	Start of 1st year	Start of 2d year	Start of 3d year	End of 3d year
I	*	*	*	2.75
II	*	*	3.60	3.00
III	*	1.50	2.33	3.00
IV	1.20	2.67	3.50	3.00
V	1.75	2.08	2.45	2.60
VI	1.80	3.00	2.78	†
VII	2.33	3.00	†	†
VIII	2.25	†	†	†

*Preceding period of research.
†Research period terminated.

evasiveness. In the use of evasiveness in psychotherapy, lack of linear change would seem to be the exception rather than the rule.

This linear trend over time contrasts with the lack of linear trend in the responses concerning the challenge of authority on the ward (table 6). Two of the four cohorts that were interviewed at the start and at the end of their third year increased in evasiveness during that period and two decreased. During the first year of residency also, two of the four cohorts that were interviewed at the beginning of their first and second years decreased and two increased their scores. Only one cohort—the one that entered O'Brien in 1960—shows a straight increase in evasiveness between the beginning of the first year and the beginning of the third. Here linear change tends to be the exception rather than the rule.

Table 6. Mean evasiveness scores in regard to ward authority, by cohort and year of residency

Cohort	Start of 1st year	Start of 2d year	Start of 3d year	End of 3d year
I	*	*	*	3.75
II	*	*	2.60	3.67
III	*	4.00	3.11	3.80
IV	3.25	3.89	4.50	4.33
V	2.43	4.08	4.00	3.63
VI	4.20	3.50	4.00	†
VII	4.33	3.88	†	†
VIII	5.00	†	†	†

*Preceding period of research.
†Research period terminated.

It would seem that insofar as evasiveness is a manner of coping with ambivalence, it occurs more often in the activity system of the ward. As a coping mechanism in the activity system of psychotherapy, it seems to be at the same time a learned technique.

The fact that the linear trend of evasiveness in psychotherapy is not followed consistently to the end of the third year of residency, as column 4 of table 5 shows, provides additional evidence that what has been called "evasiveness" is part of the learning process of psychotherapy. These scores at the end of residency gain relevance if they are compared with the responses of the senior staff who were interviewed four times during the period of the research.

Supervisors of therapy were asked, "If a therapy patient were to ask your resident whether he has supervision, what would you want him to say?" Administrators of wards were asked, "If a patient on your ward were to say to the resident, 'You're a nice person to talk to but you have no authority anyway, you're no help to me,' how would you want him to handle it?" Their answers were scored on the evasiveness index. It turns out that at the end of their last year the residents' scores of responses to the hypothetical threat to their competence in psychotherapy approximate the scores of their supervisors of therapy more closely than at any earlier time. The latter scored fairly consistently over the four years, 3.00, 3.00, 2.93, and 2.69, respectively (table 7). It is noteworthy that the two cohorts who at the beginning of their third year exceeded the supervisors' recommended measure of evasiveness (scoring 3.60 and 3.50, respectively) decreased their evasiveness score by the end of the year. Conversely, the two cohorts who scored significantly below their seniors at the beginning of their third year (2.33 and 2.45, respectively) increased their scores by the time their residency terminated. Thus at the end of residency those who had exceeded their seniors and those who had stayed behind came closer to their teachers' scores than they did previously. Their final scores not only tended to

Table 7. Mean evasiveness scores in regard to supervision of therapy during the third year of residency, compared with supervisors' scores

Cohort	Residents, start of 3d year (Jun)	Supervisors of therapy (Oct of same year)	Residents, end of 3d year (Jun of next year)
II	3.60	3.00	3.00
III	2.33	3.00	3.00
IV	3.50	2.93	3.00
V	2.45	2.69	2.60

Table 8. Mean evasiveness scores in regard to clinical administration during the third year of residency, compared with clinical administrators' scores

Cohort	Residents, start of 3d year (Jun)	Clinical adminis- trators (Oct of same year)	Residents, end of 3d year (Jun of next year)
II	2.60	2.82	3.67
III	3.11	2.50	3.80
IV	4.50	2.82	4.33
V	4.00	4.43	3.63

match those of their leaders (table 7) but in addition came closer to one another.

This trend in the relation between the residents' scores and those of the clinical administrators does not appear in the activity system of the ward during any one year of residency (table 8).

If one compares the residents' scores in both activity systems with their status superiors in these systems by time of interview, we find that, in contrast to the psychotherapy situation, residents tend to exceed the psychiatrists in charge in their evasiveness scores three times out of four (table 9). The fact that their status superiors do not tend to advise them to use evasiveness in the same measure as they are disposed to do is additional evidence for the fact that this manner of coping is not merely an application of a skill to be learned.

In this research it is possible to compare not only statistical categories of responses of residents with those of their status supe-

Table 9. Mean evasiveness scores for two activity systems, by year of interview and status position

| Year of research | WARD | | | | PSYCHOTHERAPY | | | |
| | Clinical administrators | | Residents | | Supervisors of therapy | | Residents | |
	Score	N	Score	N	Score	N	Score	N
Year 1	2.82	11	3.48	21	3.00	12	2.14	22
Year 2	2.50	10	3.25	28	3.00	10	2.34	29
Year 3	2.85	10	4.10	30*	2.93	14	2.64	36
Year 4	4.43	7	3.93	30*	2.69	13	2.77	35

*Some residents who were at the end of their last year of residency were not asked the question concerning their authority on the ward. This was because after the first two years of research the training program was changed to the effect that some residents would spend their last year at another affiliated hospital while continuing their supervised psychotherapy with patients at the center.

riors. We can compare the responses of each resident with those of his or her supervisors of therapy and those of his or her superiors on the wards during the period preceding the interview. Averaging the evasiveness scores of residents for the June and December interviews and comparing them with those of their status superiors obtained in October, we find that in each interview series residents tend to be less evasive than their supervisors of therapy (table 10) in regard to this activity system.

In contrast, in regard to the ward situation residents tend to be more evasive than their own psychiatrists in charge of their wards in two out of the three interview series.

While the findings in two interview series lend additional support to the inference that evasiveness on the ward exceeds any measure of technique taught by seniors, they are contradicted by the results of the last interview. This raises the problem of the deviant case and presents a challenge to the explanatory model of this chapter.

If one compares the results of year 4 of the research in regard to the ward situation presented in table 10 to the year 4 results for clinical administrators presented in Table 9, it appears that, in contrast to the supervisors of therapy, the senior staff of the wards have significantly increased their evasiveness during that year. Hence, one must conclude that the "deviance" that appears in the last row of table 10 is not so much a result of a *decrease* in the residents' evasiveness during that year as of an *increase* in the administrators' evasiveness. This circumstance provides the opportunity to examine once more the sociological roots of evasiveness.

Table 10. Comparison between residents' evasiveness scores* and those of their own status superiors, in two activity systems

Year of research		Ward situation	Psychotherapy
Year 2	Residents more evasive	15	8
	Residents equally or less evasive	4	18
Year 3	Residents more evasive	15	11
	Residents equally or less evasive	5	16
Year 4	Residents more evasive	3	13
	Residents equally or less evasive	17	15

*Average scores for interviews given in June and December of the indicated year.

Between October of year 3 and October of year 4—that is, between the two interview series with senior staff—two major events occurred in the hospital. In January of year 4 a new post was created, that of director of the hospital. The new director had been a clinical administrator who had already been named "director of hospital affairs" in July of the previous year, with the assignment of taking over administrative duties from the psychiatrist-in-chief. His new title in January of year 4 put him in command of both administrative and patient-related activities. Symbolic of the importance of the event is the fact that by the end of the month this new director had taken over the office of the psychiatrist-in-chief, on the main floor of the administration building.

The second event occurred in September 1963, when a newly created post of clinical director in charge of ward psychiatry was filled by a man from outside the hospital who had previous experience in hospital psychiatry. Thus the responsibilities assumed up to that year by the psychiatrist-in-chief were now divided among the three posts.

Previously, the psychiatrist-in-chief had wanted clinical administrators to exercise complete authority over their wards. This was in accordance with the medical ethic governing physicians' authority over their patients. Being a strong personality, the psychiatrist-in-chief was able to control his staff by appealing to their conscience without having to make decisions by fiat. When the leadership of the hospital was changed to consist of three persons rather than one, there was no explicit intention to change the authority structure. However, the new clinical director found himself in a position of great responsibility without the authority to make any changes or explicitly to interfere with the treatment of patients on the wards beyond making recommendations that might or might not be followed.[20]

When he took office in September of year 4, he tried to exercise what he thought were his status prerogatives. He made demands on the staff that had never been made before, such as insisting on everybody's presence at all staff meetings and taking an active part in ward policy. Six weeks after his arrival, which was during the period in which the interviews were conducted, the news was circulated that "for the first time in eight years a clinical administrator found his order reversed." However, no official decisions to limit the authority of administrators were made explicitly. Insecurity set in among the clinical administrators; while continuing to live up to the prescriptions of the old regime, they did not know whether to expect interference or counterorders. The frequency of rumors apparently exceeded that of events. At that time I was informed by a leading member of the staff that "the administrators are very upset," that "they had formed a group [for the first time] to discuss mutual problems," and yet that "they all sold out; I'm not certain whether the group will continue."

During the period of the last interview with members of the senior staff, these psychiatrists found themselves in a condition of structural ambivalence similar to that faced by the residents. They were to treat patients according to the best of their judgment, yet they did not know whether they had the full authority to do so. The increase of their own evasiveness score when answering a question regarding their expectations of residents seems to reflect the threat that they themselves experienced in regard to their own authority on the ward.

The data presented in this chapter lead me to conclude that evasiveness, in addition to being part of psychotherapeutic technique, is a response to sociological ambivalence. When, especially in the diagnostic culture of a psychiatric hospital,[21] the term *ambivalence* is used to explain behavior, it remains focused on the psychological level and becomes an accusatory label. Residents (and patients and nurses as well) are often accused of being "ambivalent about authority." This is a case of borrowing from psychoanalytic terminology in a way that obscures the social roots of behavior and misdirects our focus. If, instead, we recognize that this is a case of *sociological* ambivalence—that is, one in which contradictory expectations face a status occupant—attention is directed to the possibility of changing the social structure.

Changes in the social structure are resisted because they imply a redistribution of authority with an accompanying threat to prerogatives, privileges, and rights associated with status positions. Status holders develop mechanisms of defense for themselves that serve the status quo. This is how the personality system and the social system are articulated through the structure of roles.[22]

Just as sociological ambivalence has its source in the social structure, mechanisms of defense against this ambivalence are also elaborated through structural properties of the system; and like the defenses of the ego, sociological mechanisms of defense, in addition to serving to *re*press what is not to be legitimately *ex*pressed, serve at the same time to satisfy some needs of the system as it is defined. For example, it will be remembered that residents often refer to status superiors as "consultants." This is a denial of the ambivalence stemming from hierarchic arrangements through substitution of a term denoting a society of equals for one denoting subordination. But at the same time it strengthens the normative system by legitimizing a highly valued colleague relationship in the medical profession.

Hence, the denial serves at the same time the purpose of anticipatory socialization.

Similarly, the type of evasiveness that is used to resist acknowledgment of sociological ambivalence and hence helps prevent awareness of its structural source is borrowed from a technique that is a legitimate part of treatment in the hospital. Sociological ambivalence is denied through a pattern that is made to appear legitimate because it is borrowed from the highly valued psychoanalytic technique. Status holders use values that underlie the practice of psychotherapy when dealing with their own structural position. In this way, values are used as *ideology*, as Mannheim defined the term—that is, as an unwitting disguise of the nature of a situation, a disguise that serves to maintain the status quo.[23] Values are being used to justify behavior at the same time that they help cover up the source of the ambivalence.

7
Consensus and Dissensus, Norms and Counternorms

If the preceding chapter ended with the suggestion that values may help justify behavior and cover up sources of sociological ambivalence, it must also be borne in mind that values may themselves be a source of such ambivalence. True, values provide a common outlook and thus help unify people in different positions and with different perspectives who might otherwise remain divided by these differences. But this fact itself, paradoxical as it may seem, is in turn a source of contradictions. For example, some values associated with psychoanalytically oriented therapy may help unify O'Brien's staff, but they may at the same time be incompatible with task requirements on the wards as they are defined in the hospital.

It is not only residents, who occupy the contradictory statuses of students and practitioners, who find themselves in a condition of sociological ambivalence. Psychiatrists of senior rank, who do not have to face this particular ambiguity, also face contradictions, such as those between the ideals of the profession and the requirements of everyday tasks. While it is reassuring to them that shared values unite them in the same professional universe, they may also find it more difficult to reconcile these shared values with some contradictory expectations of performance. The use of authority, the subject matter of the previous chapter, again seems to be the pivotal point on which other values center. Yet it will turn out this time that the clinical administrators are probably more conflicted than the residents.

There is consensus at O'Brien about the attributes of an ideal psychiatrist, even when these attributes may somewhat contradict

120

each other. There is general agreement that psychiatrists ought to be permissive, yet also that they ought to be decisive and assertive. When it comes to assessing themselves in terms of these ideals, differences emerge among occupants of different status, as if for some of them the various ideals were not quite compatible.

During three consecutive yearly interviews, psychiatrists at O'Brien were presented with lists of adjectives and asked to indicate which of these were attributes of the "ideal psychiatrist," and also which applied to themselves.[1] Subsequently, for purposes of analysis, the adjectives were grouped into clusters that were named: "intellectual flexibility," "nonauthoritarianism," "assertiveness," and "self-confidence." An additional cluster consisting of adjectives expressing "dispassionateness" and "involvement" will be discussed in the next chapter.[2]

Intellectual Flexibility, Nonauthoritarianism and Assertiveness

Most senior psychiatrists, as well as O'Brien's residents, agree that the ideal psychiatrist has the qualities that make for "intellectual flexibility,"[3] although only the supervisors from outside the hospital were unanimous in so stating. When reporting their self-assessments,[4] however, clinical administrators seem to be less sure than their

Table 11. Average self-image scores for adjectives related to "intellectual flexibility" and "nonauthoritarianism," by status and time of interview

| | Residents | | | | | | |
	Start of 1st year	Start of 2d year	Start of 3d year	End of 3d year	Ad*	HS	OS
"Intellectual flexibility"							
Year 2	76	80	75	93	74	58	86
Year 3	45	76	91	80	61	70	89
Year 4	80	67	73	85	63	80	93
Year 5	94	87	80	79	not interviewed		
"Nonauthoritarianism"							
Year 2	94	84	88	75	38	50	50
Year 3	80	79	75	84	56	63	86
Year 4	92	45	77	95	45	86	79
Year 5	100	85	78	83	not interviewed		

*Ad = administrators; HS = supervisors within the hospital; OS = supervisors outside the hospital.

higher-status colleagues both inside and outside the hospital, and also less sure than the residents at each stage of residency, that they live up to what seems to be considered the norm (table 11).

Nevertheless, the deviant responses of clinical administrators are so rare that it seems safe to say that the lack of "intellectual flexibility" is not felt to be a serious problem for O'Brien's psychiatrists of whatever generation. The small departure of the clinical administrators would not be worth reporting if it were not for the fact that their deviation from the norm increases when it comes to attributes about which there seems to be some incompatibility between stated values and everyday practice. Throughout this book it has been shown that hospital practice is fraught with ambivalence because of the contradictory norms that guide the treatment of mental patients—that is, the desirability of a therapeutic alliance in the therapeutic relationship, and the use of some measure of coercion in the clinical management of patients. Thus psychiatrists have a thin line to tread lest assertiveness on the wards turn into authoritarian behavior, or so that their nonauthoritarian values do not interfere with their effectiveness on the wards. The respondents agree that the ideal psychiatrist is assertive, yet not authoritarian or domineering. Nor should a psychiatrist be dictatorial or stern, even while remaining decisive. Thus, although there is not always complete unanimity on either subject, it is generally held that both "nonauthoritarianism" and "assertiveness" are desirable traits.

The contradictions inherent in these norms should be most pressing for those who have to apply them in their everyday behavior—that is, the clinical administrators. This is, indeed, the case. Clinical administrators score lowest in their self-assessments on "nonauthoritarianism" in all three interviews (table 11).

It is those who are closest to the "ground of operation" who are most likely to report that they do not live up to the ideal. We are reminded of the familiar fact that in all organizations people who are removed from workaday reality can afford to be more permissive. It is well known that operators in industry blame the foreman more readily than a higher supervisor for being "authoritarian." What is interesting here, however, is that respondents themselves report some failure to live up to expected nonauthoritarianism. This becomes understandable when we realize that people who have to be concerned with the details of their subordinates' behavior, and who have to observe this behavior, tend to be more concerned with discipline than people whose interests lie in the more general sphere of attitudes or broad goals.[5] Since clinical administrators are responsible for daily events on the wards, and since their goal is to avoid disturbances coming from patients, perhaps we should find it more remarkable that they still are able to maintain in their own minds the ideal of nonauthoritarianism, as they do.

One would expect that residents would suffer most from these contradictions, since they are lowest in the hierarchy and are therefore closer than the clinical administrators to the ground of operations. But residents exercise hardly any authority on the wards, as was made clear in the previous chapter. Indeed, they do not frequently see themselves as having traits that would violate the norm of nonauthoritarianism. Insofar as their authority is problematic to them, this is more likely in regard to its use than in regard to refraining from its use. From the frequency of the residents' statements of intention to evade the issue of authority in relation to patients, we should expect that they would have no problem seeing themselves as being permissive. This, indeed, seems to be the case, as table 11 shows.

Few residents, at each stage of residency, report not having the attributes making for nonauthoritarianism, and they exceed their seniors in their perceived conformity to this ideal.

The measure of ambivalence that results from contradictory expectations seems to be directly related to the frequency with which expectations are put to a test. Ambivalence would seem to be greater as direct use of authority is less avoidable.

In regard to assertiveness residents seem to be less sure of themselves than in regard to nonauthoritarianism. Yet, while more of them report behavioral departure from this norm than from the norm of nonauthoritarianism, it is noteworthy that it is the clinical administrators, again, who most often score lower on self-reported assertiveness than either the other senior psychiatrists or the residents (table 12).

Since they are called upon to make practical decisions on the wards much more frequently than either the residents or the higher-

Table 12. Average self-image scores for adjectives related to "assertiveness," by status and time of interview

Year of research	Residents						
	Start of 1st year	*Start of 2d year*	*Start of 3d year*	*End of 3d year*	Ad*	HS	OS
Year 2	13	49	29	63	13	58	67
Year 3	−10	21	80	22	11	44	78
Year 4	67	20	46	39	14	71	86
Year 5	60	33	33	19	not interviewed		

*Ad = administrators; HS = supervisors within the hospital; OS = supervisors outside the hospital.

echelon psychiatrists inside or outside the hospital and thus have to be decisive about many more details than their colleagues, one would have expected clinical administrators to score higher than other psychiatrists on adjectives expressing "assertiveness." But on each of the adjectives that make up this cluster—"well-organized," "assertive," "decisive," and "not passive"—more clinical administrators than other senior status occupants tend to see themselves as deviating from the norm. It seems that the demands made upon their assertiveness exceed their self-perceived capability of meeting them in the face of contrasting demands for flexibility and nonauthoritarian behavior.

As to the "outside supervisors," clearly some ambivalence as regards these values exists for them as well. Indeed, some of them tend to see themselves as not conforming to the norm of "nonauthoritarianism." Even private practitioners feel they cannot completely dispense with some use of authority, be it only in the extreme situation when they decide to hospitalize a patient, and although such decisions may be made with considerable reluctance. While private practitioners feel free from organizational constraints and can therefore go much further than ward psychiatrists in granting immunity to their patients, they do not feel entirely exempt from the occasional use of coercion or from firm decisions that interfere with the patients' lives. It is doubtful, however, that such authoritative decision making puts a private practitioner in an ambivalent situation comparable to that of the ward administrator.

Nor is assertiveness a serious problem for psychotherapists because they avoid situations in which assertiveness would contradict the self-image of being supportive. As one outside supervisor explained:

> In general I would like to keep my interference at a minimum and I would merely try to persuade the patient away from something that I think is unreasonable. . . . The ideal is for the therapist to be alert in order to prevent certain crises from occurring. Most of the time, if they occur, usually they don't happen in the therapist's presence, and other people move in anyway.

One mechanism that helps in dealing with contradictory expectations is to live up to them at different times. This is related, of course, to the mechanism of insulation from observability referred to earlier.[6] Should a psychotherapist make the decision to hospitalize a patient, and thus interfere in the patient's life directly, the psychotherapeutic relationship is temporarily given up. Should the therapist continue to see the patient in psychotherapy after that time (which happens rarely at O'Brien), the supportive stance can be taken up again in the setting of the "therapeutic triad" described in chapter 3.

Moreover, the private office presents an "aseptic" atmosphere in which, because of the limited contact with each patient and the insulation from organizational demands, a psychotherapist can construct reality in accordance with the values that are shared with other professional colleagues. The supervisor of therapy quoted just above explained how he arranged for a patient's hospitalization:

> For example, [this patient] for weeks had sort of been threatening me with a crisis, some melodramatic action in order to call out what her husband is doing to her, what her parents are doing to her. She was going to develop some real dramatic crisis. I tried to avert that by pointing out that there were ways out, and if she couldn't find the solution, then she ought to take some time for the hospital, to get away from and meditate on the situation. Well, it turned out she took my advice, and instead of what she had previously done, made a suicidal attempt, she very casually called me up. I made arrangements in the hospital so that she came under her own steam very quietly.

The assertiveness this psychotherapist uses in "pointing out" to his patient the need for "taking some time for the hospital" does not seem to be problematic to him because he can easily reconcile his persuasive manipulation with his supportive behavior. And he can "pass the buck" because he sees the patient only three times a week for one-hour sessions. This is very different from the situation faced by the clinical administrator, who spends much time on the ward and is responsible for his patients' behavior there. As one administrator put it: "In dealing with the patients for six hours [a day], you cannot choose between methods of management and small affairs, and you really . . . need an example of decision making in order that [the patients will pull] themselves together and not make extremely bad social errors." While having to deal with patients on the ward puts lofty values to a test on a daily if not hourly basis, we note how this administrator reconciles his assertiveness with nonauthoritarian language. He speaks of the need to provide "an example of decision making," yet refers to what would be considered misbehavior of patients as "social errors."

In such an ambiguous situation mechanisms develop for dealing with dilemmas, and one of them is the choice of words. One of the arguments current at O'Brien that help reconcile the contradiction between therapeutic values and decision-making behavior is that patients ought to be protected from their impulses. That is, psychiatrists at O'Brien *account* for their use of authority by reference to its therapeutic effect. As Scott and Lyman express it, "An account is a linguistic device employed whenever an action is subjected to valuative inquiry. Such devices are a crucial element in the social order since they prevent conflicts from arising by verbally bridging the gap between action and expectation."7 Thus a language that borrows from psychodynamic theory is used to legitimize apparently contradictory practices.

Cognitive Dissonance and Self-confidence

Those familiar with psychological literature will recognize that an *account* is an attempt to deal with what Festinger has called *cognitive dissonance.*8 It is important to note, however, that such a psychological state arises from the structural circumstance that people's task requirements do not permit them to live up to shared values; that is, it arises under conditions of *contradictory expectations.*

There was occasion earlier in this book to point out that a conflict could arise between occupants of different status positions precisely because they shared the same values. This time, reference is not to conflicts between status occupants but to internal role conflicts within one type of status occupant. The role conflict that results from cognitive dissonance derives from the fact that O'Brien does not have two subcultures based on the division of labor. All O'Brien's psychiatrists are part of the same prestige structure. As in the medical profession generally, this structure assigns higher prestige to private practitioners, and in psychiatry the higher prestige goes to psychoanalysts. Consequently, clinical administrators orient their own values toward those of the more prestigeful private practice of psychoanalytically oriented psychotherapy. They tend to want to be like psychoanalysts in upholding the ideals of intellectual flexibility and permissiveness. Yet, this produces cognitive dissonance with the behavior that is expected of them on the wards.

This seems to be an example of how cognitive dissonance may derive from the structural circumstance that people in specific social positions face expectations that are at odds with the values they share with another group. Whether the psychological attribute is always derived from a structural property cannot be said with certainty at this point; yet, in this case it seems to derive from a situation in which there is what Morris Rosenberg has called *contextual dissonance.*9 That is, the norms governing everyday behavior are dissonant with the values governing the psychoanalytically oriented profession, which provides the social context of hospital psychiatry at O'Brien and which is highly valued. Therefore, clinical administrators reconcile their own tasks with the values of the psychoanalytic profession by making reference to the therapeutic effect of impulse control.

Contextual dissonance helps explain not only the account that clinical administrators give of their behavior but also their relatively low self-image. Comparing themselves to their higher-status colleagues, they know that they cannot be so permissive, nor can they consistently afford the intellectual flexibility that their outside colleagues report themselves to have. In trying to live up to these values, they find themselves less assertive. At each interview, fewer of the administrators than of the other two types of psychiatrists report being "decisive."

It is not surprising, therefore, that over the years fewer and fewer clinical administrators report being "self-confident." Although there is a fair amount of agreement that the ideal psychiatrist is "self-confident," differences among status occupants again become marked in regard to self-assessment. In each of the three yearly interviews, almost half of the clinical administrators express lack of "self-confidence." For each of the adjectives making up this cluster, clinical administrators are more likely than the other senior psychiatrists to note their "shortcomings." Fewer of them than of the other senior status occupants say that they are "relaxed" or "self-confident," and more of them are likely to say that they are "anxious" or "dependent," in each of the three yearly interviews (table 13).

It seems that those who are close to the day-to-day management of the lives of patients feel that they are not always capable of living up to the norm. Whether or not the relatively low degree of "self-confidence" they report is related to this can only be conjectured. At the other extreme, psychiatrists who are not part of the hospital and who have knowledge of O'Brien's patients only through their supervisees (at the same time that they are dealing with their own patients in private offices) and who, as will be remembered, are more likely to see themselves as being "intellectually flexible," "nonauthoritarian" and "assertive" tend to rate higher on "self-confidence" than either

Table 13. Average self-image scores for adjectives related to "self-confidence," by status and time of interview

Year of research	Residents				Ad*	HS	OS
	Start of 1st year	*Start of 2d year*	*Start of 3d year*	*End of 3d year*			
Year 2	.22	.17	.17	−.13	14	60	45
Year 3	−.50	.04	.65	.22	11	56	64
Year 4	.50	−.05	.00	.17	9	71	71
Year 5	.20	.40	.22	.15	not interviewed		

*Ad = administrators; HS = supervisors within the hospital; OS = supervisors outside the hospital.

group of colleagues within the hospital (although some of them also seem to see themselves as lacking in this trait). "Self-confidence" seems to be inversely related to the closeness of one's responsibility within the field of operation.

The level of reported self-confidence is equally low for the residents. It is worth looking at what happens during the last year of residency. The cohorts that have a low score in "self-confidence" at the beginning of the third year hardly improve by the end, but the one cohort that had a relatively high self-confidence score finds it significantly reduced at the end of the third year (table 14). By the time they are ready to leave, the residents' self-confidence is close to the low level of the administrators' (table 14). Similarly, the residents' assertiveness takes a dip during the third year. These figures seem to indicate that the level of self-confidence of those who work on the wards is remarkably low.

One thing stands out from the discussion of selected values at O'Brien: administrative psychiatry does not seem to have become completely integrated into the psychoanalytically oriented social context, as the advocates of clinical psychiatry hoped when they instituted it five years before this study began. We note not only the repeated tendency on the part of clinical administrators to score lower than the other psychiatrists on attributes that are considered desirable, but also the seeming increase over time in the gap in reported self-assessment between the clinical administrators and the other psychiatrists. It is noteworthy that the higher-status hospital psychiatrists, those who have been called the norm bearers of the

Table 14. Changes in residents' self-image scores for adjectives related to "assertiveness" and "self-confidence" during the last year of residency

	Change in cohort III*		Change in cohort IV†		Change in cohort V‡	
	*From B§ to E**		*From B§ to E**		*From B§ to E**	
"Assertiveness"	29	22	80	39	46	19
"Self-confidence"	17	22	65	17	0	15
Year of research	2	3	3	4	4	5

*Consisting of residents who began their last year of residency when the list of adjectives was first administered (that is, the second year of the research).
†This cohort had entered O'Brien when the research first began; residents in this cohort are one year "younger" than those of the previous cohort.
‡This next youngest cohort had entered O'Brien in year 2 of the research.
§ Beginning of third year of residency.
**End of third year of residency.

organization, seem to move away from the clinical administrators in their self-assessments and toward the outside supervisors—that is, the psychoanalysts in the community.

Discrepancies and Differences: Changes over Time

Enough has been said about the difficulties that clinical administrators seem to experience in living up to expectations for the "ideal." There is more disagreement among them than among the other psychiatrists about whether or not the ideal psychiatrist is "intellectually flexible," "nonauthoritarian," and "self-confident," but those who do not hold these norms are so few that this difference would hardly be worth mentioning were it not for the marked differences in self-assessments between the administrators and their colleagues. In all three yearly interviews, administrators score lower in their self-assessments on "nonauthoritarianism," "assertiveness," and "self-confidence," and two times out of three they also score lower on "intellectual flexibility."

Several trends seem to emerge:

1. Administrators seem to move farther away from the norm as time goes on; that is, from the first to the second interview there is increased *discrepancy* between the scores obtained for the "ideal" and those obtained for self-assessments.
2. Outside supervisors move farther away from clinical administrators: there is an increased *difference* in self-assessments between these two types of authority holders (figure 11).
3. Hospital supervisors tend to move from self-assessments that resemble those of the administrators toward those of the outside supervisors: thus there is an increased *difference* between hospital supervisors and administrators between year 3 and year 4 of the research (figure 11).

At the same time that clinical administrators depart more from the norm in their self-assessments, outside supervisors report themselves to be drawing closer to the norm. And as if these outside supervisors were exercising a pull on the hospital supervisors (or perhaps as if administrators were pushing them), by year 4 differences between the two types of hospital psychiatrists had increased, differences between administrators and outside supervisors had also continued to increase, and hospital supervisors moved closer to outside supervisors.

What has happened at O'Brien? We know from the previous chapter that in year 3 of the research there was a crucial change that seemingly caused administrators to feel more ambivalent about their authority on the wards. This aspect of their performance would, of course, affect all the attributes expressed by the "clusters," and especially their self-confidence. But what about the hospital supervisors?

It would seem that between year 3 and year 4 the higher-status psychiatrists at O'Brien changed reference groups—that is, oriented themselves toward the outside supervisors, who saw themselves as living up to the norms of the profession more and more as time went on. Hospital supervisors came closer to their outside colleagues in year 4 than at any other time before.

The question arises whether the change in the organizational structure had affected not only the administrators, so as to increase their ambivalence, but also the outside supervisors and hospital supervisors, so as to turn them away in some measure from expecta-

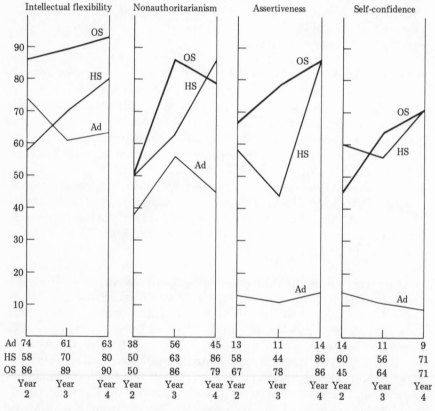

Figure 11. Successive self-assessments on four clusters of attributes, by status position

tions inherent in hospital psychiatry. This, indeed, seems to have happened.

Because of the consecutive appointments of a former clinical administrator to the posts of director of hospital affairs and director of the hospital, respectively, clinical administrators during year 3 of the research were less under the control of the psychiatrist-in-chief, who was firmly committed to psychoanalysis. The change in leadership was symbolized by a change in the morning conference, which was moved into a more formal setting and was now scheduled to take place every other day instead of every day. While the psychiatrist-in-chief continued to attend these meetings, he no longer did so regularly, nor did he any longer regularly read off, at the end of the meetings, the names of clinical administrators he wanted to speak to. That is, there was a weakening of the leadership that stood for synthesizing psychoanalytic principles with administrative psychiatry.

This change increased the ambivalence inherent in administrative psychiatry, because O'Brien continued to be psychoanalytically oriented. The prestige structure of the profession, especially in this academic milieu, continued to assign highest status to psychoanalysts. All senior staff, supervisors of therapy as well as clinical administrators, at each interview assigned psychotherapy and its supervision the first two ranks in usefulness for learning.

The new appointment of a director of the hospital could not remove the hospital from psychoanalytically oriented psychiatry, not only for the reason mentioned above, but also because its higher-status staff, the hospital supervisors, were with one exception members of the Psychoanalytic Institute, as were the outside supervisors, some of whom held such positions at the institute as membership in admissions committees.

Under the new circumstances, hospital supervisors, those who both approved of and hoped to influence hospital psychiatry and yet were oriented toward the psychoanalytic profession, seemed to have oriented themselves more toward their colleagues on the outside. In reporting their own attributes, they seemed to see themselves more and more the way the outside supervisors saw themselves. This trend, which begins in year 3 but comes to a head later, is illustrated in figure 11.

There seems to be increasing separation between the clinical administrators and the other psychiatrists at O'Brien. Though the data are in no way conclusive, they lend themselves to the speculative inference that this separation helped the psychoanalysts among the staff to increase their self-confidence at the expense of the self-confidence of the administrators, as the last graph of figure 11 seems to imply.

That hospital supervisors became oriented toward the outside finds further evidence in the fact that, as the next chapter will show, they are the only ones who report in years 3 and 4 being much less involved than they would like to be.

8
Involvement and Detachment

While it is difficult to strike the right balance between being "assert-ive" yet not "domineering," there is little doubt that the first is "good" and the second "bad," not only for psychiatrists but for all professionals, and in the culture at large. However, there is one set of attributes about which no such unanimity exists. Should a psychi-atrist be dispassionate, neutral, and reserved? Or should a psychiatrist be involved?

At none of the three yearly interviews did psychiatrists of any status position agree on whether or not the ideal psychiatrist was detached, dispassionate, reserved, neutral, nondirective, or imper-sonal. Their opinions were clearly divided on the subject, even though the majority usually expressed itself in favor of involvement. This is not, I believe, because these traits are of no importance to O'Brien's psychiatrists, but because each trait, and its opposite as well, could be considered desirable.

These attributes resemble the incompatible expectations facing medical practitioners, who must have what Merton et al. have called "detached concern."[1] They argue against the view, mainly held by Parsons, that the role expectations of a professional are to be "affectively neutral."[2] Merton and Barber proceed to show that "the structure of the physician's role" consists, in contrast, of a *"dynamic alternation of norms and counternorms."* The authors state:

> The physician is taught to be oriented toward *both* the dominant norm of affective neutrality (detachment) and the subsidiary norm of affectivity (the expression of compassion and concern for the patient). That is why ... we have treated this part of the physician's role not as one of affective neutrality

133

(with only idiosyncratic departures from this norm) but as one involving "detached concern," calling for alternation between the instrumental impersonality of detachment and the functional expression of compassionate concern. As physician and patient interact, different and abstractly contradictory norms are activated to meet the dynamically changing needs of the relation.[3]

Merton and Barber emphasize that these conflicting norms are not happenstance or matters of choice for practitioners according to their personal or psychological inclinations. What is at stake here is that the "conflicting norms are built into the social definition" of the role.

The implication of this theory is, of course, that status occupants have to exercise their own judgment as to which occasions within the same relationship with a patient require one or the other stance. This conceptualization of social role leaves the individual considerable leeway for interpretation. Role expectations, then, do not refer to a specific type of behavior but to a mind set or attitude of the practitioner. Much training is needed for the psychiatrist to learn to make his judgments "spontaneously." I have argued elsewhere that for some roles there is a wide range of choice for conformity because behavior is guided not by specific prescriptions but by the actors' internal dispositions. Seen in this light, the sociological conception of living up to role requirements refers to a greater rather than to a lesser degree of freedom of choice.[4] It is therefore not suprising that on such controversial matters as "to be or not to be involved," O'Brien's psychiatrists make different choices at different times.

In year 2 of the research, all clinical administrators at O'Brien said that the ideal psychiatrist was "involved," while their other colleagues did not attain such unanimity. A year later, the higher-status hospital psychiatrists were the only ones to share this view unanimously. One year later still, it was the outside supervisors' turn to share this ideal without exception. Consistent with their tendency to favor "involvement" over time, hospital supervisors more and more rejected "detachment"; outside supervisors, a majority of whom had favored "detachment" during the first interview, were more likely than not to reject it the second and third times. In contrast to these two types of psychiatrists, but consistent with their own changing view about "involvement," the clinical administrators who saw "detachment" as an ideal attribute increased in number in year 3. In support of the Merton–Barber hypothesis, it seems that neither detachment nor involvement is being accepted exclusively of the other attribute. A supervisor of therapy makes this clear:

I think the therapist should be a human being. . . . Certainly [neutrality] has a degree of usefulness in that it prevents people from interfering too much. . . . But often the therapist acts like a zombie, because it's not neutrality for the therapist to show interest in what the patient is saying . . . or to direct it in a certain way.

No doubt, residents learn about *detached concern* at an earlier stage in their training. One of them describes an attitude expected of all physicians.

I think that a psychiatrist, like any professional, has to get involved with the patient; to be empathetic. . . . Probably a certain amount of distance, a certain amount of professional aloofness is required, healthy skepticism that promotes a therapeutic relationship. . . . It is vitally important to be involved with the patient.

The notion of detached concern would seem to refer to what I would like to call an *ambinormative* expectation, because, as Merton and Barber also imply, the two elements have become fused into one. This is how one supervisor commented on the need for neutrality in a psychiatrist:

It is both true and false. True in the sense that it is not our business to make judgments or to seduce . . . or to influence what it is the patient is trying to tell us. . . . But it is false if one interprets it as being nonresponsive as a human being . . . it is false if it means that one should not basically have a very encouraging attitude about people, and if you can't have it, you shouldn't treat them.

The felt need for an ambinormative attitude tends to be more intense for psychiatrists than for other physicians or professionals generally, mainly because in psychotherapy the social relationship between physician and patient is itself part of treatment, and mental illness more than any other illness concerns social and therefore moral behavior.

Since the social relationship is itself part of treatment, psychotherapists more than other professionals have to consider the effect of their words on a patient's feeling. The supervisor who was heard saying "it is not our business to . . . influence what it is the patient is trying to tell us" provides an illustration of the difference between the behavior expected of a psychotherapist and that expected of other professionals: "If one greets a patient heartily and remarks upon the beauty of the weather, one has already influenced a patient who may want to tell you how terribly depressed he felt that day. You have already shut off one line of communication." Clearly, no other professional relationship precludes talk about the weather! Another supervisor echoes: "The therapist should not contaminate what the patient has to tell him by his own idiosyncrasies or his own personality." This means, however, that psychotherapists must control their feelings, including those aroused by the patient's personality, so that unguarded reactions will not adversely affect the therapeutic relationship. This is what in psychoanalytic terminology is called "countertransference," and it is what one of the hospital psychiatrists had in mind when he said that a psychotherapist should "not fall into a reaction pattern." There seems to be general agreement that the therapist should not "impose his own neurosis and biases and prejudices on the patient," in the words of one supervisor. Says a clinical administrator who thinks a psychiatrist ought to be "dispassionate," "You have to accept [the patient] for what he says. If he wants to talk about shit, then he wants to talk about shit. If he wants to talk about sugar, that's OK too."

This administrator implies that he withholds judgment about the appropriateness of such talk, but such issues become a little more "iffy" if one follows the suggestion of the supervisor who said that "the therapist favors one kind of workup instead of acting out." How is it going to be decided whether the patient who "wants to talk about shit" is or is not acting out?

Where a violation of strongly held moral values is at stake, there often is more than mere concern, there is real involvement. A hospital psychiatrist expressed this tersely when he said that a psychiatrist should be neutral "in the same sense that a judge is neutral. I could think of arguments for the judge not being neutral in respect to law and order."

Similarly, a clinical administrator felt that a psychiatrist has a moral role, which view seems opposed to that of the outside supervisor who said, "It is not our business to make judgments"; yet, he adds: "I don't think [the psychiatrist] can be entirely morally neutral, because realistically the morality of the [psychiatrist] and the morality of reality are not necessarily dissimilar. In reflecting morality, the psychiatrist can't be really neutral."

This type of involvement differs from the more morally neutral concern of the physician, just as having to be "dispassionate" differs from the detachment required for professional objectivity. Here not only objectivity but the total therapeutic relationship is at stake.

In spite of the fact that all psychiatrists tend to agree that they are to be both "dispassionate" and "involved," certain trends can be discerned in the combined scores these adjectives received. Except for the first interview series, clinical administrators are somewhat less likely than the other psychiatrists to see involvement as an ideal. This tendency becomes stronger in the respondents' self-assessments (table 15). In all three interviews, clinical administrators are less likely than their colleagues of whatever status to see themselves as being "involved" and more likely to see themselves as "dispassionate." This is especially true for the adjectives "involved," "not uninvolved," "impersonal," and "directive," for which they receive more often than not a score lower in self-image than their colleagues. In contrast, the outside supervisors report being "involved," "not uninvolved," "not detached," and "not impersonal" more frequently than either type of psychiatrist within the hospital (see appendix C, tables 32, 33).

These differences are surprising, since we know that ward psychiatrists are more likely than the others to interfere in the patients' everyday behavior—that is, to be "directive" rather than "neutral." But in regard to both their ideal and their self-image, they report leaning toward noninvolvement more than the other respondents do. In contrast, the outside supervisors, who are primarily engaged in private practice and have least occasion to direct their patients'

Table 15. Average self-image scores* for adjectives related to "dispassionate involvement," by status and time of interview

Year of research	Residents						
	Start of 1st year	*Start of 2d year*	*Start of 3d year*	*End of 3d year*	Ad†	HS	OS
Year 2	.33 (=)‡	.28 (+)	.34 (+)	.61 (+)	.11 (=)	.20 (+)	.50 (+)
Year 3	.07 (−)	.50 (+)	.41 (+)	.49 (+)	.19 (+)	.36 (+)	.43 (+)
Year 4	.59 (+)	.27 (+)	.21 (+)	.58 (+)	.11 (+)	.27 (−)	.52 (+)
Year 5	.42 (+)	.76 (+)	.21 (+)	.40 (+)	not interviewed		

*The scoring was done in the direction of "involvement," since more often than not the choice was made in favor of this attitude.
†Ad = administrators; HS = supervisors within the hospital; OS = supervisors outside the hospital.
‡The signs =, −, and + indicate whether the score was equal to or lower or higher than the corresponding normative score. A difference of 1 or 2 points was considered equal.

behavior in an immediate sense, are the ones who most frequently report that involvement is an ideal attribute, and even more frequently that they have it themselves.

There is no ready explanation for this paradox, and what follows must therefore remain highly speculative. Yet it is worth reflecting on this matter.

It would be tempting to say that for clinical administrators, who are part of the hospital bureaucracy, being "dispassionate" and not "involved" reflects the impersonal relationships characteristic of bureaucratic structure. The administrator who said it is all right to let the patient "talk about shit" also said that a psychiatrist has to be "dispassionate to some degree, but accepting." He added: "I don't think you have to indicate to a person that you like him." Yet, although this administrator seems to be somewhat impersonal in his approach, generally there is no strong evidence in the data of a bureaucratic stance on the part of clinical administrators. This explanation would be *ad hoc*—that is, not integrated with the analysis presented so far.

However, it will be remembered that in the previous chapter reference was made to the notion of "what is problematic," and I believe the same notion can be applied here.

People are likely to emphasize not what they take for granted but what is problematic for them. Melvin Kohn has called attention to this fact in his studies on class differences in parental values.[5] He found that if middle-class respondents do not mention cleanliness as being important as often as working-class respondents do, it is not because they care less about it but because, given the hygienic conditions of middle-class homes and the greater availability of comfort and leisure there, cleanliness is no problem; since it is taken for granted, it is not mentioned as an important value. It would, however, be mentioned by those for whom the scarcity of the value could become a risk. Similarly, the psychiatrists in the present study seem to emphasize that which is likely to get them into trouble.

The notion of the problematic has already been referred to in regard to the surprising finding that clinical administrators see themselves as being less assertive than their colleagues see themselves as being, although their own ideal in this regard is hardly lower than the others'. This type of behavior is problematic to them because in their work on the ward assertiveness may interfere with the nonauthoritarian stance which is the norm in the social context of psychoanalytically oriented psychiatry. Similarly, it is not that clinical administrators are less involved with their patients; it is quite plausible, however, that their involvement is problematic because it may interfere with the dispassionateness which is also a role requirement.

For therapists who do not deal with patients on hospital wards, involvement as they define it is not a problem. For them, noninvolvement may be the problem. We have heard the supervisors of therapy say that a psychiatrist should not be a "zombie" but should be human and encouraging. Considering that a session with any particular patient is over after 50 minutes and that they do not see this patient again for another 48 to 72 hours, there is little risk of overinvolvement for them. For ward psychiatrists, by contrast, who have to be alert to their ward patients whom they must control, overinvolvement becomes a risk. The emphasis on aloofness has been noted elsewhere in organizations where the close proximity and visibility of people in different status positions would otherwise present a problem for the exercise of discipline. Homans notes that on a warship the captain is not supposed to play cards with his crew, for fear that he might not be objective in exercising discipline.[6]

Of all attributes said to pertain to a psychiatrist, "involvement" seems to be the most problematic of all, and it seems to be even more problematic for residents than for the senior staff. That the discrepancies between the ideal and self-assessments more often than not are higher for residents than for the senior staff (table 16) seems to make sense if we consider that noninvolvement of emotions is considered the most difficult thing to learn.

Table 16. Discrepancies between "self" and "ideal" in regard to "dispassionate involvement,"* by residency cohort and time of interview

Year of research	Cohorts									
	II	III	IV	V	VI	VII	VIII	Ad†	HS	OS
Year 2	39 (+)‡	14 (+)	7 (+)	1 (=)	x§	x	x	2 (−)	13 (+)	34 (+)
Year 3	xx	28 (+)	10 (+)	32 (−)	17	x	x	13 (+)	14 (−)	21 (+)
Year 4	xx	xx	16 (+)	19 (+)	29 (+)	18 (+)	x	4 (+)	28 (−)	7 (+)
Year 5	xx	xx	xx	34 (+)	7 (+)	38 (+)	18 (+)	not interviewed		

*The scoring is in the direction of "involvement."
†Ad = administrators; HS = supervisors within the hospital; OS = supervisors outside the hospital.
‡The signs =, −, and + indicate whether the descrepancy was equal to or in the direction of less or more involvement than the norm.
§x = residents not yet in residency; xx = residents no longer in residency.

Indeed, while all professionals, and especially physicians, have to come to terms with the contradictory demands that they be both detached and concerned, the self-control that is needed to maintain this stance in psychoanalytically oriented therapy surpasses that of other professions. Allen Wheelis[7] has described in great detail how the psychoanalyst gets involved in the most intimate thoughts and feelings of patients while remaining so detached that he cannot even look into the patient's face during the therapeutic hour. Wheelis believes that becoming a psychoanalyst is a matter of psychological predisposition, that to be a psychoanalyst one has to have a personality that enjoys both closeness and aloofness, that engages in a sort of "withdrawal and return," at one and the same time. Be this as it may, the training itself helps bring about this type of "double bind" in young practitioners.

To be sure, training in psychoanalytically oriented psychiatry is not so demanding, psychologically speaking, as training in psychoanalysis, where the personal analysis is supposed to develop the candidate's awareness of unconscious feelings and fantasies, not only in order better to comprehend the unconscious feelings and fantasies of patients, but in order to be able continuously to exercise the necessary self-control over involvement with patients' emotions. Yet, even short of a personal analysis, the recruit to psychoanalytically oriented psychiatry is continuously admonished to avoid "transference"—that is, infusion of one's own emotions into the course of therapy. A good number of the residents—about half of them—were encouraged by some senior staff members to go into a personal analysis. And even short of that, the supervision residents receive is much concerned with the residents' own anxieties.

Erik Erikson likens the training of the psychoanalyst to the training of a monk. He says: "Psychoanalysts in training must undergo a training procedure which demands a total and central personal involvement, and which takes greater chances with the individual's relation to himself and to those who up to then have shared his life, than any other professional training except monkhood."[8] Erikson speaks of psychoanalytic training as of training for a "new kind of asceticism," and he speaks of the therapeutic relationship as one of "interpersonal austerity." And even though psychiatric residents at O'Brien are not (or not yet) in psychoanalytic training, the "combination of the personal, the professional, and the organizational" Erikson also mentions is like a massive impingement on the trainees' personality, helping to instill in them the self-control without which they will not be able to exercise the art as it is conceived by the senior practitioners.

It now becomes understandable why "involvement" is such an issue with both senior psychiatrists and residents at O'Brien, and why they all tend to report that they are more "involved" than they would like to be. For what is problematic is how to remain "dispassionate" when confronting their own engagement with the emotional problems of their patients.

It was argued earlier that there is a constant danger of a coalition between the psychotherapist and the patient, and that much of O'Brien's social dynamics of interaction with clinical administrators is to be understood from that perspective. A "coalition" of the therapist with the patient is undesirable from the vantage point of the supervisor of therapy, who watches a resident's "transference." But it is also a danger to the very organization of the treatment triad of patient, therapist, and clinical administrator. This is how the personal, the professional, and the organizational reinforce each other to impress on the trainee the dangers of "overinvolvement"— while at the same time the pronouncement that "a psychiatrist ought to be involved" is part of the rhetoric of O'Brien's leaders.

It should be clear by now that the training situation in this type of mental hospital is one of psychic intensity. It is therefore not surprising that psychiatrists, young or old, who work day in, day out in this social context should be especially vulnerable to organizational instability. The events and changes that occurred after the first year and a half or so after the research was begun, and the concomitant changes in the interactional system, are the subject of analysis in the next chapter.

9
Suicide and the Relational System

Shortly after the beginning of year 2 of the research, it was being said that "massive paranoia had broken out among the residents." About a month later, a patient committed suicide. This was followed by five suicides in the next five months—six suicides in all during these six months. To top it off, less than three months later a resident took his life. The hospital was shaken.

The crisis indicated by these events was remembered some eight years later by one staff member who called it "the most traumatic time I had ever known at this hospital." By this time he could have remembered another "traumatic time" as well. Almost four years after the first suicide wave there were two consecutive patient suicides in the early summer, which turned out to be the prelude to a bad winter. Another suicide in November, three in December, and two during the first two months of the new year brought the six-month toll to six suicides.

The second suicide wave occurred one and a half years after the data collection for this research was terminated. Other suicides had occurred during the period of the research, usually more than one at a time, but never quite so many as during the two periods mentioned above.

Special note: An earlier version of this chapter appeared under the title "Suicide and the Relational System: A Case Study in a Mental Hospital" in the *Journal of Health and Social Behavior* 17 (December 1976): 318–27 and has been used here by permission of the American Sociological Association.

I am indebted to Donald Light and Stephen Cole for valuable suggestions on an earlier draft of this chapter, and to Judith Tanur for important statistical advice.

A Sociologist at Work

As Philip Hammond, among others, has shown,[1] research usually does not proceed as smoothly as some research reports would have us believe. Unexpected events during the research or on the research site may distort the data or may lead to the exploration of new issues that could not have been foreseen in the research plan. The research reported here was not intended initially to study the behavior of patients, nor could the planning of the research have taken into account any unexpected happenings. However, care was taken to keep a "calendar of events," recording occurrences such as suicides as well as organizational changes in the hospital. I decided a year after the data collection was terminated to examine my data and records for clues related to the waves of suicides.

At that time I visited the hospital for the purpose of obtaining some follow-up information. I found grave consternation, especially among the residents, for three suicides had occurred that month.

During these conversations remarks were dropped about the general quality of life at O'Brien. When I asked an old-time clinical administrator to identify some of the new residents for me, he answered: "It's perhaps a sign of the times that I don't know them. I only know one, the one who works with me on [my ward]." A third-year resident reacted in a similar way: "I don't know if I know them. This one over there, he could be Dr. A., but I'm not sure. You know, the residents all look alike this year, I can't tell one from the other."

I could no longer believe that the suicides were merely the result of the mental conditions of patients. I noticed that these accidents had occurred in "clusters," and I also knew that the hospital had gone through some organizational upheaval.

Suicides do, of course, occur in mental hospitals now and then because of the preselection of patients: people who threaten or attempt suicide are considered to be in need of hospitalization. And no matter how watchful a staff and how strict the constraints in the form of locked doors, five-minute checks, escorts, the removal of sharp objects, and the time and energy spent on assuring the effectiveness of these constraints, patients now and then find the means to kill themselves if they are strongly motivated to do so.

Whatever the psychological explanations are of an individual suicidal act, they do not account for "clusters" of suicides. Since we can assume that the number of suicidal patients is more or less randomly distributed in the hospital over time, it behooves the sociologist to ask whether there are some social-contextual features that distinguish periods of high incidence of suicide from periods of low incidence.

We should not rule out the possible explanation that suicides are at least in part a result of *imitation* once a first suicide has taken place.[2] It is impossible to test this hypothesis here, but assuming that this is valid, one would have to ask why there should be more imitation at one time than at another (six suicides in a row rather than two). While this may be due purely to chance, such a conclusion should be the result of lack of empirical information to the contrary.

Ever since Durkheim, the sociological explanation of rates of suicides which says that they are related to conditions of *anomie*— that is, conditions in which the social bonds in a group or society are relatively weak—has stood ground on the aggregate level despite attempts from time to time to refute Durkheim's explanation.[3] Whether we take the large body of work by Porterfield or such analyses as those of Gibbs and Martin, or of Henry and Short, rates of suicide have proved to be associated with *weakness in relational systems.*[4]

Sociological studies of suicide have to be limited to large populations because of the relatively rare occurrence of the event. Therefore, the *process* by which a weak relational system gets translated into this type of individual behavior is largely unknown. A mental hospital offers the opportunity to study within a delimited universe the regularity of social events associated with such individual acts even if their occurrence is relatively rare. While it remains difficult to formulate generalizations from findings within a small universe and from a small number of cases over a limited time, insights can be gained about the relation between repeated individual acts and some specified interactive processes.

My hypothesis is that suicide waves among patients in a hospital tend to occur under conditions of weakened relations among the staff. This differs slightly from Durkheim's proposition that suicides occur under conditions of anomie in that I speak here of two different populations. I intend to trace suicides of patients not to anomie on the wards where they reside, but to anomie among the psychiatric staff, who are distributed over all the wards in many different buildings and in the administration building and who spend much of their time away from patients.

I am encouraged in formulating my hypothesis by a finding by Stanton and Schwartz, who showed in two major papers and again in their book *The Mental Hospital*[5] that collective disturbances among patients could be traced to unspoken and unrecognized disagreements among the staff. They did not, however, show *how* the staff's latent disagreements are translated into heightened anxiety in patients (if we may assume, as I think we may, that collective disturbance is an indicator of anxiety).

A concept suggested by Philip Slater may help us probe deeper into this matter. Slater speaks of *social anxiety*[6] as a phenomenon arising among members of a group if they sense that the group's safety, however defined, may be endangered. As I read him, he means that group members may become anxious collectively if relationships within the group threaten the normative pattern. Social anxiety would be distinguishable from individual anxiety in that it occurs collectively and in that its source lies in the social-structural arrangements rather than within the personality, although, to be sure, individuals cope in different ways with threats of social disturbance, and, conversely, individual states of anxiety may be aroused by the social environment.

The notion of social anxiety can help us to interpret the findings of Stanton and Schwartz about the relation between staff disagreements and patients' collective disturbances. The nonrecognition or denial of disagreements introduces contradictory elements into the colleague relationship in that it is an avoidance phenomenon among people who are expected to cooperate with one another as members of a caring team. These contradictory tendencies constitute cross-pressures for the persons involved; we are sensitized by sociological theory[7] and have empirical evidence from voting studies[8] that cross-pressures lead to indecisiveness and withdrawal. It should not be surprising if patients react with social anxiety—that is, with a sense that their safety is threatened—to manifestations of withdrawal from one another by those whose care constitutes their only hope.[9] The discovery by Stanton and Schwartz that patients' collective disturbance can be traced to latent disagreement among the staff should be amended to read that it is an expression of social anxiety as a result of the weakening of the staff's relational system.

Therefore, in dealing with patients' repeated suicides as a form of collective disturbance, attention is directed toward patterned interactions among the staff that would be indicators of the strength of the relational system.

Ebb and Flow of Interaction

Selected Meetings with Residents

During the follow-up interviews, a resident said: "The residents are not important. We are supposed to have weekly conference with Dr. X every Wednesday. The first-year residents haven't seen him yet, they came in July 1st. Every week he canceled. When three patients killed themselves in one week, then he came." Later, at lunch, the same resident spoke about the suicides as "crisis" in the hospital and "mass disaster," adding: "You'll be interested to know that Dr. X has canceled again. This is the fourth time. What we need is another suicide. [Smiles uncomfortably.]"

Dr. X was an authority figure because of his position in the hospital as senior supervisor and his reputation as a psychiatrist and academician. I suddenly became aware of how important his meetings with residents were to them. There was much emotion in what was said and the strong implication of a causal link between the omission of these meetings and the suicides of patients.

Although it seemed farfetched to suppose that patients would commit suicide because a leader had failed to meet with residents, I felt that such failure might well be an indicator of a weakening of social relations in the hospital. I decided to find out how the residents' feelings compared with reality. I asked Dr. X whether he would object to my looking at his appointment books. He was startled by my question and made it clear that he could guess what I was after, thus indicating that he himself had some feelings about the relation between his failure to meet with residents and the occurrence of the suicides. Yet, he responded generously, saying that I should see his secretary. I obtained his appointment books for the six years since the start of the research.

The strong feelings expressed by the resident about the lack of meetings with a leader of the hospital were sufficient reason for investigating whether these feelings were based on reality. It also makes sociological sense to ask whether some indications of strength or weakness in the relational system can be found in the fluctuating frequency of important meetings with residents, as one type of opportunity for interaction among them. It will be remembered that in their work with patients at O'Brien there are few opportunities for residents to communicate among themselves and to develop solidarity. Usually only one resident is assigned to a ward. In the few instances when two residents were on the same ward they were assigned to different patients, although in these rare cases there was some opportunity for them to participate together in hall meetings with the administrator, nurses, and aides. It has also been shown that the structure of treatment discouraged interaction among the residents in relation to their common patients. Meetings of residents are therefore valuable devices to induce interaction.

Occasions for residents to meet with one another arose naturally at the didactic exercises conducted by individual members of the senior staff acting as teachers. These meetings were a source of support for residents not only because of the instruction and leadership they provided but because they made discussions among residents possible, both during and after the meetings. They also provided a chance for the leaders of the hospital to give social and moral support to residents, a support all the more needed in view of the largely individualistic nature of their work.

What added weight to the importance of these meetings over and above their usefulness for residents is that training has a control function in the organization. It helps those in authority to obtain knowledge about ongoing activities. At meetings, residents not only reveal their own performances but tell about hospital life. To be in control of training means to be in control of the hospital, if training sessions are used properly. Failure to meet with the residents deprives an authority holder of knowledge needed for his control over the treatment pattern of patients.

It turns out that the two longest suicide episodes, those of years 2 and 6, were each preceded by a drastic reduction in the frequency of meetings between the senior supervisor and the residents (figure 12). Moreover, onsets of suicides tended to correspond to the frequency with which meetings were held (table 17). Four of the five onsets occurred during periods in which the meeting rate did not exceed the median. In turn, in the three periods when meeting rates were much above the median, there was no onset of suicide.

Similarly, the *direction of change in frequency of meetings* also seems to be associated with the onset of suicides (table 18). In none of the four periods when the frequency of meetings increased was

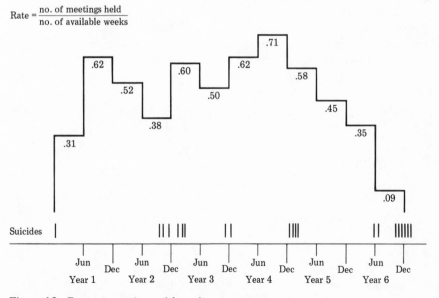

Figure 12. Rate of meetings with senior supervisor

Table 17. Number of periods of low, medium, and high frequency rates of selected meetings, by suicide rates

	Frequency rate of meetings			
	Below median (.50+ below)	*Slightly above median (.51-.60)*	*Clearly above median (.61+)*	*Average frequency rate*
Suicide onsets	4	1	0	.39
Suicide episodes continued	0	1	1	.61
No suicide	1	1	2	.57

there a suicide; conversely, all five onsets occurred during periods when the frequency rate had decreased.[10]

The two heaviest suicide periods—that is, those in which there were six suicides or more—were preceded by long periods in which there were no meetings at all (figure 13). Before the crisis broke out in year 2, Dr. X had not met with the residents since the middle of June. He held the first meeting the last week in October, a week after the first suicide of that wave. Similarly, preceding the crisis that started with a suicide in November of year 6, no meetings had been scheduled with the residents since the end of April. The senior supervisor held his first meeting after the third suicide had taken place in December.

Yet, in contrast to these two periods when failure to meet with residents preceded the highest suicide waves of those years, there were two other periods where such association was absent. During the second part of year 4 there was a series of four suicides that was not preceded by a no-meeting period. At that time, Dr. X's meetings were held regularly. The other is the obverse case: During the year in which the research was begun, the senior supervisor saw the residents only once in almost half a year between the last week of March and

Table 18. Half-yearly direction of change in frequency of selected meetings, by onset of suicide episodes

	Frequency rate of meetings	
	Decreases	*Increases*
Suicide onsets	5	0
Suicide episodes continued	0	2
No suicides	2	2

the second week of September, a period that was not followed by any suicides that fall or the following winter.

If we are to attach any importance to the coincidence between the absence of meetings and the highest suicide waves, the two instances

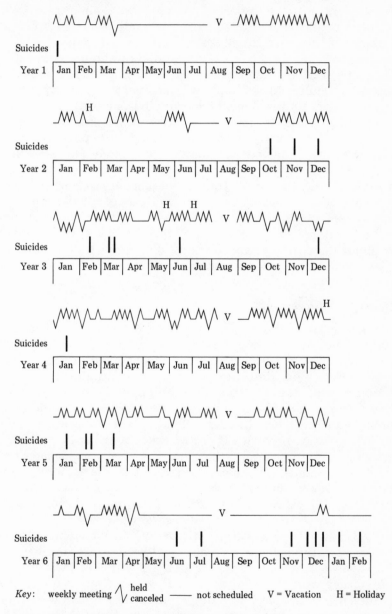

Figure 13. Significant meetings with residents

when these phenomena do not coincide should teach us more about the meaning, if any, of the omission of meetings that preceded the two worst crises. It would seem highly exaggerated if not absurd, indeed, to claim that the lives of some patients depend merely on the frequency with which a leader, no matter how admired, meets with those who are in charge of treatment. Granted that such meetings are important for the morale of the junior staff, common sense or intuition would tell us that some other things could have been going on in the hospital at these crucial times. Some other factor affecting the social structure—for example, organizational instability defined in terms of staff turnover—could account independently for a reduction in the number of meetings with residents and for patients' suicides; in this case, failure to meet could have an independent effect, or the two phenomena could be completely independent of each other.

Assuming, first, that low frequency of meetings is a manifestation of a more general condition of anomie, there should be other manifestations of this condition. Therefore, before examining some structural features of the hospital at that time, and before saying more about the two "deviant" periods, it is useful to turn attention to the behavior of the residents themselves.

Participation of Residents

The meetings of residents with Dr. X were regarded as the most important didactic exercise. The second most important didactic exercise was the "problems conference," conducted by the director of residency training. He continued these meetings after his resignation from his post (but not from the hospital) in the spring of year 3. He attached much importance to them because he was proud of the form he had given them. Residents took turns at consecutive conferences in presenting problems they had encountered in their work, in therapy or on the wards, and the other residents present played the roles of "consultants" in the cases presented. These gatherings were conducted weekly, and only very few—five in the course of five years—were ever canceled. No meetings took place during August; sometimes they were omitted in July as well—that is, during the first month, also called the month of orientation, for incoming residents.

Because the problems conferences, unlike the meetings with the senior supervisor, were held regularly, the question of their differential frequency cannot be raised here. However, there is a record of the residents' attendance, for the problems conferences were taped regularly during the five years of the research. Figure 14 shows that

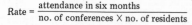

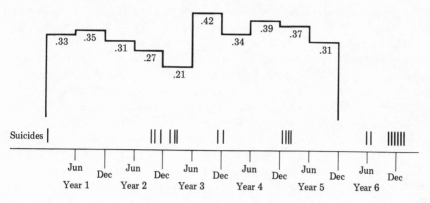

Figure 14. Rate of participation in problems conferences

both suicide waves were preceded by a gradual decline in the participation of residents at these conferences.

A comparison of the average half-yearly participation of residents at problems conferences for the five years and the frequency trend of meetings with the senior supervisor shows a similar trend (figure 15). Attendance at problems conferences began to decline in the first half of year 2 of the research, at a time when the frequency of meetings also began to decline; and attendance at conferences continued to decline through the first half of year 3. At that time (this was a half

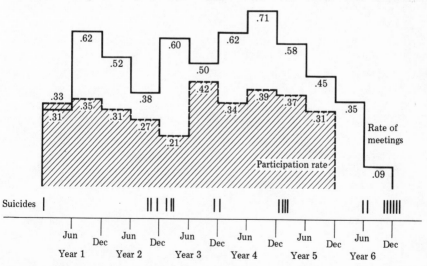

Figure 15. Rate of meetings with senior supervisor and participation in problems conferences

year following the suicide of a resident, it will be remembered), attendance increased significantly. Later, just as the meetings began to decline in frequency during the first half of year 5, attendance at problems conferences again began to decline as well.

This is surprising, for it seems logical to assume that residents, busy as they are with patients and meetings, and indeed complaining continuously about the overload of conferences and didactic exercises of all sorts, would use the free time made available by the omission of some meetings to attend others. But to argue this is similar to arguing that the tide of the Atlantic should be high in Europe when it is low in America and vice versa. Such a pseudological argument would be based on the assumption that there is a limited amount of water available that spills in either the one or the other direction, just as there would be a limited amount of time available that is used either for some meetings or for others. In fact, just as the flow of water is the result of a third force—the mutual attraction of bodies—frequency of interaction is not necessarily determined by the allocation of limited resources. There is a third force

Table 19. Comparison between attendance at conferences and frequency of meetings, in number of months

Attendance at conferences	Frequency of meetings	
	High	*Low*
Year 1		
High	4	2
Low	0	3
Year 2		
High	2	1
Low	2	5
Year 3		
High	2	3
Low	2	4
Year 4		
High	5	3
Low	2	1
Year 5		
High	4	1
Low	1	4
Total		
High	17	10
Low	7	17

that can mobilize or demobilize resources. This "third force" is the attraction of people to one another—that is, their *relational strength*.

A closer look at the coincidence between the two instances of withdrawal will bear this out. When attendance at problems conferences is compared, month by month, with the frequency of meetings over a period of five years (table 19), it turns out that there is a tendency for a coincidence between the monthly frequency of important meetings (about which the decision rested with the senior supervisor) and the monthly attendance at problems conferences (about which the decision rested with the residents). In 17 (63 percent) of the 27 months in which conference attendance was high (above .30), frequency of meetings was also high (above .50); during 17 (71 percent) of the 24 months when conference attendance was low, frequency of meetings was low as well (table 19).

The tendency is not always equally strong, but in all five years for which data are available the coincidence is more likely to occur than not (table 20).

Ebb and Flow in the Composition of Staff

If we assume that the low ebbs of interaction as manifested in the low frequency of meetings and low participation of residents in problems conferences are indications of weakness in the relational system, the next question is whether some organizational instability lay at the roots of these phenomena.

Turnover in Leadership

One thing stands out for both fatal years, 2 and 6, as figure 16 shows: in these years, there was a high turnover among the leader-

Table 20. Coincidence between frequency of meetings and attendance at conferences

Year of research	Number of months in which the two frequencies	
	coincide	do not coincide
	(both high or both low)	
Year 1	7	2
Year 2	7	3
Year 3	6	5
Year 4	6	5
Year 5	8	2
Total	34	17

154   *Suicide and the Relational System*

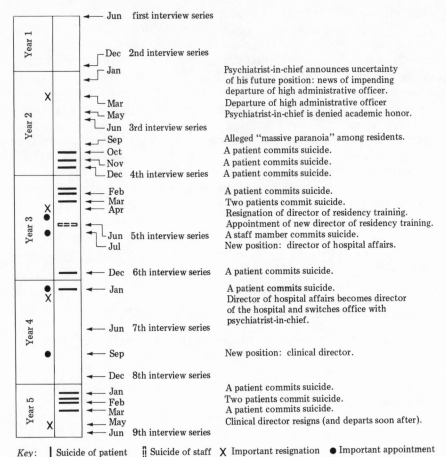

Figure 16. Calendar of events during research period, years 1–5

ship. In each of these years, and only in these years, a top administrator occupying one of the three highest positions left the hospital. In March of year 2 a top administrator, who had been a psychiatrist at O'Brien for many years, left the hospital. In year 6, also in March, the clinical director left. Although he had been in the hospital for less than two years, he too had occupied one of the three leading positions.

Both of these springs preceded periods during which the senior supervisor did not meet with residents for 3½ months or more and coincided with a tendency on the part of residents to withdraw from problems conferences. It is in regard to turnover of leadership that these periods differ from the one in which the failure to meet with residents was *not* followed by patients' suicides.

In addition, in these two springs, unlike the one other time when the senior supervisor omitted meeting with residents for a long period, there were restlessness and anticipation of further turnover among the staff. In year 2, around the time when the top administrator prepared to leave, there were expectations of other departures as well. Rumor had it that the psychiatrist-in-chief intended to resign. Although the rumor turned out to be false, he did indeed seek to alter his position in the hospital all during year 2, as he himself stated publicly at an all-staff meeting at the end of that year. And by July of year 3 he had delegated most of his administrative responsibility to a newly appointed director of hospital affairs, who subsequently became director of the hospital.

In year 2 residents were directly affected by turnover in the leadership in another way. At that time, the director of residency training, who had held this post for six years, was preparing for his resignation, which he handed in in April of year 3. A new director was then appointed.

One important aspect of resignations, as of other changes in status within an organization, is that the date of their occurrence has to be considered the culminating point of a period of preparation, characterized by doubts, unease, and dissatisfaction.[11] When the psychiatrist-in-chief divested himself of administrative responsibilities in order to devote himself to research, it was a year and a half after he had announced to the staff that he hoped to change his present role "in order to do more interesting things in the hospital." He did not accompany this statement by anything more specific about this change in role. For a year and a half there was uncertainty at O'Brien about the role he intended to play. In turn, when the director of residency training decided to resign his post, in April of year 3, it was according to his own account, after a year of deliberation with himself. He said when he was questioned about the matter, "I hesitated because basically this involves a sense of failure. . . . It was difficult to realize that there was nothing I could do to change the system, and that they'll get along just as well, or just as badly, without me." He added: "I knew all along that I would make more money and have more leisure if I went into private practice."

The decision to leave an organization is often an admission of failure or of uselessness, an admission few professionals are likely to make lightly. Depth of commitment is probably one determinant of the time it takes to make the decision to separate, and that commitment increases with time spent in the organization. The longer one has been in an organization that demands investment of internal dispositions, the more commitment one has to it; and the stronger the commitment, the harder it is to leave the organization—ignoring, for the sake of the argument, the pull exerted by opportunities for advancement elsewhere.

In addition to the variable of time spent in the organization, the variable of level of responsibility is associated with the length of time it takes to make the decision to leave: the higher the level of responsibility, the more difficult it is to drop it.

A third variable affecting the length of time for deciding to leave an organization or to drop a specific task is the amount of idealism involved when the task was first taken on. Several leading personalities in the hospital, and several of those at lower rungs of the hierarchy as well, had started their work there in the firm belief that they had a new manner of treatment: they would combine the best psychoanalytic technique with the best that is known of milieu therapy, and these treatment methods would be informed by the best talent and the most humane approach. And all these qualities would be put at the service of training new generations of psychiatrists. In short, the leaders of the hospital were convinced that they could combine the best treatment situation with the highest of academic standards.

The two changes in leadership within the hospital by men who had been the enthusiastic initiators of a new method of treatment six years earlier were part of the social disturbance at O'Brien for the previous year, ever since the departure of the "old-timer" top psychiatrist in year 2. It will be remembered that my field notes include the notation that in year 2, a month before the onset of the large suicide wave, rumor had it that "massive paranoia had broken out among the residents." A year later, one of the residents recalled this period: "[I remember] last year, when the whole question of [the psychiatrist-in-chief] staying or not staying, and so forth, was going on, there were all sorts of pieces of information that was filtering down about it, but none of the residents knew what the hell was going on about the hospital, about their chief." And this was the time, it will be remembered, when important meetings with residents failed to occur for three and a half months.

As to the second wave of six suicides, there is less information available because observation and data collection had ceased a year and a half earlier. But one fact stands out: the then clinical director, who had joined the hospital 18 months earlier, suddenly resigned in the spring of year 6. As far as I know, no rumors preceded this resignation. Although he had not been a mainstay of the hospital for a long time, his sudden intention to depart caused consternation. Right after the announcement of his impending departure, patients picketed the administration building with signs demanding that he stay.

Also at that time, the first director of residency training, who had led the problems conferences and who had resigned from his post in year 3, prepared to leave O'Brien for good. And the then director of residency training prepared to resign from his post in the near future. His relationships with residents had deteriorated by that time (they called him a "company man"). He himself told the researcher in year 6 (after the first suicides of that wave): "I'm afraid I have withdrawn also. I haven't given the residents the support they need."

It seems that the omission of meetings with residents coincided, both in year 2 and in year 6, with organizational instability and that the senior supervisor's failure to meet with residents for a long stretch of time in both these periods was a manifestation similar to the low participation of residents at problems conferences (figure 17). It is quite possible that under conditions of organizational instability residents were especially vulnerable to the failure of their senior supervisor to meet with them. This is indeed how we could interpret the indignant feelings expressed by the resident quoted earlier.

This interpretation of the residents' vulnerability makes sense from both the psychological and the sociological perspective. Psychologists or psychiatrists would say that this was a period of generalized "separation anxiety." From the sociological point of view, departures or absences of people in leadership positions mean that there is a vacuum among the socializing agents who guide the younger members in their endeavor to emulate and absorb the values that govern the organization. With the loss of leaders the organization loses socializers. And this may indeed create social anxiety in those who are there to learn and absorb the new values. It deprives the new recruits to the profession of role models for orientation toward the organization and the profession.

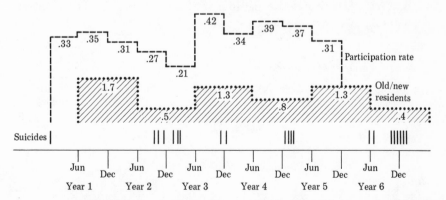

Figure 17. Rate of participation in problems conferences and ratio of old/new residents

If this reasoning is correct we should consider not only the possible impact made by the senior staff but more generally the presence in the organization of "veterans" in relation to new recruits. Residents are socialized not only by senior staff members but also by one another. Opportunities for new residents to watch and discuss with older residents exist mainly at the meetings and conferences, which serve as didactive exercises. These opportunities must be all the more valuable since the residents hardly need to interact with one another in regard to their treatment of patients.

The notion that residents get support and learn from one another, together with the proposition enunciated earlier that older people in the organization serve as socializers, leads us to the examination of the ratio of older to younger residents at various times.

Turnover of Residents

In an article entitled "The Regeneration of Social Organization," Kenneth McNeil and James D. Thompson point out that the ratio of veterans to newcomers can "affect the understanding of both meanings and routes of communication"[12] and call attention to the importance of this ratio for the socialization of new recruits. Older residents help younger residents improve both their competence and their sense of self in regard to their competence, as Emily Mumford has shown.[13] This proposition can be tested here.

Table 21 shows the number of new residents entering in July of each year compared with the number of older residents and the number of patients' suicides that year. Table 22 presents the rank order of both events. The coincidence is striking.

Perhaps one can now understand better how a weak relational system induced residents to withdraw from highly valued conferences. Figure 18 shows the parallel trends of residents' participation at problems conferences and the ratio of old to new recruits. It also

Table 21. Turnover of residents

Year of research	New residents entering	Old residents remaining	Old/new ratio	No. of suicides
Year 1	7	11	1.7	0
Year 2	13	7	0.5	6
Year 3	10	13	1.3	2
Year 4	12	10	0.8	4
Year 5	9	12	1.3	1
Year 6	14	6	0.4	7

Table 22. Rank order of yearly old/new residents' ratio compared with rank order of suicides

	Rank order of ratio	Old/new ratio	Rank order of no. of suicides	No. of suicides	
(high)	1	(1.7) (year 1)	1	(0)	(low)
	2.5	(1.3) (year 2)	2	(1)	
	2.5	(1.3) (year 3)	3	(2)	
	4	(0.8) (year 4)	4	(4)	
	5	(0.5) (year 5)	5	(6)	
	6	(0.4) (year 6)	6	(7)	

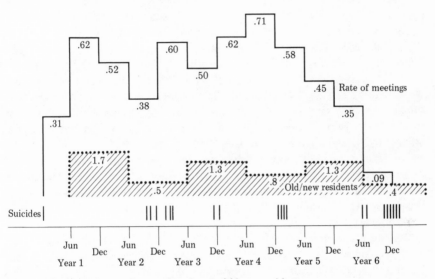

Figure 18. Rate of meetings and ratio of old/new residents

shows how the low O/N ratio corresponds to suicide waves among patients.

Some additional information regarding the problems conferences is in order here. By presenting a problem, a resident makes him- or herself vulnerable to the criticism of peers, especially when these are officially cast in the role of "consultants." This may be an opportunity for them to "cool the mark out"[14]—that is, to convince the presenter that the problem is not really his or her own but one emanating from the patient or from other people in the organization. To the extent that the conference fulfills this function, to that extent it is an occasion for mutual support. However, the "consultants" may also unite in their criticism and thus make the problems

conference an anxiety-provoking occasion, as in the following ex-
cerpt from my field notes:

> Dr. H. [a first-year resident] presented the case and he said the boy was a
> psychopath and so on, and then made himself appear as if he did not know
> what he was doing, and so the whole group jumped on him, so much that
> [the director of training, who led the conference] even tried to rescue him
> and support him. At the next conference, Dr. H. was asked did he have a
> problem, and he said, "No." Asked about this in the interview with the
> researcher, he explained, "I didn't want to be a masochist again."

The problems conference, then, always involves a risk to the
residents' egos. Even in their role as consultants they may be crit-
icized by some of their peers, or by the director of training himself in
the presence of their peers. The dynamics of the conference, as it had
been set up, were such that everyone confronted the immanent
threat of loss of face. To be sure, tactics of "conferencemanship"
were used, such as, in the words of one resident, an occasional "pat
on the back." But such supportive behavior is based on a claim of
superiority. Older residents at conferences are buffers between the
authority of the leader and the "greenness" of the newcomers. If
there are relatively few older residents, the newcomers to the
organization feel more vulnerable. It would stand to reason, therefore, that in times when there are relatively few older residents at the
hospital, the younger residents feel more anxious about conferences
and tend to participate less for that reason.

The sense of insecurity would, of course, be strengthened when a
leader departs from the hospital or when another leader fails to see
the residents in his or her supervisory capacity. Returning, then, to
the meetings with the senior supervisor, it is now appropriate to turn
attention to the "deviant cases"—those periods in which frequency
of meetings and the suicide rate were *not* shown to be inversely
related.

It will be remembered that just prior to the beginning of the
interviewing for this project, failure to meet with residents was not
followed by nor did it coincide with patients' suicides. Figure 18
shows that at that time the old/new ratio was high—almost two to
one. Conversely, the four suicides at the beginning of year 5, which
occurred during a period of high meeting frequency, took place when
the old/new ratio had dropped to less than one to one. Hence it
seems that it is under conditions of a low old/new ratio and not
under conditions of a high old/new ratio that the frequency of the
senior supervisor's meetings with residents is inversely associated
with the occurrence of patients' suicides.

It is not possible, given the limitations of the data, to conclude that the association between meeting frequency and suicides is spurious, or whether not meeting with residents has an additional impact under conditions of a low old/new ratio. We can only speculate that when there are few older residents who can act as agents of socialization, it is a bad time for staff members to relax their own efforts. As McNeil and Thompson also point out, "As the proportion of members who need . . . information increases, *socialization should consume a greater portion of the total activity of the organization*"[15] (emphasis added); that is, more meetings rather than fewer would be indicated.

What took place at O'Brien, however, is the opposite. Instead of devoting a greater portion of its total activity to socialization at times when the ratio of old to new residents was lowest (and when the organization suffered from leadership turnover), the organization devoted *less* time to residents. The hospital was busy reorganizing its leadership, and an authority holder in the hospital, probably both busy with and worried about these matters, failed to hold his expected meetings with residents.

These coinciding factors—low frequency of meetings, turnover among the senior staff, and the ratio of older to new residents—all of which are conditions in which residents are deprived of the presence of socializers, may well have had a cumulative effect in producing the sort of anxiety that comes with a fear of incompetence. As Stotland and Canon state, if there are no means available for individuals to raise their sense of competence, they "would be in a state of considerable anxiety. . . . One way that this anxiety can perhaps be reduced is by escaping the situation physically or psychologically."[16] Could it be that residents withdraw not only from problems conferences but from patients as well?

Unfortunately I have no data that could answer the question of the residents' behavior with patients, so that in interpreting the relation between suicide waves and the indicators (or producers?) of weakness of the relational system, I can only speculate. I am helped in this by the findings of Stotland and Kobler, who interpret a high suicide rate in another hospital as due to a decrease in optimism among the staff.[17] They describe how a previously optimistic milieu had deteriorated to a collective feeling of helplessness. The authors conclude that if staff members have no hope of getting patients better, the patients can be driven to acts of despair.

This is a plausible explanation. Precisely what the process is by which a weak relational system of the staff gets translated to patients—whether through withdrawal from them, or by conveying lack of self-confidence and competence, or by yet a third factor—cannot be specified here. But my findings, which support those of Stanton and Schwartz and of Stotland and Kobler, seem to indicate that, in some ways yet to be found out but perhaps not so mysterious, the quality of relations among the staff does get transmitted to patients.

Even without any firm conclusions, the events described here suggest a horror story. Two periods of social disorganization characterized by departures, rumors of departures, and preparations for departures at the top level of the organization coincided with a drop in the proportion of "veteran" residents, a drop in the frequency of an important type of regular meeting with residents, and a drop in the residents' own attendance at a regular conference—both of these considered the most important didactic exercises at this training center. The two periods that were thus most characterized by a substantial weakening of the relational system carried in their wake the two strongest suicide waves of patients in five years. It does not seem exaggerated to conclude that the social organization of the staff is as important a part of treatment as clinical decisions and therapy— a tentative conclusion to be sure, but one that has implications for organizational policy and sociological theory.

10
Social-structural Determinants of Anomie

The crises discussed in the previous chapter occurred in the context of weak relationships, especially among the residents, and a breakdown in the centralized leadership on which the organization rested. The social system of O'Brien was vulnerable because its members, especially the residents, were more or less working on their own; nor was there a compensatory mechanism that would foster interaction among them. It will be remembered that the analysis of triadic relationships revealed that, as a result of contradictory expectations, residents tended to communicate little with one another about their common patients. This tendency could not be counteracted in a social context that failed to provide mechanisms for solidarity.

Solidarity among members of an organization can develop in several ways. People may have to cooperate for the accomplishment of tasks; that is, they may find themselves in a condition of *instrumental interdependence*. They may also get together in small groups over coffee, in their "own" lounge or some other gathering place; that is, they may engage in *primary interaction*. Or they may, especially if they occupy similar status positions, organize as an "interest group" oriented toward specific goals and issues and seeking representation in committees or with decision makers; that is, they may be engaged in *instrumental association*. Each of these structural arrangements was weak at O'Brien.

Instrumental Interdependence

The concept of instrumental interdependence is similar to Durkheim's notion of organic solidarity. Such solidarity develops in complex organizations where people in different positions, and often with different types of specialized interests, are dependent on one another for their task performance. Such interdependence, which fosters interaction, is the result of division of labor and specialization in modern society. However, work at O'Brien is so organized that interdependence among the various practitioners is curtailed at all status levels and in both activity systems—that is, in psychotherapy and on the wards.

It is not surprising that there is little professional interdependence in the practice of psychotherapy because of the individualized character of this activity and because of its confidential nature. It will be remembered that residents have a proprietary attitude in regard to their therapy patients, whom they rarely discuss with one another. Nor do they exchange informal information about their supervisors, because the supervisory relationship is considered a private one. Residents report in interviews, and the director of residency training has confirmed this, that they do not talk to others about their supervisory sessions or about their supervisors.

The converse is also true: supervisors need not be concerned with any residents but their own supervisees; they are interested in happenings in the hospital only when their residents are affected through some ward policy concerning a particular therapy patient, and even then they try to refrain from interfering. If they do come upon the stage, it is for a hospital "drama"—that is, for negative reasons—because a situation is considered so serious and so much in need of a corrective that a resident alone cannot handle it.

It stands to reason that, in contrast to the system of psychotherapy, work on the ward would offer residents more opportunity for interaction. At least for some time during the day a resident, a clinical administrator, nurses, and aides operate in full visibility of one another, either on rounds or, sometimes and on some halls, in hall meetings. While each ward is an intensive interactive system, a resident on a ward does not have a companion in a similar status position with whom he or she can share work or attempts at problem solving. Each of the wards operates, as someone in the hospital said, as an "independent kingdom." Each clinical administrator is in charge of his or her own hall and has full autonomy to manage it. Patients show that they are aware of this situation by sometimes referring to their administrator as "the count" or "the baron."

This autonomy of ward psychiatrists derives from the medical ethic which dictates that physicians have full decision-making power in regard to their patients. At O'Brien the psychiatrist-in-chief wanted to be considered the psychiatrists' "supervisor" and "consultant," not their director—a euphemism which did not prevent him from being a stern taskmaster. This arrangement is, at times, quite a burden for the clinical administrators because it lays them open to blame by the psychiatrist-in-chief *post hoc*, after things have gone wrong. Since nobody is to tell an administrator what to do or what should have been done, the responsibility for mishaps falls on each individually. Arrangements such as this provide a structural source for feelings of guilt.

A similarity suggests itself between this structural arrangement and the normative structure of Calvinism, according to which individuals find guides for action only in their own faith. In identifying the structural arrangement that fosters feelings of guilt I am suggesting a link between the sociological and the psychological explanation of suicide. To the sociological insight that suicide rates are higher in Protestant than in Catholic societies because of the lesser social cohesion among Protestants,[1] we can now add that in a social structure in which individuals are left to make their own judgments of right and wrong they are led to blame themselves, not some external authority. The internal guilt this produces is fertile ground for depressive states.

Not only the social structure of the hospital but its value system as well presents some similarities with Calvinism. The insistence on the need for "internal" changes in patients and the negative connotation given to what is called *"only* a social recovery" remind one of the insistence on individual faith in Calvinist dogma, in contrast to the emphasis on good works in the Catholic religion; the injunction that a patient first recognize being sick before being able to profit from therapy reminds one of the Calvinist insistence on the recognition of a *state* of sin, in contrast to the acknowledgment of *acts* of sinning in Catholic dogma. Psychoanalytic theory lends itself well to a secular Calvinist interpretation.

Thus at O'Brien the professional orientation with its value commitment, together with the social-structural arrangement favoring autonomy, make the organization vulnerable to anomie in that they reduce external support for individual practitioners by limiting the occasions during task performance when practitioners could be of assistance to one another.

Indeed, clinical administrators have to be in touch with one another only occasionally, as when a patient has to be transferred to another hall. Once the patient is transferred, no more interaction is needed between the two ward administrators or the two ward residents. Only if by chance a patient who has been on more than one hall is presented at a case conference do the different administrators who appeared in the patient's hospital history report at the conference.

Hence in their work on the wards residents hardly interact with other residents. As we know, they do interact with nurses and aides, as well as with their own administrators, although most residents feel that the administrator is not sufficiently available to them for the purpose of teaching and discussion. However, residents do not need to consult much with one another for the performance of their tasks. There is usually only one resident on a hall, and in the rare cases when two are assigned to the same hall the patients are divided between them so that the residents need not consult with each other about the same patients. They have reason to be together only if and when hall meetings are being held.

Thus, the social arrangements are such that many of the relationships are self-contained. Figure 19 compares this system with the traditional hierarchical system. In this figure, each patterned interaction between status occupants is plotted.[2] Part A shows what the interactive pattern would be if interaction were to go up the hierarchical ladder, as it does in most hospitals; part B shows the interactive pattern at O'Brien.

In the hypothetical situation plotted in part A of figure 19 the resident in the role of therapist would interact with the supervisor of therapy, the therapy patient, and the patient's assistant administrator on the ward. In relating to the supervisor, the resident would profit from the latter's interaction with the patient's clinical administrator. And in the role of assistant administrator, the resident would interact with the ward patients and their resident therapists. In the latter relationship he or she would profit from the knowledge the resident

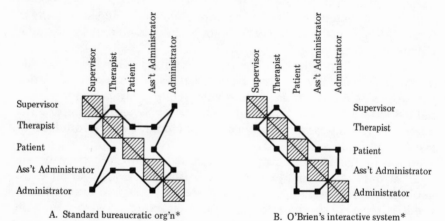

A. Standard bureaucratic org'n*

B. O'Brien's interactive system*

*Limited to the relations between patient and physician.

Figure 19. Two forms of organization

therapists transmit from their own supervisors. Thus in the hypothetical situation, there is interdependence between the various actors.[3]

Part B of figure 19 represents the existing state of affairs at O'Brien: the resident therapist interacts with the therapy patient in a nonobservable dyadic relationship, and with the supervisor of therapy in a similarly closed relationship. The latter, in turn, does not see the resident's patient. In the activity system of psychotherapy, the patient's role-partners and those of the resident therapist hardly interact with one another, as they would be expected to do by virtue of their common interests. The patient's two activity systems are not integrated through cross-communication between the patient's role-partners. In other words, the resident therapist, who remains the focus of this analysis, is isolated from the patient's role-partners on the ward. Indeed, in the graphic representation in part B of figure 19 it looks as if it is up to the patient, at the center, to integrate the activity systems. We can now speculate why it is felt at O'Brien that patients "manipulate their psychiatrists": patients are implicitly encouraged to do so because they are the ones on whom there is some latent pressure to accomplish integration.

One can look at figure 19 for its purely graphic presentation. It appears that O'Brien's interactive system is a bottleneck, whereas the standard form of bureaucratic organization appears to be branching out. As now seems to be the case, it is largely up to the patients to integrate the system. Yet, they have no leverage to defend themselves if accused of "manipulation." In the traditional form of organization, residents would be the ones who help integrate and who would profit from interaction with diverse role-partners. Thus, a system that starts out being very complex, as described in chapters 4 and 5, ends up, because of unanticipated avoidance patterns as well as the authorized form of organization, being *de facto* restricted in its daily functioning.

The lack of instrumental interdependence in the residents' work is paralleled by relatively little interdependence in regard to training and learning such as there usually is in general teaching hospitals. Usually, relay teaching goes down the hierarchical ladder: the chief resident teaches the younger residents, and they in turn teach interns and medical students; the latter are taught by interns as well.[4] Conversely, questions and information-seeking go up the same ladder. In contrast, at O'Brien there is no status gradation between residents. Whether they are in their first, second, or third year of training, no distinctions are being made between them in regard to type of work, privileges, or obligations. While such an arrangement may convey the impression of equality, it also conveys the message that older residents cannot claim recognition for more knowledge and skill than younger residents. Residents seem to be aware of this, as the following second-year resident explained to the interviewer: "I had the impression . . . that there is a terrific static force here at [O'Brien] in that one is expected to remain always at a particular level of development. A patient is always expected to perform at the same level and so is a psychiatric resident. . . ." This is a case of "negative democratization."[5] It makes all residents equally dependent on their superiors and supervisors.

It is not that under these conditions of "negative democratization" residents at O'Brien failed to learn from one another, but that they have less occasion to learn from one another than they otherwise would. To be sure, the fact that there is little instrumental interdependence between residents in regard to work or training does not mean that they don't see one another. On the contrary, they are together a lot. Almost every day there is one or another meeting or conference or lecture, during which all "equalized" residents learn from a more mature psychiatrist. Every week there is a case conference at which one or another patient is discussed. Usually a resident presents the case. This is an all-hospital meeting, to which all psychiatrists, social workers, psychologists, social scientists, nurses, and aides are invited. (While residents do participate somewhat in the discussions, they often defer to senior staff, since here, as elsewhere, participation in discussions is status-graded.[6] On these occasions residents tend to be cast in a passive role.)

We have seen in the previous chapter that the ratio of older to newer residents seems to be important for the process of socialization. Residents give each other support by the mere fact that they share the same position in the hierarchy of the organization, and older residents can articulate for the younger ones some of the sources of their distress. This type of support takes place in their primary relations. It may be that it is precisely because of weak instrumental interdependence that emotional interdependence is all the stronger. While the primary relations among O'Brien's residents are not as effective as they could be, they do offer some opportunities for immediate gratification and immediate mutual support, as do the meetings and conferences at which residents spend time together. The importance of such didactic settings has been shown in the previous chapter. Yet, even these are not as effective as they could be.

Primary Interaction

Meetings and conferences can enhance solidarity if they are so structured as to encourage spontaneous interaction among the participants. Most, though not all, meetings and conferences were not of this kind. But even formal meetings and conferences can enhance solidarity if they are followed by informal discussions in primary groups. Yet, "bull sessions" after the formal meetings were not part of O'Brien's culture. Old-timers in the hospital recall nostalgically that in the past the patient-staff coffee shop was used as a meeting place after lectures, for psychiatric staff across the hierarchy, and especially for residents; they bemoan that "at present," in spite of the fact that the new coffee shop is more spacious and more centrally located, residents are rarely seen there.

Two occasions furnish the main possibilities for informal interaction: the morning report and lunch.

After the morning report, the psychiatrist-in-chief speaks to staff—mainly to clinical administrators. Residents may or may not be present at some of these conversations. Social workers talk with administrators and residents about matters of admission or workup or issues concerning patients' families. Some administrators may talk to their own ward residents at that time, and administrators or residents may check with their colleagues from other halls in regard to some patients' transfers.

Small groups of residents sit with one another at lunch; they may be joined by some senior psychiatrists, social workers, psychologists, and social scientists, who mix freely with one another (while nurses and aides tend to be grouped among themselves). In such mixed gatherings, conversations tend to be social or intellectual. Often talk will turn to political issues. Since the staff is highly intellectual, this type of conversation is rewarding for everyone, in addition to providing much-needed rest from a stressful and cerebral professional activity; and it helps residents to avoid discussing patients, although they may do this from time to time. One or another psychologist, and more frequently a social worker, will insist on "talking shop." A favored topic at lunch, especially if a social scientist is present, is "gripes and grievances," basically concerning the way residents are being treated by the powers that be.

At the hospital, residents don't have a lounge—nor does anyone else, for that matter—as is usual in most hospitals. Repeatedly, year after year, they have asked for one, but they were told that there was no space available or that a lounge would not serve any useful purpose. When the issue came up again in the fall of 1962, the new director of residency training, although he had said that he was determined "to make this hospital a happy place for residents," said that the "lounge issue" was a trivial one and surely not the "real" source of the residents' discontent. Although he was well trained and well read in matters sociological, he did not realize that the importantance of a lounge lies not only in its physical existence but in the moral legitimacy for informal gatherings which its existence symbolizes.

Hence, there is little communication between residents both because there is little instrumental interdependence and because there are relatively little opportunity and legitimacy for informal interaction.

Instrumental Association

The third type of arrangement that fosters solidarity, *instrumental association*, tended to operate in an ineffective way. When the research for this study was begun, residents wanted to be recognized formally as a body with its own peculiar interests. They started to meet once a week for lunch. They were not encouraged to do so by the senior staff, but they were not prevented from doing so either. At their request, the psychiatrist-in-chief met with them weekly in order to, in his words, "listen to their opinions." These regular meetings with the psychiatrist-in-chief lasted from the second week of September of year 1 to the second week of April of year 2. Also during that year the psychiatrist-in-chief declared himself willing to "listen," as he put it, to the residents' spokesperson, who was to represent them to him.

However, this spokesperson was never given any formal status or task. He was not put in charge nor was he consulted in regard to the rotation of residents for patients' admissions and workups, the scheduling of which was in the hands of the social service. Not then, and never during the years of the research, was a representative of the residency group invited, let alone appointed, to any committee meetings, including those of the Residency Education Committee.

Under these conditions, the weekly meetings of residents were in some respects similar to the gripe sessions at lunch in the all-staff cafeteria: they were a setting for venting grievances without expectation that something would be done about them. Like the gripes over lunch, they led neither to action nor to change. They served as a safety valve of sorts but not as a meaningful problem- or goal-focused exchange of information. They provided some immediate gratification and some immediate solidarity but did not encourage sustained collective action. Hence this "instrumental association" could hardly be instrumental. If it fostered solidarity, it was a solidarity of discontent, not of action.

At O'Brien none of the three settings for generating solidarity and providing opportunities for communication was sufficiently effective. With little instrumental interdependence, few occasions for primary relations, and a politically weak instrumental association, residents found themselves in a vulnerable position. They depended on the top leadership for communication and support.[7] In periods when they got it, they were in a position—as they should be—to act as intermediaries between the powers that be and the patients.

This dependence on the top leadership throws light on the events discussed in the previous chapter. There it was argued that residents tended to be deprived of the support they needed for developing and maintaining a feeling of competence when they did not meet with the senior lecturer and when psychiatrists in top positions left the hospital. This interpretation now gains significance. If residents were vulnerable to an interruption of communication with the top leadership and to being largely left to their own devices, it would seem to be because their "own devices" were too weak to enable them to maintain sufficient moral strength to give patients in turn the reassurance needed in their own anxiety-ridden condition.

This was an atmosphere ripe for gossip and the spread of rumors among residents as well as among patients, an expression of the anxiety that was being passed on. O'Brien unwittingly fostered social anxiety.

The Flow of Communication and the Structure of Leadership

It was common knowledge among the staff that news about real or imagined events traveled fast among patients. Some people believed that "not only do patients know everything that goes on in the hospital, but they know things even before the staff hears about them." It was suspected that information was being gathered and passed on by the "rubbish team"—the patients who were in charge of emptying the wastepaper baskets in the staff offices. Be this as it may, an explanation can be found in some structural components of the organization.

It is possible to single out two structural conditions for the spreading of rumors and information. There must be an interest in both obtaining and communicating information, and there must be opportunities for doing so.

Subordinates generally are most interested in those who have authority over them, since the latter are in a position to make decisions that affect the subordinates' lives. Decisions that are made about the staff, or generally decisions affecting changes in the organization, also impinge upon the lives of subordinates in some way or other. And since psychiatrists in this hospital serve as "high-status authorities" or "high-status friends," patients have special personal interest in them.

Patients, like low-status occupants generally, lack the authority that would legitimize the interest they have in other status occupants. Largely for this reason, the authority holders are insulated from observability by subordinates. It follows that the subordinates' interest in authority holders is not focused—that is, that subordinates will try to obtain any information they can. That their curiosity is not functionally specific, but is, rather, diffuse accounts in part for the spread of gossip and rumor. Gossip often is a concomitant of a situation in which a role-partner is interested in another status occupant but this interest is not backed up by legitimate authority or by a legitimate right to observe behavior.[8]

Unfocused interest in what goes on among authority holders develops at several levels in the hierarchy; just as patients are interested in what goes on among the psychiatric staff generally, residents are most interested in what goes on among the senior psychiatric staff. And in both types of status occupants such interest will increase with a rise in anxiety level caused by social stress.

Subordinates are interested not only in obtaining information concerning status superiors but also in passing it on, whether the information is important or trivial, as when rumors travel about the personal lives of authority holders. A patient who can boast of knowing about a psychiatrist's courtship or other personal matters makes a claim among peers of being "in." That is, the knowledge obtained by subordinates about their superordinates is often used for status enhancement among peers.

The pretense of being "in" is especially important for people whose low social positions entitle them to few such claims and even more so when the social system is "mobility-blocked." In this case the low level of visibility of the higher status groups combined with subordinate status produces a felt need to "pass" vicariously across the actually impassable status lines. It is for this reason that gossip flourishes in hospitals generally.[9]

Both residents and patients at O'Brien were most interested in obtaining and in passing on information concerning happenings "above." But in one respect patients were in a better position to fulfill this desire: they were less hampered than residents were by pressures of avoidance. The restrictions of opportunities for communication that were shown to exist for residents did not exist in the same measure for patients, who had ample opportunities to pass on fears, rumors about anticipated events, and reports, mostly distorted, of actual happenings. These opportunities arose regularly because life on the halls is centrifugal—that is, patients are expected and encouraged to leave the halls often for various activities and therapies. Patients from different halls meet on their trips to and from and during occupational or recreational therapy, group therapy, the coffee shop, or their walks on the grounds, unaccompanied or accompanied by an escort, as the case may be, and bring back to their respective halls the news obtained on these excursions. With much interest among patients in exchanging information and much occasion for such exchange, communication flows relatively freely at this level.

In sharp contrast, among staff, and especially among residents, interest in communicating about patients is limited, as analysis of the treatment structure has shown, and opportunities to communicate are limited also. However, just as patients are interested in obtaining information about goings on among the staff, so residents are much interested in finding out about the higher echelons, especially among those who are insulated from their observation. The degree of one's interest in another person can be said to be in direct relation to the difference in status positions they occupy and in indirect relation to the higher-status person's visibility. Hence, there will be a tendency to develop rumors and to engage in gossip among residents also, and as with patients this tendency increases with stress. We remember that informal interaction among residents takes place during lunch and at haphazard moments. Since the residents are very much preoccupied with themselves, these talks frequently concern their own situation in relation to those in authority. It is these authority figures, not so much the patients, who are the subject matter of conversations.

With little solidarity among residents, little interest and little opportunity to communicate work-relevant information, but much interest and some opportunity to communicate gripes, grievances, and rumors, there would be the possibility to turn interest into goal-directed behavior and the thirst for rumor into fact finding under one condition: strong central leadership.

We know from studies of power relations and from such diverse social scientists as Tocqueville and Simmel[10] that a situation where subordinates are status equals but have relatively little in common and relatively little contact with one another lends itself well to central domination. At O'Brien, pluralistic ignorance and lack of power encourage the centralization of authority. However, at the same time that such a structure lends itself to central domination, it is also dependent on it. For it is mainly through a central authority that information can reach the subordinates and their own activities can be coordinated and given meaning. Residents have to rely on central leadership for information and for guidance in their tasks, as well as for support in their endeavors.

Under these circumstances the most useful leadership would be provided by two central figures: a high-status authority and a high-status friend. Residents would then be part of a natural triad in which their subordinate position and their lack of contact among one another would be compensated for by the task-oriented guidance they receive from one of these central figures and the emotional support they receive from the other.

The Absence of a Natural Triad

The organization provided a strong task-oriented leader. However, he was so strong that he impaired the functioning of the high-status friend, and hence made the residents even more dependent on himself.

When the psychiatrist-in-chief took his position at O'Brien some four years before the beginning of this research, he brought with him a psychiatrist of great talent to become the director of residency training. The latter was to develop the residency program, do the necessary work for the recruitment of candidates, and chair the Residency Education Committee. He went about these tasks with great devotion and made himself readily available to residents who turned to him with their problems.

The arrangement had all the potentialities of becoming a natural triad, which is one, it will be remembered, in which a low-status subordinate refers to both a high-status authority and a high-status friend—that is, to both an instrumental and an expressive leader, respectively. The latter gives support and in this way alleviates the tension created in the authority relation between the task leader and his followers.

For such a triad to function, the high-status authority and the high-status friend must be in some relation with each other, but there must not be too much interaction between them. Interaction, as we know, may increase sentiments and strengthen bonds, or it may intensify a conflict where it exists. Either of these outcomes would threaten the independent effectiveness of the two leaders.

The natural triad can operate only within a value system that tolerates some conflict and some incipient coalition within it. This is the case in the therapeutic triad described in chapter 3, in which a patient relates to both a clinical administrator as his high-status authority and a psychotherapist as his high-status friend. There is little opportunity for alliance between these two and there is some toleration of conflict between them. Similarly, some measure of coalition between the patient and the therapist is tolerated to safeguard the "therapeutic alliance."

But in the top leadership of O'Brien there was no norm that would proscribe an alliance between the two high-status role-partners and induce tolerance of some measure of coalition between the high-status friend and the subordinates.

The psychiatrist-in-chief expected to have a clear-cut alliance with the director of residency training. He could not have tolerated any conflict with him or any divergence of interest stemming from their different positions. We know that if the natural triad is to operate effectively, conflict is endemic in the relationship between the two high-status role-partners. This is because the high-status friend appears to be in coalition with the low-status subordinate. Indeed, the effectiveness of the expressive leader depends precisely on some measure of alliance with the subordinate. But so does, in the long run, the effectiveness of the high-status authority, because he benefits from the fact that the support the subordinates receive relieves the tension that would otherwise accumulate between him and them.

At O'Brien, the social structure did not provide the arrangements and the value system that limit the exercise of authority, prescribe the tolerance of conflict and coalitions, and thus keep the expressive leader from threatening the power of the instrumental leader. Hence the director of residency training was obliged to do his best to assure the psychiatrist-in-chief of his complete loyalty and devotion. As a result, the tension between the latter and the residents did, indeed, accumulate, for the director of residency training was not in a position to help relieve it. By year 2 of the research the residents' main complaint was expressed in the often-used phrase that "in this hospital we have governance through the superego." This was the time when, it will be remembered, in keeping with the jargon of the diagnostic culture prevalent in a mental hospital, rumor had it that "massive paranoia had broken out among the residents."

That the failure of the director of residency training to be a high-status friend to his residents was not a personal one is shown by subsequent events, when at the end of year 2 this director resigned and the position was taken by a young and promising psychiatrist who had been a resident at this hospital five years earlier. The newcomer started out in his position enthusiastically and with the statement: "I am intent on making this hospital a happy place for residents." He gave the residents much of his time, saw them regularly both in groups and individually, and invited their confidence with his wisdom and with his friendly and jocular personality. In spite of this, residents recognized that "he identifies too much with the hospital," and it did not take long for them to dub the new director of residency training "a company man." Apparently an alliance between him and the high-status authority was unavoidable under the circumstances. The tension between the chief authority holder and the residents did not get the relief it could have gotten had the director of training been more independent of the psychiatrist-in-chief and thus been able to develop a closer relationship with the residents. Without such alleviation, the system depended on one strong leader, and it functioned reasonably well in spite of tensions, as long as he was visibly the coordinator and guide in the daily activities of the hospital.

Leadership and the Morning Conference

There was a fit between this centralized structure and the way in which the psychiatrist-in-chief saw his role. He had high aspirations for the hospital and was well qualified to put them into effect. He had studied problems of hospital milieu in great detail, was a psychoanalyst of some reputation, and had high academic standards. He wanted to make O'Brien a model for both milieu therapy and psychotherapy and an important academically oriented psychiatric training center as well. He insisted on excellence both in the care of patients and in teaching. To bring this about, he made it his task to be completely informed about all aspects of hospital life, as well as to make all the important decisions, with the help of some committees that functioned in advisory capacity. He was a stern taskmaster both for the senior psychiatric staff and for residents.

A good example of how he made his weight felt in centralizing information and getting it disseminated was the way he led the morning conference, an innovation he had brought to the hospital when he assumed the position about four years before the beginning of this research. This was an all-staff gathering which took place daily at 8:30 A.M. Nurses from all the halls gave reports about what they considered important in the behavior of patients during the previous 24 hours. This presentation took up most of the time and was followed by brief reports from occupational and recreational therapists; then the chief of social service reported about the census and about expected admissions for that day; a few residents reported on admissions during the previous day or night; and ward administrators reported discharges. The conference ended with miscellaneous announcements and was followed by informal gatherings of small groups of staff members. This gave everyone the opportunity who needed it to get some business done. It was the one time of day when everyone was around.

This meeting was both instrumental and symbolic. It served to provide information, however briefly, about the salient events on the halls during the night and to keep the psychiatrist-in-chief posted on happenings in the hospital. It made it possible for him to confer with ward administrators after the conference—an opportunity which he amply used. It was standard procedure for him to announce at the end of each meeting the names of those psychiatrists he wanted to see immediately following this gathering.

The meaning of the morning conference was also symbolic. One social scientist on the staff called it the "morning prayer."[11] Everyone was expected to be present and punctual, so as to indicate commitment to the organization irrespective of whether some instrumental purpose was being served. Even those whose work had nothing to do with the life of patients—as was the case, for example, with social scientists—were expected to attend. This was the daily occasion for visibility of everyone to all.

The meeting served as a means of social control not only of staff activities but also of commitment to the organization. Strict punctuality was one of the ways in which such commitment was to be expressed. The psychiatrist-in-chief, always punctual himself, seated himself in such a way as to have the door in his visual purview, noting those who came late. He did not hesitate occasionally to reprimand chronic latecomers personally or to make public statements about the professional importance of punctuality.

The morning conference symbolized for the whole staff the psychiatrist-in-chief's control over all aspects of the organization. He was proud of this meeting, which he rightly considered "his" creation. And its importance indeed becomes apparent as a way of compensating for what we know about the relative lack of communication among psychiatrists in regard to their patients—lack of communication dictated by the structure of treatment, as has been shown. The formal way in which reports were made every morning, akin to military procedure, would seem to be adequate for a system in which there are strong pressures for limiting communication. Here, news was presented economically, under the supervision of the psychiatrist-in-chief, who occasionally even subtly censored the manner in which this was done, as when he frowned at the use of humor at the expense of patients. The psychiatrist-in-chief's central control imprinted itself in the minds of all.

Clearly, the social organization of the hospital rested almost entirely on the strong leadership of the psychiatrist-in-chief. When he became less available and curtailed his own activities, a state of anomie set in from which O'Brien never entirely recuperated during the duration of the research.

It will be remembered that in year 2 there was a 3½-month period during which the senior supervisor abandoned his meetings with residents. It was just before then, in the spring of year 2, that the nature of the morning conference was radically changed, because of commitments of the psychiatrist-in-chief outside the hospital. From the cozy atmosphere of the patients' library, which was furnished with armchairs and couches, and which was adjacent to the psychiatrist-in-chief's office, it was now transferred to the auditorium, at the other end of the building, with all members of the staff sitting in rows and constituting an audience for the nurses, who reported from their seats on the stage. No longer was the conference held at 8:30 A.M., which had provided the occasion to check on everybody's punctual arrival in the morning. It was now held at 11 A.M., thus interrupting the staff's professional activities.

It was not long before the conference was rescheduled to be held only three times a week instead of daily. To be sure, these changes symbolized a relaxation of rigid control, but there were no structural arrangements made in its place to intensify interaction among the psychiatric staff. On the contrary, other little changes further contributed to the loosening of bonds. For example, at the time when the morning conference was held in the patients' library, the mail was distributed in the psychiatrist-in-chief's secretarial office. This meant that people coming in at 8:30 in the morning all stopped there before entering the adjacent conference room. When the morning conference was moved out of the patients' library, the location of the mail was changed to the secretarial pool on the second floor. Staff members came at all times during the morning to collect their mail. Reception of mail was no longer an occasion to say "good morning."

These occasions for loosening social ties were brought about just after one of the top leaders of the hospital had left the organization, an event reported in the previous chapter.

A system that depends for its operation on one strong leader is more vulnerable to the impact of such events as departures and general turnover among prestigious staff members. What Merton had to say in "The Ambivalence of Organizational Leaders" is peculiarly applicable to O'Brien: "The leadership did not have the versatility to shift from one to another style as changing circumstances require[d]." It "managed to keep communication among the others in the system to a minimum." It was indeed "effective for a while." Yet, "particularly for organizations in a democratically toned society, extreme and enforced dependence upon the leader means that the organizational system is especially liable to instability."[12] It is against the background of this centralized leadership, with its concomitant failure to encourage patterned mechanisms of independent interaction, that the impact of the events described in the previous chapter must be understood.

An attempt has been made to clarify the effects of social structure on the behavior of an organization's members. To be sure, psychological factors were at stake, and not least among them were social anxiety and lack of self-confidence among the residents. I have tried to show, however, that these psychological traits, especially if they are attributes of people who share similar positions in the organization, derive in large part from the structured pattern of relationships.

There are, of course, many individual differences in the manner of coping with strain or living up to the expectations of role-partners; and there are individual differences in the manner of coping with the rights and obligations of leadership. Many people "survive" under the worst circumstances; some people succumb to the best. To say that social structure helps determine the behavior of individuals is to say what in familiar terms is meant when one says that some situations bring out the best in people, others the worst. While people react to structural constraints as individuals and according to their individual predispositions, it is also true that each has many different kinds of predispositions. The best predispositions are mobilized in some situations, the worst in others. Social structures appeal to individual predispositions in selective fashion.

Socialization is always a difficult process. Recruits to a new profession and to a new organization are required to become somewhat different from what they have been so far. They are also required to show that they can perform to the satisfaction of their seniors according to varied and often contradictory criteria, not always defined. Finally, every new status in the status sequence of promotions also constitutes a demotion: from being seniors in medical school—that is, among the most advanced and knowledgeable of all students—medical students are *promoted* to internship within a hospital, where they are the youngest, the novices among the house staff. After a year of initiation to medical practice, the intern becomes a resident. Entering a mental hospital means entering a world vastly different from the hospitals known heretofore. The new recruit to the specialty is a greenhorn: promotion to residency status is at the same time a demotion to the lowest rung of professional experience.

These attributes all residents have in common, irrespective of their individual psychologies. The manner in which the path is prepared for passing the hurdles will have a determinate influence on the manner in which the "socializees" develop that security of self-image which is the mark of the mature professional. The constraints of social structures constitute the parameters of the outcome of the socialization process.

Appendix A

(Chapter 1)

The Research Design

From June 1960 through July 1964, a total of 260 interviews were conducted with residents and a total of 109 with senior members of the staff. The interviews with the senior staff were conducted once a year (in October) as follows:

	N
Year 1 (Oct)	25
Year 2 (Oct)	26
Year 3 (Oct)	30
Year 4 (Oct)	28
Total	109

The interviews with residents were conducted twice each year, in June (and July) and December (and January) as follows:

	N
Year 1 (Jun)	22
Year 1 (Dec)	17
Year 2 (Jun)	30
Year 2 (Dec)	26
Year 3 (Jun)	36
Year 3 (Dec)	26
Year 4 (Jun)	38
Year 4 (Dec)	29
Year 5 (Jun)	36
Total	260

Figure 20 shows the research plan for interviews with residents. The horizontal rows indicate that residents were interviewed at the beginning of their second year (which was the end of their first year)

Int. no.	1 B	1 M	1 E 2 B	2 M	2 E 3 B	3 M	3 E	Total
1-1	IV 5		III 8		II 5		I 4	22
1-2		IV 5		III 8		II 4		17
2-1	V 8		IV 9		III 9		II 4	30
2-2		V 8		IV 9		III 9		26
3-1	VI 5		V 12		IV 10		III 9	36
3-2		VI 5		V 12		IV 9		26
4-1	VII 6		VI 10		V 13		IV 9	38
4-2		VII 6		VI 10		V 13		29
5-1	VIII 5		VII 10		VI 9		V 12	36
Total	29	24	49	39	46	35	38	260

Key: B = Beginning of academic year   E = End of academic year
M = Middle of academic year   I-VIII: Roman numerals indicate the cohort.

Figure 20. Research plan for interviews with residents

How to read the research plan: The columns indicate length of residency; thus, all those in the first column are beginning first-year residents, those in the second column are first-year residents in the middle of the first year, those in the third column are residents who are at the end of their first year that is, at the beginning of their second year, and so on.

The rows indicate the residency structure at any time. The diagonals from left to right indicate the history of the same cohort. They show that at some times some residents joined an older cohort, at other times one or another resident dropped out; yet the diagonals make it possible to follow the same cohort over time.

(1E 2B), in the middle of their second year (2M), at the end of their second year (which was the beginning of their third year) (2E 3B), in the middle of their third year (3M), and at the end of their third year (3E), which marks the end of residency. The first column at the left shows the year of the research and the number of the interview in the particular year: thus, in the entry "1-2," the "1" indicates the first year of interviews, and the "2" indicates the second interview given in that year (December).

The horizontal rows show the social structure of residency at a particular interviewing time: this yields comparisons between residents who were at the hospital at one time. For example, interview number 1-1 was administered in June of year 1 of the research to

182 *The Research Design*

four categories of residents: those who were at the end of their third year of residency (cohort I), those who were at the end of their second year or the beginning of their third (cohort II), those who were at the end of their first or the beginning of their second year (cohort III), and those who were at the beginning of their first year (cohort IV). Arabic numerals show the size of each cohort at the time of interview.

Going down the columns: the first column at the left (1B) lists all interviews with those in their first year of residency; 1M, with those in the middle of their first year; 1E 2B, with those at the end of their first year, which is the beginning of cohorts of first-year residents who entered O'Brien between 1960 and 1964. The totals of each stage of residency are given in the bottom row.

The Roman numerals on the diagonals from left to right show the cohorts that were followed during their training: two cohorts (IV and V) were followed from the beginning of their residency through three years. Two other cohorts were interviewed five times; two cohorts were interviewed three times; and two cohorts were interviewed once each.

Figure 20 shows that each year some residents came to the hospital at the beginning of their second year of residency. These residents could be followed only from that point; that is, there is no material regarding their first year of residency. On the other hand, there is some mortality during the third year of residency because some residents left the area. An attempt was made to follow those who did which was partially successful. One resident went to New York; two investigators each took a trip to New York to interview him during the regular interview periods. One resident who went to San Francisco was interviewed there once. Two residents who went abroad sent their responses to the interview schedule by mail. In these last three cases the interview was repeated only once after they left because it was felt that their spatial and temporal detachment from the training center would impair the comparability of their answers after that.

Restrictiveness Scores

Figure 21 shows the scores related to a distinctive aspect of the research: suicides of patients and willingness of both junior and senior staff to restrict patients in order to prevent harm to themselves and others.

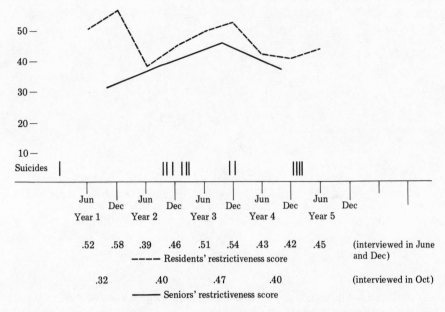

Figure 21. Restrictiveness scores of residents and seniors, by time of interview and occurrence of suicides

Appendix B

(Chapter 1)

Schedule for
Interviews with Residents

1. Tell me a bit about some of the problems you've encountered in your training these last six months.

I. WARD WORK

2. Do you look upon your work on the ward primarily as a service to the hospital or primarily as an opportunity to learn psychiatry?

3. When you are on duty or on call, do you look upon your work primarily as service or primarily as an educational opportunity?

4. Do you consider some ward assignments more desirable than others?

   4a. [*If yes*]: In what respects?

5. If you were made administrator of a ward, how would you run it?

6. If you are called to a ward, your own or someone else's, while on call, to handle a difficult situation such as a patient's emotional outburst or some acting out, are you inclined to make a decision immediately about how to handle the patient or do you talk to somebody before making a decision?

   6a. [*If "talk to somebody"*]: To whom do you talk?

   6b. [*If "make a decision immediately"*]: Have you ever felt it would be a good thing if you could talk to somebody? Who?

7. How important is it for an administrator to be present on the ward most of the day? Very important? Not important?

   7a. How about the assistant administrator? Should he spend most of his day on the ward? About half a day? Or should he only check with the ward from time to time?

8. Is it a good idea for an administrator to spend some time in the living room

184

with patients, or is it preferable not to associate with patients in such an informal manner?

8a. How about the assistant administrator?

9. What do you think is the most difficult part of clinical administration?

   9a. With whom do you discuss this?

10. Here is the first of several lists we shall be using. This one has only a couple of statements on it. Please indicate to what extent you agree or disagree with each of them. That is, do you wholly agree, agree with qualifications, disagree with qualifications, or wholly disagree? Please feel free to make comments and qualifications.

    [*Supply a copy of the following list.*]

    1. A patient's activities have to be closely supervised to prevent him from doing harm to himself and others.
    2. The main reason for evaluating a patient's discharge plans carefully is the risk involved in the harm he might do to himself and others.

11. In regard to the care of patients on the ward, do you think that in some respects you have too little responsibility?

    11a. Are there other respects in which you have too much responsibility?

    11b. Has this always been true since you've been at O'Brien?

12. If a patient on your ward tells you "You're a nice person to talk to, but you have no authority in this place and you're no help to me," how do you feel?

    12a. What do you say to the patient?

13. In the past year, have you ever been involved in a change of therapists for a patient whom you administered?

    13a. [*If yes*] : Tell me about it.

14. How many administrators have you worked with at O'Brien?

    14a. [*If only one*]: If you could continue working with him [*or* her], would you choose to?

    [*If no*] : Is there any other administrator you would like to work with?

    14b. [*If more than one*] : Whom have you most enjoyed working with?

    [*Probe*] : Who do you think is better qualified as an administrator?

    14c. [*If more than one*] : Whom have you least enjoyed working with?

15. If you had the choice of another administrator, whom would you try to get?

16. Here is a list of adjectives, some of which may and some of which may not describe the administrators you've mentioned. Please check off those that apply to each. I've labeled each copy of the list with a name.

    [*Supply a copy of the Adjective Checklist for each administrator the respondent has mentioned in answering questions 14 and 15.*]

Adjective Checklist		
rebellious	dispassionate	neutral
flexible	vague	practical
opinionated	narrow	lucid
compassionate	courageous	anxious
manipulative	dictatorial	well-organized
domineering	detached	stern
enthusiastic	involved	reflective
decisive	accommodating	cold
uninvolved	consistent	self-confident
communicative	impersonal	evasive
inflexible	idealistic	authoritarian
passive	reserved	easygoing
distant	erratic	pedestrian
relaxed	nondirective	assertive
doctrinaire	approachable	dependent
warm	directive	insightful
reliable	impatient	

17. About how much time a week do you spend in "administrative supervision" with your present administrator?

   17a. Would you like to spend more time, or less, or is it about right as it is?

II. ADMISSIONS AND WORKUPS

18. In regard to admissions procedures and workups, do you feel that at your level of training you are given too much or too little responsibility, or just the right amount?

19. Suppose a patient were admitted to another ward and then transferred to your ward. Would you agree or disagree with the opinion that the administrator of the ward to which the patient was admitted is the only person who has to be talked to in regard to your plan for management of that newly admitted patient?

20. Some people feel that the main problems about admissions is having to deal with so many different people—patient, relatives, social worker, nurse, and so on. Do you agree strongly, or moderately, or do you disagree?

   20a. Why?

21. Do you agree that it is not necessary for a psychiatrist to talk to a patient's relatives about his history if the history can be obtained from the records or from the patient himself?

22. How important is it to talk to the referring physician of a newly admitted patient?

   22a. Why?

III. PSYCHOTHERAPY

23. Do you look upon your psychotherapy with patients primarily as an

opportunity to help patients or primarily as an opportunity to learn psychiatry?

24. It has often been said that a psychotherapist should be neutral with his patient. How do you interpret such a statement?

25. Should a psychotherapist never visit his patient on the ward outside therapeutic hours, or should he visit if the patient asks him to?

    25a. Should he visit the patient occasionally on his own initiative?

26. If a patient says, "Psychotherapy won't help me anyway," how do you feel?

    26a. What if he says, "You're only a resident, but I don't mind helping you out in your training; you have to learn"?

27. If your patient in psychotherapy asks his nurse whether you have supervision, what would you like her to answer?

    27a. If the patient asks you this directly, what do you say?

28. A resident in another hospital was heard to say, "I learned a basic rule of therapy from a patient who, after he had been successfully treated, said to me, 'Just listen to the patient; don't listen to his family.' " What do you think of this statement?

29. About what sorts of things do you communicate with the administrator of a patient you have in therapy?

30. How many patients do you have?

    30a. Describe them briefly, please, mentioning any change that may have taken place since the time you started therapy.

31. Here is a list of twenty-six kinds of patients. Please indicate how easy or difficult you think it would be for you to treat each of them. That is, do you think it would be especially easy, no different from treating other patients, more difficult than treating other patients, or especially difficult? If you don't know, you may indicate that too.

    [*Supply a copy of the following list.*]

    1. A patient very much like you, like a young doctor, for example, in status and education
    2. A patient you have known outside, or whose family you have known outside
    3. A patient who is psychologically very much like you
    4. A patient who reminds you of a member of your family
    5. A patient so extremely talkative that he rarely permits you to talk
    6. A patient who refuses to talk in the interview
    7. A patient who expresses his hostility through action
    8. A patient who cannot talk coherently
    9. A patient who questions your competence as a psychiatrist
    10. A patient previously in therapy with a senior person in the profession
    11. A patient of the opposite sex
    12. A patient much older than you
    13. A homosexual patient of the same sex
    14. A homosexual patient of the opposite sex
    15. A patient of high professional status, like a well-known psychiatrist
    16. A patient whose progress is extremely slow

17. A geriatric patient
18. A patient less than twenty years old
19. A patient who is very promiscuous sexually
20. A Harvard professor
21. An acute catatonic schizophrenic patient
22. A chronic paranoid schizophrenic patient
23. A patient in a manic phase of excitement without paranoid feelings
24. A psychotic depressed patient who is suicidal
25. A hysterical patient
26. A patient with a serious physical disorder

31a. Do you remember discussing any of these with your supervisor? Please put a check by the ones you've discussed.

31b. Do you think there would be any marked differences in the ease or difficulty of treating these patients in clinical administration, as compared to psychotherapy? If so, note in red what the differences would be.

32. Would you prefer to treat a hospitalized or an unhospitalized patient?

33. Do you think a patient's psychotherapist should be consulted if administrative changes are planned for the patient?

   [*Probe for examples.*]

34. Does the way in which a patient is administered on the ward sometimes create difficulties in therapy?

   34a. [*If no*]: Are you sure you can't remember even a small instance where this was so?

   34b. [*If yes*]: Tell me about a concrete situation that you remember.

   [*Ask the next two questions in reverse order if the respondent's previous answer makes this desirable.*]

35. Have you found that the separation between therapy and administration sometimes creates some difficulties for the psychotherapist? If so, give me an example.

36. Have you found that the separation between therapy and administration sometimes makes things easier for the psychotherapist? If so, give me an example.

37. If you are concerned about some administrative decision concerning a patient whom you have in psychotherapy, what do you do?

   37a. [*If no mention of supervisor*]: Can your supervisor ever be of any help in such a case?

   37b. When was the last time you had such a concern? Tell me about it.

38. Has anyone on the hospital staff other than your supervisor ever interfered in any way in some psychotherapy that you were conducting?

39. In the past year, have you ever had to stop psychotherapy with a patient against your wish?

   [*If yes, probe.*]

40. What do you think is the most difficult thing to learn in psychotherapy?

40a. With whom have you discussed this?

41. So far in these questions we have tried to cover some problems relating to both administration and therapy. Can you make a rough estimate about which of these two areas is more important for your training?

41a. If it were decided to train residents in only one of these two areas at a time, which one would you take up first?

41b. Why?

IV. SUPERVISION

42. How many supervisors have you had since you came to O'Brien?

42a. [*If only one*]: If you were to get another patient, would you like to get another supervisor, or would you prefer to stay with your present one?

[*If "get another"*]: What other supervisor would you like to work with?

42b. [*If more than one*]: Whom have you most enjoyed working with?

42c. [*If more than one*]: Whom have you least enjoyed working with?

[*Probe*]: If you had to restrict yourself to only one supervisor, whom would you select?

43. If you had the choice of another supervisor, whom would you try to get?

44. Let's return to the list of adjectives we used earlier; they may or may not describe the supervisors you've mentioned. Please check off those that apply to each. I've labeled each copy of the list with a name.

[*Supply a copy of the Adjective Checklist for each supervisor the respondent has mentioned in answering questions 42 and 43.*]

45. In regard to your work with supervisors, do you find that you have enough time to discuss all therapy problems that you have an urge to discuss, or does it seem that there is never enough time?

45a. [*If "never enough time"*]: Since you cannot discuss the whole content of a therapy session with your supervisor, what kind of problems do you find most important to take up with him? Please try to formulate this by referring to your last session with your supervisor or with one of your supervisors.

45b. [*If "enough time"*]:Was this always true? Does it take some skill or effort to fit it all in?

V. TRAINING

46. Do you think your professional skills in regard to either therapy or administration have improved over the last six months?

46a. [*If no*]: How do you account for this?

46b. [*If yes*]: In what way?

47. Do you think your salary is adequate considering

47a. your status in the profession?

47b. your level of training?

47c. your services to the hospital?

47d. your personal needs?

47e. the value that training has for you?

48. If you were in charge of the resident training program in this hospital, what changes in the program would you make?

48a. If you were made a resident representative on the training committee, what [other] things would you recommend?

48b. [*Probe if necessary*]: Do you consider any parts of the present training program superfluous?

49. Are there facilities or personnel of the hospital not fully utilized for training purposes?

50. How do you think other residents feel about the training program or about specific exercises?

51. Here is a list of thirteen learning situations. Please rank them according to their usefulness to you as a trainee in psychiatry, using a scale from 1 (not very useful) to 7 (very useful). Use a red pencil for hypothetical, black for actual.

[*Supply a copy of the following list.*].

1. Workup with patients
2. Group psychotherapy
3. Admission procedures
4. Supervision of group psychotherapy
5. Interviewing patients on the ward
6. Observing a senior's interview with a patient
7. Sessions with supervisor of psychotherapy
8. Hall meetings with patients
9. Meetings with the whole ward staff
10. Psychotherapy with patients
11. Opportunity to observe individual psychotherapy through a one-way screen
12. Giving shock therapy
13. Engaging in research activities

52. Do you think that staff case conferences in this hospital should be open to all nonmedical as well as medical personnel, or do you think it would be preferable if they were restricted to medical personnel only?

52a. How about morning conference?

53. Are you now receiving or do you intend to receive psychoanalytic training?

53a. [*If yes*]: Why, in your opinion, is it important for you to receive psychoanalytic training?

54. Have you had in the past, do you have now, or do you intend to have a personal analysis?

55. After you finish your formal training, do you intend to give most of your working time to a hospital or to private practice?

56. Besides hospital work [*or* private practice], do you contemplate doing any other type of work in the future?

[*Probe*]: Work in the community? Teaching? Research? Writing?

56a. Have you always felt this way?

VI. RELATIONS WITH OTHERS

57. During these last six months, have you sometimes felt that your clinical judgment surpassed that of another resident?

57a. [*If yes*]: When was the last time?

57b. [*If no*]: How about problems conference?

58. During these last six months, have you ever felt that your clinical judgment was not so good as that of another resident?

58a. When was the last time?

59. Here's the adjective list again, to apply to yourself this time.

59a. Please check off, on this copy, the adjectives that describe you as you are now, in your role as resident psychiatrist.

[*Supply an Adjective Checklist labeled "real self."*]

59b. Now, please check off on this copy the qualities you would *like* to have ultimately, in your future role as psychiatrist.

[*Supply an Adjective Checklist labeled "ideal self."*]

60. Here is a list of ten criteria that you probably use in evaluating your colleagues. How much importance do you attach to each of these attributes? Please rank them on a scale from 1 (not very important) to 7 (very important).

[*Supply a copy of the following list.*]

1. Extensive knowledge of facts
2. Ability to get along with colleagues
3. Skill in diagnosis
4. Ability to establish rapport with patients
5. Ability to work effectively with nurses
6. Determination to keep informed about research and literature
7. Therapeutic skill
8. Willingness to take risks
9. Willingness to accept the existing state of affairs, even in the face of disagreement
10. Skill in clinical administration of patients

61. Who among the senior staff with whom you have worked or whom you have listened to this year do you think of as your best teacher?

62. Who among the senior staff whom you know do you think of as the best psychotherapist?

63. During this year, have you sometimes felt that your clinical judgment about a particular case surpassed that of a senior staff member?

63a. [*If yes*]: When was the last time?

VII. GENERAL QUESTIONS

64. Do you think that mental illness is like other types of illness, or do you think that there are significant differences?

    64a. [*If "significant differences"*] : What are they?

65. At a staff conference at another hospital, a resident said, "Hospitalization is a catastrophe in a patient's life and should be avoided at all costs." To what extent do you agree or disagree with this statement?

    [*If necessary, probe*]: Please explain your reasons.

66. Here is a list of seven statements. Please indicate whether you agree or disagree with each. If you feel that a simple "agree" or "disagree" answer does not represent your complete idea on the subject, please make comments and qualifications.

    [*Supply a copy of the following list.*]

    1. It is better to give a patient shock therapy if there is a reasonable expectation of improvement than to make him go through a lengthy process of psychotherapy.
    2. Shock therapy should be avoided even at a high cost, since even a remarkable improvement brought about in this way cannot be relied upon as much as little improvement brought about in psychotherapy.
    3. Shock therapy is helpful under some circumstances to enable the patient to profit from psychotherapy.
    4. Since drugs help to calm a patient but do not really constitute therapy, their use should be very limited.
    5. Since drugs help to calm a patient, they should be used freely, since such calming often has important beneficial consequences.
    6. Drugs are helpful under some circumstances to enable the patient to profit from psychotherapy.
    7. Since the beneficial effects of drugs have been amply substantiated, they constitute the most hopeful method of treatment.

67. Do you find it easy or difficult to treat a patient who has had electric shock?

68. Do you find it easy or difficult to treat a patient who has been given or is being given tranquilizing drugs?

69. Here is a list of four statements. Please give an order of importance to each, using a scale from 1 (not very important) to 7 (very important), and please make comments freely.

    [*Supply a copy of the following list.*]

    1. A psychotherapist should never be late for an appointment with a patient.
    2. A patient must realize that he is sick before he can be successfully treated.
    3. A patient's complaints should be interpreted in reference to his illness.
    4. A psychotherapist must remember that mental patients tend to distort reality.

70. To what extent do you agree with the idea that a patient's lateness for an appointment is due mainly to his underlying resistance to see the therapist?

71. If a patient were to say "I feel sicker here in the hospital than I feel at home," how would you interpret his statement?

72. What are you most likely to do when you find yourself with a couple of free hours when you're on duty?

73. Here's our last list: nine statements about the contacts between residents and various people in this hospital. Please indicate by each statement whether you think that residents have opportunities for such contacts not often enough, often enough, or too often.

    [*Supply a copy of the following list.*]

    1. Residents here have informal contacts with senior members of the staff.
    2. Residents here have formal contacts with senior members of the staff.
    3. Residents here have informal contacts with each other.
    4. Residents here associate with each other in task-oriented activities.
    5. Residents here can visit the library.
    6. Residents here see patients informally.
    7. Residents here see patients in a structured setting.
    8. Residents here have formal contacts with the nursing staff.
    9. Residents here have informal contacts with the nursing staff.

74. When you are at home, do you ever find yourself worrying about your work?

    74a. [*If yes*]: What do you worry about, for example?

    74b.   When was the last time?

    74c.   To whom did you talk about it?

75. Do you ever get indignant about anything that happens in the hospital?

    75a. [*If no*]: How do you account for that?

    75b. [*If yes*]:When was the last time?

    75c.   With whom did you talk about it?

76. If a medical student were to ask you what he should read to find out what psychiatry is all about, what would you recommend to him?

    [*If necessary, explain*]: That is, a student who is contemplating specializing in psychiatry.

77. This is the end of the interview. Is there anything about your work here, or specifically about your training, that you would like to add?

Appendix C

(Chapter 7)
Normative and Self-Image Scores on Five Clusters of Adjectives

In the interviews conducted in year 1, all respondents were asked to describe a good psychiatrist. They were also asked to describe the psychiatrist at O'Brien they admired most and the one they admired least. From these descriptions, lists of adjectives were compiled. Some obvious synonyms were then eliminated, and some adjectives were added. This yielded a total of 126 adjectives, which were used in the 1961 interviews. Subsequently, these lists were reduced to 50 adjectives to eliminate duplications and to make the task of checking them off less tedious for respondents.

In the analysis reported here, only the shortened lists were used. The adjectives that were eliminated were subsequently eliminated from the lists that had been checked off in 1961.

The adjectives were grouped in several factors, of which the first three could be called "rapport," "assertiveness-permissiveness," and "detached concern." The adjectives that are part of these factors—labeled I, II, and III—are shown in table 23. Out of these factors, five clusters of adjectives were constructed.

The first cluster, "intellectual flexibility," consists of the adjectives in factor I except those marked with an asterisk (*) and a dagger (†). Those marked with an asterisk occur again in factor II. Those marked with a dagger seem to refer specifically to some feeling state of insecurity. They were used to form a second cluster, "self-confidence."

The third cluster, "nonauthoritarianism," consists of those adjectives in factor II that express this trait: not dictatorial, not domineering, not authoritarian, not stern. The fourth cluster, "assertiveness,"

195

consists of those adjectives that express this trait: well-organized, assertive, decisive, and not passive. Asterisked adjectives were eliminated to avoid duplication.

The fifth cluster, "dispassionate involvement," consists of all the adjectives making up factor III except the one asterisked, which was eliminated to avoid duplication.

Normative and self-image scores on these five clusters of adjectives are given in tables 24-33.

Table 23. Adjectives grouped by factors of "rapport," "assertiveness-permissive-ness," and "detached concern"

Factor I: rapport	Factor loadings	Factor II: assertiveness-permissiveness	Factor loadings	Factor III: detached concern	Factor loadings
Flexible	.74	Assertive	.78	Involved	.64
Warm	.70	Decisive	.69	Uninvolved	−.69
Approachable	.65	*Self-confident	.61	Detached	−.68
†Relaxed	.63	*Lucid	.53	Directive	.66
Communicative	.62	Well-organized	.52	Neutral	−.66
Insightful	.62	Authoritarian	−.60	Dispassionate	−.62
Reliable	.61	Domineering	−.57	Impersonal	−.62
Practical	.55	Dictatorial	−.56	*Distant	−.49
†Self-confident	.55	Stern	−.53	Reserved	−.47
Compassionate	.54	Passive	−.41	Nondirective	−.44
Lucid	.54				
Consistent	.53				
Inflexible	−.80				
Narrow	−.81				
*Dictatorial	−.72				
Cold	−.76				
Distant	−.69				
Vague	−.68				
Evasive	−.66				
Erratic	−.65				
†Anxious	−.63				
Doctrinaire	−.61				
Impatient	−.59				
*Authoritarian	−.59				
*Domineering	−.58				
*Stern	−.51				
Pedestrian	−.57				
†Dependent	−.52				

Table 24. Normative scores for adjectives related to "intellectual flexibility," by time and position in the hospital

	Year 2			Year 3			Year 4		
	Ad*	HS	OS	Ad	HS	OS	Ad	HS	OS
Flexible	100	100	100	100	75	100	100	100	100
Warm	100	100	100	100	100	100	100	78	100
Approachable	100	100	100	100	100	100	100	100	100
Communicative	100	100	100	100	100	100	100	100	100
Insightful	80	100	100	100	100	100	100	100	100
Reliable	80	100	100	100	100	100	100	100	100
Practical	100	100	100	100	100	100	100	100	100
Compassionate	100	67	100	100	100	100	100	100	100
Lucid	100	67	100	100	100	100	100	100	100
Consistent	100	100	100	100	50	100	82	78	100
Not inflexible	60	67	100	56	50	100	82	100	100
Not narrow	100	100	100	100	100	100	100	100	100
Not cold	80	67	100	100	100	100	100	100	100
Not distant	80	67	100	78	50	10	100	78	100
Not vague	80	67	100	78	75	100	100	100	100
Not evasive	100	67	100	78	75	100	82	100	100
Not erratic	80	67	100	100	100	100	100	78	100
Not doctrinaire	20	33	100	78	100	100	82	100	100
Not impatient	40	67	100	100	50	100	82	56	100
Not pedestrian	80	100	100	78	100	100	64	100	100
$\bar{X}$	85	82	100	92	86	100	94	93	100
N	10	6	5	9	8	6	11	9	7

*Ad = administrators; HS = supervisors within the hospital; OS = supervisors outside the hospital.

Table 25. Self-image scores for adjectives related to "intellectual flexibility," by time and position in the hospital

	Year 2			Year 3			Year 4		
	Ad*	HS	OS	Ad	HS	OS	Ad	HS	OS
Flexible	100	100	100	100	100	100	100	75	100
Warm	75	60	100	100	75	100	64	43	100
Approachable	100	100	100	56	100	100	64	100	100
Communicative	50	60	67	56	50	100	82	71	71
Insightful	100	100	100	78	100	100	100	100	100
Reliable	100	60	100	100	100	100	100	100	100
Practical	100	100	67	56	100	100	64	100	100
Compassionate	100	20	67	100	100	100	82	100	100
Lucid	100	60	100	35	50	100	64	43	71
Consistent	50	60	100	33	25	100	09	14	100
Not inflexible	75	60	100	78	75	100	82	100	100
Not narrow	75	20	67	78	50	100	100	100	100
Not cold	75	100	100	100	100	100	45	100	100
Not distant	50	60	67	78	50	100	45	100	100
Not vague	75	60	100	56	75	100	09	71	100
Not evasive	75	20	100	56	75	100	27	100	100
Not erratic	75	20	100	11	50	71	82	71	71
Not doctrinaire	50	60	100	56	75	43	82	100	100
Not impatient	−25	−20	−20	−33	00	−43	−09	14	100
Not pedestrian	75	60	100	33	50	100	64	100	43
$\bar{X}$	74	58	86	61	70	89	63	80	93
N	10	6	5	9	8	6	11	9	7

*Ad = administrators; HS = supervisors within the hospital; OS = supervisors outside the hospital.

Table 26. Normative scores for adjectives related to "self-confidence," by time and position in the hospital

	Year 2			Year 3			Year 4		
	Ad*	HS	OS	Ad	HS	OS	Ad	HS	OS
Self-confident	80	100	100	80	100	100	80	100	100
Relaxed	60	100	100	78	75	100	100	100	100
Not anxious	60	67	100	100	75	100	82	78	100
Not dependent	40	67	100	78	75	100	82	100	100
$\bar{X}$	60	84	100	84	81	100	86	95	100
N	10	6	5	9	8	6	11	9	7

*Ad = administrators; HS = supervisors within the hospital; OS = supervisors outside the hospital.

Table 27. Self-image scores for adjectives related to "self-confidence," by time and position in the hospital

	Year 2			Year 3			Year 4		
	Ad*	HS	OS	Ad	HS	OS	Ad	HS	OS
Self-confident	80	100	100	56	75	100	27	100	71
Relaxed	−50	20	−20	−33	00	43	−45	14	71
Not anxious	−25	20	00	−56	75	43	−27	71	43
Not dependent	50	100	100	78	75	71	82	100	100
$\bar{X}$	14	60	45	11	56	64	09	71	71
N	10	6	5	9	8	6	11	9	7

*Ad = administrators; HS = supervisors within the hospital; OS = supervisors outside the hospital.

Table 28. Normative scores for adjectives related to "nonauthoritarianism," by time and position in the hospital

	Year 2			Year 3			Year 4		
	Ad*	HS	OS	Ad	HS	OS	Ad	HS	OS
Not dictatorial	80	100	100	100	100	100	100	100	100
Not domineering	80	100	60	100	100	100	82	100	100
Not authoritarian	40	100	100	100	100	100	82	100	100
Not stern	60	67	60	100	100	67	64	100	100
$\bar{X}$	65	92	82	100	100	92	82	100	100

*Ad = administrators; HS = supervisors within the hospital; OS = supervisors outside the hospital.

Table 29. Self-image scores for adjectives related to "nonauthoritarianism," by time and position in the hospital

	Year 2			Year 3			Year 4		
	Ad*	HS	OS	Ad	HS	OS	Ad	HS	OS
Not dictatorial	50	60	33	78	75	100	82	100	100
Not domineering	50	60	67	56	50	100	45	100	100
Not authoritarian	50	20	33	33	75	100	27	100	100
Not stern	00	60	67	56	50	43	27	43	14
$\bar{X}$	38	50	50	56	63	86	45	86	79

*Ad = administrators; HS = supervisors within the hospital; OS = supervisors outside the hospital.

Table 30. Normative scores for adjectives related to "assertiveness," by time and position in the hospital

	Year 2			Year 3			Year 4		
	Ad*	HS	OS	Ad	HS	OS	Ad	HS	OS
Well-organized	60	100	100	100	100	100	82	100	100
Assertive	60	67	20	100	100	67	64	100	33
Decisive	100	100	100	100	100	100	100	100	100
Not passive	78	67	60	78	100	100	82	100	100
$\bar{X}$	75	84	71	95	100	92	82	100	83

*Ad = administrators; HS = supervisors within the hospital; OS = supervisors outside the hospital.

Table 31. Self-image scores for adjectives related to "assertiveness," by time and position in the hospital

	Year 2			Year 3			Year 4		
	Ad*	HS	OS	Ad	HS	OS	Ad	HS	OS
Well-organized	00	20	67	−78	00	71	−45	43	100
Assertive	00	100	33	78	75	71	45	71	71
Decisive	50	60	67	33	50	71	09	100	71
Not passive	00	50	100	11	50	100	45	71	100
$\bar{X}$	13	58	67	11	44	78	14	71	86

*Ad = administrators; HS = supervisors within the hospital; OS = supervisors outside the hospital.

Table 32. Normative scores for adjectives related to "dispassionate involvement," by time and position in the hospital

	Year 2			Year 3			Year 4		
	Ad*	HS	OS	Ad	HS	OS	Ad	HS	OS
Involved	100	33	60	33	100	67	45	78	100
Not uninvolved	60	00	20	56	75	33	45	78	67
Not detached	60	00	−20	56	50	00	27	78	67
Not neutral	20	00	20	−11	75	33	−27	50	67
Not dispassionate	−20	00	−20	−56	−75	00	−45	33	00
Not impersonal	20	33	60	33	75	67	64	78	67
Not reserved	−20	00	20	−56	25	00	−64	33	33
Not nondirective	00	00	−60	−11	50	00	−09	33	33
Directive	−100	00	60	11	75	00	27	33	−33
$\bar{X}$	13	07	16	06	50	22	07	55	45

*Ad = administrators; HS = supervisors within the hospital; OS = supervisors outside the hospital.

Table 33. Self-image scores for adjectives related to "dispassionate involvement," by time and position in the hospital

	Year 2			Year 3			Year 4		
	Ad*	HS	OS	Ad	HS	OS	Ad	HS	OS
Involved	75	60	67	11	100	100	−27	71	100
Not uninvolved	25	20	67	33	75	100	27	43	100
Not detached	50	20	33	78	75	100	45	71	71
Not neutral	25	60	100	56	25	43	27	43	43
Not dispassionate	00	20	60	11	−50	−14	09	−14	43
Not impersonal	00	60	67	33	100	100	09	71	100
Not reserved	−25	−100	−20	−11	−75	−71	−27	−71	−14
Not nondirective	−50	20	20	−33	25	43	09	14	71
Directive	00	20	60	−11	50	−14	27	14	−43
$\bar{X}$	11	20	50	19	36	43	11	27	52

*Ad = administrators; HS = supervisors within the hospital; OS = supervisors outside the hospital.

Notes

Chapter 1. **Introduction**

1. Robert K. Merton and Elinor Barber, "Sociological Ambivalence," in *Sociological Ambivalence and Other Essays*, by Robert K. Merton (New York: Free Press, 1976), pp. 3-31.

2. Harvey L. Smith, "Psychiatry in Medicine: Intra- or Inter-professional Relationship?" *American Journal of Sociology* 63 (November 1957): 285-89.

3. Adolf Meyer, "The Rise to the Person and the Concept of Wholes or Integrates," *American Journal of Psychiatry* 100 (April 1944): 100-106.

4. See John C. Whitehorn, "The Individual Psychiatrist and Social Psychiatry," *American Journal of Psychiatry* 108 (July 1951): 1-6: "There is going on in American psychiatry a specifically sound development of social psychodynamics. We have gained a partial grasp of the interpersonal dynamics and the intimate social meanings of personality disorders, and we have been learning to use with some success our limited understanding of these social implications for the care and treatment of patients."

On the specific tasks of psychiatrists in World War II, see Albert Deutsch, "Military Psychiatry: World War II, 1941-43," in *One Hundred Years of American Psychiatry* (New York: Columbia University Press, 1944), pp. 367-84. On the importance of psychotherapy in military practice, see Thomas A. C. Rennie and Luther E. Woodward, *Mental Health in Modern Society* (Cambridge, Mass.: Harvard University Press, 1948), pp. 35-37. See also the *Report of the Special Commission of Civilian Psychiatrists*, by Leo H. Bartemeier, Lawrence D. Kubie, Karl A. Menninger, John Romano, and John C. Whitehorn, covering "Psychiatric Policy and Practice in the U.S. Army Medical Corps, European Theater, April 20 to July 8, 1945": "The disruption of group unity is, in the main, a primary causal factor, not a secondary effect, of personality disorganization"; excerpted in the *Journal of Mental and Nervous Diseases* 104 (October 1946).

W. C. Menninger writes about both the focus on social aspects of mental illness and the integration of psychiatry into medicine. In "Psychiatric Lessons from World War II," *American Journal of Psychiatry* 103 (March 1947):

577-86, he writes that psychiatry for the postwar world includes "learning anew the importance of the group ties in the maintenance of mental health." In *Psychiatry in a Troubled World* (New York: Macmillan, 1948), p. 7, he also writes that the integration within army medicine "was one of the chief factors that helped psychiatry out of its isolationism."

5. Without engaging in a discussion of the value of any of the currently available techniques in psychiatry, it should be noted that the distribution of these techniques marks the prestige grading in the profession. Psychotherapy, especially where it is closely linked to psychoanalysis, is expensive and takes a long time. The use of drugs is cheap and quick. Although a combination of techniques is used in most hospitals, they provide the basis for prestige grading. No claim is being made here for the association between the prestige of a technique and its effectiveness. The point is that, as Hollingshead and Redlich have shown, the use of psychoanalytically oriented psychotherapy is associated with the class positions of patients; see August B. Hollingshead and Frederick C. Redlich, *Social Class and Mental Illness: A Community Study* (New York: Wiley, 1958).

6. See Rose Laub Coser, "Laughter among Colleagues," *Psychiatry* 23 (February 1960): 81-95.

7. Renée C. Fox, "Training for Uncertainty," in *The Student Physician*, ed. Robert K. Merton, George G. Reader, and Patricia L. Kendall (Cambridge, Mass.: Harvard University Press, 1957).

8. Charles Kadushin, "Power, Influence and Social Circles: A New Methodology for Studying Opinion Makers," *American Sociological Review* 33 (October 1968): 685-99.

9. Commenting on the training of psychiatrists, Lawrence S. Kubie is reported in the *New York Times* (April 5, 1964) to have said that "the average psychiatrist treating a severely disturbed person is like a doctor just out of medical school performing delicate brain surgery."

10. See R. A. J. Asher, "The Dangers of Going to Bed," *British Medical Journal* (December 13, 1947): 967: "Rest in bed is anatomically, physically and psychologically unsound. Look at a patient lying long in bed. What a pathetic picture he makes! The blood clotting in his veins, the lime draining from his bones, the scybala stacking up in his colon, the flesh rotting from his seat, the urine leaking from his distended bladder, and the spirit evaporating from his soul"; quoted by Leon Lewis and Rose Laub Coser in "The Hazards of Hospitalization," *Hospital Administration* 5 (Summer 1960): 25-45.

11. Erving Goffman, "Total Institutions," in *Asylums* (Garden City, N.Y.: Doubleday, Anchor Books, 1944).

Chapter 2. Psychiatric Residents at Work

1. When, after the third year of the research had begun, the then new director of the hospital announced that his policy would be community oriented, I made the prediction that this would mean a rise in status for the social

service and for its chief. The chief social worker indeed prided herself on having the director's ear. The following incident is noteworthy. Residents reported that when the staff cafeteria was being remodeled and enlarged to include a second room, the director of the hospital intended to have this room reserved for MDs only. He later changed his mind, so the story went, because this would make it impossible for him to talk business with the chief of the social service over lunch. The story was never verified, but the point here is that this is how the importance of the chief of social service was perceived by the residents. It is also noteworthy that it was at that time—that is, in year 3—that the senior staff increased its ranking of admission procedures on a scale of learning usefulness.

2. See Rose Laub Coser, *Life in the Ward* (East Lansing: Michigan State University Press, 1962), pp. 22–34.

3. On the patterned distribution of authority and access to observability, see Rose Laub Coser, "Insulation from Observability and Types of Social Conformity," *American Sociological Review* 26 (February 1961): 28–39.

4. Alfred H. Stanton and Morris S. Schwartz, *The Mental Hospital* (New York: Basic Books, 1954), pp. 10–11.

5. On the split between clinical administration and therapy, see ibid., esp. pp. 69–74.

6. Much has been written about the conflicts between professional standards and the requirements of bureaucratic organization. While a review of this literature seems superfluous here, related to the present problem is Arlene K. Daniels's paper, "The Captive Professional: Bureaucratic Limitations in the Practice of Military Psychiatry," *Journal of Health and Social Behavior* 10 (December 1969): 255–65. On the reconciliation between the medical value system and organizational requirements, see Mary E. W. Goss, "Patterns of Bureaucracy among Hospital Staff Physicians," in *The Hospital in Modern Society*, ed. Eliot Freidson (New York: Free Press, 1963).

7. Robert K. Merton, *Social Theory and Social Structure*, rev. ed. (New York: Free Press, 1957), p. 371.

8. Ibid., p. 377.

9. Theodore Caplow, *Two against One: Coalitions in Triads* (Englewood Cliffs, N.J.: Prentice-Hall, 1969).

10. Merton, *Social Theory and Social Structure*, p. 371.

11. Ibid.

Chapter 3. The Therapeutic Triad

1. Regarding these two functions of the mental hospital, see Talcott Parsons, "The Mental Hospital as a Type of Organization," in *The Patient and the Mental Hospital*, ed. Milton Greenblatt, Daniel J. Levinson, and Richard H. Williams (New York: Free Press, 1957), pp. 108–29.

2. See George C. Homans, *The Human Group* (New York: Harcourt, 1950), pp. 244ff.

3. Talcott Parsons, "A Sociologist Looks at the Legal Profession," *Essays in Sociological Theory*, rev. ed. (New York: Free Press, 1954), pp. 370-85. See also, by the same author, *The Social System* (New York: Free Press, 1951), esp. chaps. 7 and 10.

4. This form of mental hospital organization has been described by Alfred H. Stanton and Morris S. Schwartz in *The Mental Hospital* (New York: Basic Books, 1954).

5. Robert K. Merton, *Social Theory and Social Structure*, rev. ed. (New York: Free Press, 1957), pp. 368-80.

6. Robert K. Merton, "Discrimination and the American Creed," *Sociological Ambivalence and Other Essays* (New York: Free Press, 1976), pp. 189-216.

7. On the distinction between behavioral and attitudinal conformity, see Robert K. Merton, "Conformity, Deviation and Opportunity Structures," *American Sociological Review* 24 (April 1959): 177-88.

8. Rose Laub Coser, "Insulation from Observability and Types of Social Conformity," *American Sociological Review* 26 (February 1961): 28-39.

9. The concept is used here in a somewhat broader sense than it was by Chester Bernard. See Chester I. Bernard, *The Functions of the Executive* (Cambridge, Mass.: Harvard University Press, 1938), pp. 168ff.

10. Rose Laub Coser, "Insulation from Observability. . . ."

11. This dual approach to psychiatric treatment helps patients not only to differentiate between fantasies and reality but also to *acknowledge* their inner dispositions. Some patients who obsessively focus their attention on action and the here-and-now (that is, on concrete behavior and its immediate consequences) must first learn to involve their attitudes in their relationships and in their expectations. Learning to acknowledge internal dispositions and long-range goals and being willing and able to talk about them with a psychotherapist may precede the ability to establish a therapeutic alliance. Such an alliance is based on the ability to apply reciprocity in one's relationships by taking account of the motivations and intentions of the other person and relating these to long-range goals.

Harold F. Searles and Jacob Christ have noted—see Searles, *Collected Papers on Schizophrenia and Related Subjects* (New York: International Universities Press, 1965), p. 118, and Jacob Christ, "Psychoanalytical Treatment of a Dissociative State with Hallucinations," in *Psychotherapy in the Designed Therapeutic Milieu*, ed. Stanley H. Eldred and Maurice Vanderpol (Boston: Little, Brown, 1968), pp. 47-59—that often "the schizophrenic appears to be in some ways imprisoned in the present; his fears make him cling desperately to what is immediate." The focus is on immediate action. "People [are] not people, but tools which serve action-oriented purposes." The psychotherapist may help crystallize the acknowledgment of internal dispositions in a way that would be more difficult for a psychiatrist who must focus attention on the details of everyday behavior. Such crystallization is seen as a precondition for successful therapy in which the relation between these internal dispositions to reality can be explored.

12. Robert K. Merton and Elinor Barber, "Sociological Ambivalence," in *Sociological Ambivalence and Other Essays*, by Robert K. Merton (New York: Free Press, 1976), pp. 3–31.

13. Alfred H. Stanton, Introduction to *Psychotherapy in the Designed Therapeutic Milieu*, ed. Stanley H. Eldred and Maurice Vanderpol (Boston: Little, Brown, 1968), p. xviii.

14. Merton, *Social Theory and Social Structure*, pp. 425ff.

15. Rose Laub Coser, "Authority and Structural Ambivalence in the Middle-class Family," in *The Family: Its Structure and Functions*, 2d ed., ed. Rose Laub Coser (New York: St. Martin's, 1974), pp. 362–73.

16. Arnold W. Green, "The Middle-class Male Child and Neurosis," *American Sociological Review* 11 (February 1946): 31–41.

17. Gregory Bateson, Don D. Jackson, Jay Haley, and John Weakland, "Toward a Theory of Schizophrenia," *Behavioral Science* 1 (October 1956): 251–64.

18. Personal communication.

19. On the norm of reciprocity, see Claude Lévi-Strauss, *Les Structures élémentaires de la parenté* (Paris: Presses Universitaires, 1949); see esp. the translation of chap. 1, "The Principle of Reciprocity," in *The Family: Its Structure and Functions*, 2d ed., ed. Rose Laub Coser (New York: St. Martin's, 1974), pp. 3–12. See also Peter M. Blau, *Exchange and Power in Social Life* (New York: Wiley, 1967); and Alvin W. Gouldner, "The Norm of Reciprocity: A Preliminary Statement," *American Sociological Review* 25 (April 1963): 161–78. On the fact that every relationship must be based on some common definition, see Max Weber, *The Theory of Social and Economic Organization*, trans. A. M. Henderson and Talcott Parsons (New York: Oxford University Press, 1947), pp. 118–20.

20. Talcott Parsons, "The American Family: Its Relations to Personality and to the Social Structure," in *Family, Socialization and Interaction Process*, by Talcott Parsons and Robert F. Bales, in collaboration with James Olds, Morris Zelditch Jr., and Philip E. Slater (New York: Free Press, 1955), pp. 3–33; and Robert F. Bales and Philip E. Slater, "Role Differentiation in small Decision-making Groups," in ibid., pp. 259–306.

21. Georg Simmel, *The Sociology of Georg Simmel*, trans. and ed. Kurt H. Wolff (New York: Free Press, 1950), chap. 4.

22. Morris Freilich, "The Natural Triad in Kinship and Complex Systems," *American Sociological Review* 29 (August 1964): 529–40. See also Raymond Firth, *We, the Tikopia* (London: Allen & Unwin, 1936).

23. Marcel Mauss, *The Gift: Forms and Functions of Exchange in Archaic Societies*, trans. Ian Cunnison (New York: Free Press, 1954). See also Peter M. Blau, *Exchange and Power in Social Life* (New York: Wiley, 1964).

24. Stanton and Schwartz observed in the hospital they studied that an unresolved antagonism between two such psychiatrists did indeed help foster a collective disturbance among patients. See Alfred H. Stanton and Morris S.

Schwartz, "The Management of a Type of Institutional Participation in Mental Illness," *Psychiatry* 12 (February 1949): 13-22.

25. See Homans, *The Human Group*; idem, *Social Behavior: Its Elementary Forms* (New York: Harcourt, 1961); and Lewis A. Coser, *The Functions of Social Conflict* (New York: Free Press, 1956).

26. In regard to the formation of coalitions in triadic relationships, see Theodore Caplow, *Two against One: Coalitions in Triads* (Englewood Cliffs, N.J.: Prentice-Hall, 1969).

27. Simmel, *The Sociology of Georg Simmel.*

28. Merton, *Social Theory and Social Structure*, p. 377.

29. Stanton and Schwartz, *The Mental Hospital*, p. 73.

30. Regarding conflict as being based on common values, see Lewis A. Coser, *The Functions of Social Conflict.*

31. See Robert K. Merton, "Social Structure and Anomie," in *Social Theory and Social Structure*; see also Richard A. Cloward and Lloyd E. Olin, *Delinquency and Opportunity* (New York: Free Press, 1960).

32. See Lewis A. Coser, "Unanticipated Conservative Consequences of Liberal Theorizing," *Social Problems* 16 (Winter 1969): 263-72.

33. On the importance of work for a person's self-image and the resulting tendency of people to refer to their work in a publicly recognized and preferably esteemed occupation or professional category, see Everett C. Hughes, *Men and Their Work* (New York: Free Press, 1958), p. 43.

34. For a notable exception to the confusion that pervades most writings on the subject, see the excellent specification of the concept of alienation by Melvin Seaman, "On the Meaning of Alienation," *American Sociological Review* 24 (December 1959): 783-91. See also Dwight G. Dean, "Alienation: Its Meaning and Measurement," *American Sociological Review* 26 (October 1961): 753-58.

35. Amitai Etzioni, "Dual Leadership in Complex Organizations," *American Sociological Review* 30 (October 1965): 688-98.

36. See Hughes, *Men and Their Work.* In regard to status inconsistency as a source of anomie, see Jack P. Gibbs and Walter T. Martin, *Status Integration and Suicide: A Sociological Study* (Eugene: University of Oregon Books, 1964).

37. Regarding the notion that *relative* rather than *absolute* deprivation is a source of frustration, see Samuel A. Stouffer et al., *The American Soldier: Adjustment during Army Life*, Studies in Social Psychology during World War Two, vol. 1 (Princeton: Princeton University Press, 1949).

Chapter 4. **The Treatment Set**

1. See Peter M. Blau, *Exchange and Power in Social Life* (New York: Wiley, 1967), and George C. Homans, *Social Behavior: Its Elementary Forms* (New York: Harcourt, 1961).

2. Blau, *Exchange and Power*, p. 98.

3. Amitai Etzioni, "Dual Leadership in Complex Organizations," *American Sociological Review* 30 (October 1965): 688-98.

4. Morris Freilich, "The Natural Triad in Kinship and Complex Systems," *American Sociological Review* 29 (August 1964): 529-40.

5. On the formation of strong sentiments through interaction, see George C. Homans, *The Human Group* (New York: Harcourt, 1950).

6. On the notion of coalition as a threat to survival of triadic arrangements, see Theodore Caplow, *Two against One: Coalitions in Triads* (Englewood Cliffs, N.J.: Prentice-Hall, 1969).

7. Ibid., pp. 24f., 54.

8. Ibid., p. 9.

9. See Robert K. Merton, *Social Theory and Social Structure*, enl. ed. (New York: Free Press, 1968), pp. 422.

10. Compare this 1963 letter to the syndicated column "Dear Abby": "My next-door neighbor Laurie likes to visit with me at night because her husband works late and she doesn't like to be by herself. I am a widower and I like being friendly to her. The other night I went to visit my niece, and found out that she had a date with Laurie's husband. What shall I do? Shall I tell my niece that she is dating a married man, shall I tell Laurie about it, or shall I keep my nose in and my mouth shut?"

11. Freilich also considers the possibility of there being no relations between HSA and HSF—that is, the possibility of "unrelated roles" to balance a negative relationship. See Morris Freilich, "The Natural Triad in Kinship and Complex Systems," *American Sociological Review* 29 (August 1964): 529-40. However, I question whether "unrelated roles" can be part of a triad: if we wish to follow a geometrical model, two people who do not interact are like two lines that never meet; they are parallel. This type of relationship will be discussed in the next chapter.

12. Fritz Heider, *The Psychology of Interpersonal Relations* (New York: Wiley, 1958). For a discussion and further elaboration of this theory, see Joseph Berger, Bernard P. Cohen, L. Laurie Snell, and Morris Zelditch Jr., *Types of Formalization in Small-group Research* (Boston: Houghton Mifflin, 1962), esp. chap. 2.

13. Paul F. Lazarsfeld, Bernard Berelson, and Hazel Gaudet, *The People's Choice: How the Voter Makes Up His Mind in a Presidential Campaign* (New York: Duell, Sloan & Pearce, 1944), chaps. 6 and 7.

Chapter 5. **The Training Set**

1. There is general agreement that "administrators are talked about much more than supervisors." As another resident explained: "I think there is less tendency to discuss what goes on in supervision. It is more formal and more guarded and not out in the open." The director of residency training confirmed this on the basis of his own earlier experience when he was a resident at O'Brien and on the basis of his present experience with the residents with whom he has sustained contact.

2. Robert K. Merton, *Social Theory and Social Structure*, rev. ed. (New York: Free Press, 1957), p. 375.

3. Max Weber, *The Theory of Social and Economic Organization*, trans. A. M. Henderson and Talcott Parsons (New York: Oxford University Press, 1947), pp. 88–100; George Herbert Mead, *Mind, Self and Society* (Chicago: University of Chicago Press, 1934), pp. 152–64; and Jean Piaget, *The Moral Judgment of the Child*, trans. Marjorie Gabain (New York: Free Press, 1932).

4. See Donald I. Warren, "Power, Visibility and Conformity in Formal Organizations," *American Sociological Review* 33 (December 1968): 951–70.

5. Robert K. Merton, George G. Reader, and Patricia L. Kendall, *The Student Physician* (Cambridge, Mass.: Harvard University Press, 1957).

6. Merton, *Social Theory and Social Structure*, p. 374.

7. Rose Laub Coser, "Insulation from Observability and Types of Social Conformity," *American Sociological Review* 26 (February 1961): 28–39.

8. Although a resident has two or three supervisors, one for each patient, the several supervisors occupy a similar structural position, so that there will hardly be differing expectations emanating from structural sources. Moreover, the fact that each supervisor focuses on the resident's therapy with a different patient prevents contradictory recommendations in regard to the same patient. This does not mean that the resident is entirely free from experiencing contradictory messages in regard to his or her internal dispositions, but such contradictions are less strongly felt than if several supervisors were to give their guidance in relation to the same patient.

Chapter 6. Structural Ambivalence and Patterned Mechanisms of Defense

1. See Raymond S. Duff and August B. Hillingshead, *Sickness and Society* (New York: Harper & Row, 1968).

2. A similar dilemma exists, of course, in regard to the simultaneous activity of research and treatment. For an outstanding report about how both patients and staff cope with the problem of the use of patients as subjects of research, see Renée C. Fox, *Experiment Perilous: Physicians and Patients Facing the Unknown* (New York: Free Press, 1959).

3. From the field notes from an earlier research reported in Rose Laub Coser, *Life in the Ward* (East Lansing: Michigan State University Press, 1961).

4. See Emily Mumford, *Interns: From Students to Physicians* (Cambridge, Mass.: Harvard University Press, 1970).

5. Robert K. Merton, *Social Theory and Social Structure*, rev. ed. (New York: Free Press, 1957), p. 423.

6. Personal communication.

7. Merton, *Social Theory and Social Structure*, pp. 370–76.

8. Ibid.

9. Robert K. Merton and Elinor Barber, "Sociological Ambivalence," in *Sociological Ambivalence and Other Essays*, by Robert K. Merton (New York: Free Press, 1976), pp. 3–31.

10. Wilbert E. Moore and Melvin M. Tumin, "Some Social Functions of Ignorance," *American Sociological Review* 14 (1949): 787-95.

11. Robert K. Merton, "The Ambivalence of Scientists," in *The Sociology of Science: Theoretical and Empirical Investigations*, ed. Norman W. Storer (Chicago: University of Chicago Press, 1973), pp. 383-412.

12. See Rose Laub Coser, "Laughter among Colleagues," *Psychiatry* 23 (February 1960): 81.

13. See Martin Grotjahn, *Beyond Laughter* (New York: McGraw-Hill, 1957), esp. chap. 2.

14. At the psychiatric staff meetings where I studied the use of humor, it turned out that there was a tendency for those who were low in the authority structure to make fewer witticisms. Of 90 witticisms made by the permanent staff, 53 were made by the senior staff, 33 by the residents, and 4 by the paramedical staff. The average number of witticisms per member was 7.5 for senior staff, 5.5 for junior staff, and 0.7 for paramedical staff. This difference gains relevance if one considers the fact that junior staff had the floor more frequently. At 14 of the 20 meetings observed, a resident had the floor for about three-quarters of the time allotted because he or she gave a case presentation. The fact of having the floor did not substantially increase the number of humorous remarks by a junior member; 19 were made by residents presenting a case, 14 by those in the audience. See Rose Laub Coser, "Laughter among Colleagues," p. 84.

15. Attendants in some state hospitals use humor with patients freely; see Richard F. Salisbury, *Structures of Custodial Care* (Berkeley and Los Angeles: University of California Press, 1962). At O'Brien, the psychiatrist-in-chief explained: "I deliberately try to squelch humor during morning reports. I want to teach that patients are to be treated, not laughed at."

16. All the coding was done "blindly" by two coders. There was no agreement between them in about 10 percent of all cases. Decisions about these were made independently by a third person.

17. The fact that evasiveness tended to increase in both activity systems between 1960 and 1964 is related to changes in the social structure of the hospital. See chapter 9.

18. Bettie Arthur and Judith L. Birnbaum, "Professional Identity as a Determinant of the Response to Emotionally Disturbed Children," *Psychiatry* 31 (May 1968): 138-49.

19. Allen H. Barton, "The Concept of Property-space in Social Research," in *The Language of Social Research*, ed. Paul F. Lazarsfeld and Morris Rosenberg (New York: Free Press, 1955), pp. 40-53.

20. He resigned the post in the spring after the termination of data collection (see chapter 9). The reason given for his resignation was related to decisions concerning his personal career.

21. See Martin B. Loeb, "Some Dominant Cultural Themes in a Psychiatric Hospital," *Social Problems* 4 (1956): 17.

22. Talcott Parsons, *The Social System* (New York: Free Press, 1951).

23. K. Mannheim, *Ideology and Utopia* (New York: Harcourt, 1936), p. 49.

Chapter 7. **Consensus and Dissensus, Norms and Counternorms**

1. This part of the research design owes much to my discussions with my colleague Robert Schnitzer. Janice Stroud, the very capable assistant during this early part of the research, contributed much to our discussions.

A report about the way in which the list of adjectives was obtained is to be found in appendix C.

2. Appendix C contains an explanation of how these clusters were obtained.

3. This is based on a "normative score" computed as follows: $NS = 1 - (MI/\frac{1}{2}N)$, where MI is the number of minority responses to the ideal (dissenters) and N is the number of respondents. The reason for dividing by half the number of respondents rather than by the total is the following: if one-half of the respondents express an opinion that contradicts the other half, it must be concluded that there is no norm or no common value, and that therefore the score must be zero.

4. The formula used to compute the "self-image score" was constructed according to the same rationale: $SI = MS/\frac{1}{2}N$, where MS is the number of minority responses to the self-image question (nonconformists) and N is the number of respondents. The reason for dividing by half the number of respondents rather than by the total is the following: if one-half of the respondents see themselves as behaving or believing the opposite of the other half, there is no conformity, and this is expressed by a score of zero.

5. Rose Laub Coser, "Insulation from Observability and Types of Social Conformity," *American Sociological Review* 26 (February 1961): 28–39.

6. Ibid.

7. Marvin B. Scott and Stanford M. Lyman, "Accounts," *American Sociological Review* 33 (February 1968): 46–62. The notion is similar to the psychological concept of rationalization. This is the psychological counterpart to the Marxist use of the term *ideology* to refer to a "false" use of values to legitimize the status quo. Cf. Robert K. Merton, *Social Theory and Social Structure*, enl. ed. (New York: Free Press, 1968), p. 512.

8. Leon Festinger, *A Theory of Cognitive Dissonance* (Evanston, Ill.: Row, Peterson, 1957).

9. Morris Rosenberg, *Society and the Adolescent Self-image* (Princeton: Princeton University Press, 1965). Rosenberg found that black children in integrated schools in Baltimore had lower self-esteem than black children in the city's segregated schools, even though scholarly performance, as measured by grades, was superior under conditions of integration. However, even these improved grades did not come up to the level of the white children. Whether for this reason or for reason of color alone, these black children had lower self-esteem than children in the segregated schools of the same city. Similarly, Rosenberg found that Jews in Catholic neighborhoods had lower self-esteem than Jews in the more prestigious Protestant neighborhoods. Catholics had lower self-esteem when they lived in Jewish neighborhoods than when they lived in Protestant neighborhoods, and Protestants followed the same trend, having lower self-esteem in the presence of Jews than in the presence of Catholics. In

each case the minority seems to have compared itself with the more prestigious of the majority groups.

The process is similar to one reported in Samuel A. Stouffer et al., *The American Soldier*, 2 vols. (Princeton: Princeton University Press, 1949), where newcomers (called replacements) within veteran units were found to under-estimate their abilities compared to newcomers who were separated from veterans.

Chapter 8. Involvement and Detachment

1. Robert K. Merton, George G. Reader, and Patricia L. Kendall, eds., *The Student Physician* (Cambridge, Mass.: Harvard University Press, 1957).

2. Talcott Parsons, "Social Structure and Dynamic Process: The Case of Modern Medical Practice," *The Social System* (New York: Free Press, 1951), pp. 428-79.

3. Robert K. Merton and Elinor Barber, "Sociological Ambivalence," in *Sociological Ambivalence and Other Essays*, by Robert K. Merton (New York: Free Press, 1976), pp. 3-31.

4. Rose Laub Coser, "Role Distance, Sociological Ambivalence, and Transitional Status Systems," *American Journal of Sociology* 72 (1966): 173-87.

5. Melvin L. Kohn, *Class and Conformity: A Study of Values* (Homewood, Ill.: Dorsey, 1969).

6. George C. Homans, "The Small Warship," *American Sociological Review* 11 (1946): 294-300.

7. Allen Wheelis, *Quest for Identity* (New York: Norton, 1958).

8. Erik H. Erikson, *Young Man Luther* (New York: Norton, 1958), pp. 150ff.

Chapter 9. Suicide and the Relational System

1. Phillip E. Hammond, ed., *Sociologists at Work: Essays on the Craft of Social Research* (New York: Basic Books, 1964).

2. David P. Phillips has shown that this could be so. See "The Influence of Suggestion on Suicide: Substantive and Theoretical Implications of the Werther Effect," *American Sociological Review* 39 (June 1974): 340-54.

3. See, for example, Jack D. Douglas, *The Social Meanings of Suicide* (Princeton: Princeton University Press, 1970).

4. A. L. Porterfield, "Indices of Suicide and Homicide by States and Cities," *American Sociological Review* 14 (1949): 489-90; idem, "Suicide and Crime in Secular Society," *American Journal of Sociology* 57 (1952): 331-38; idem, "Suicide and Crime in the Social Structure of an Urban Setting: Fort Worth, 1930-1950," *American Sociological Review* 17 (1952): 341-49; and Jack P. Gibbs and Walter T. Martin, *Status Integration and Suicide: A Socio-*

logical Study (Eugene: University of Oregon Books, 1964). For the concept of strength or weakness of the relational system, see Andrew F. Henry and James F. Short Jr., *Suicide and Homicide* (New York: Free Press, 1954).

5. Alfred H. Stanton and Morris S. Schwartz, "The Management of a Type of Institutional Participation in Mental Illness," *Psychiatry* 12 (February 1949): 13-22; idem, "Observations on Dissociation as Social Participation," *Psychiatry* 12 (February 1949): 339-54; and idem, *The Mental Hospital* (New York: Basic Books, 1954).

6. Philip E. Slater, "On Social Regression," *American Sociological Review* 28 (1963): 339-64.

7. An early formulation of the effect of cross-pressures was made by Georg Simmel in "The Web of Group Affiliations," trans. Reinhard Bendix, in *Conflict and The Web of Group Affiliations*, 2 vols. in 1 (New York: Free Press, 1955), pp. 125-95.

8. Paul F. Lazarsfeld, Bernard Berelson, and Hazel Gaudet, *The People's Choice: How the Voter Makes Up His Mind in a Presidential Campaign* (New York: Duell, Sloan & Pearce, 1944). See also Seymour Martin Lipset, *Political Man* (Garden City, N.Y.: Doubleday, 1960), esp. pp. 203ff.

9. About some consequences of patients' loss of hope, see Ezra Stotland and Arthur L. Kobler, *Life and Death of a Mental Hospital* (Seattle: University of Washington Press, 1965).

10. I am indebted to Judith M. Tanur for applying the Kolmogorov-Smirnov test to this material. She took the cumulative distribution of suicides lagged three months behind the cumulative distribution of nonheld meetings and found no significant difference in the shapes of the distributions.

11. Cf. Murray Melbin, "Organization Practice and Individual Behavior: Absenteeism among Psychiatric Aides," *American Sociological Review* 26 (1961): 14-23. Melbin calls attention to the fact that "leaving a job is the outcome of a chain of experiences. . . . It is not discrete but part of a process."

12. Kenneth McNeil and James D. Thompson, "The Regeneration of Social Organization," *American Sociological Review* 36 (August 1971): 624-37.

13. Emily Mumford, *Interns: From Students to Physicians* (Cambridge, Mass.: Harvard University Press, 1970).

14. See Erving Goffman, "On Cooling the Mark Out: Some Aspects of Adaptation to Failure," *Psychiatry* 15 (1952): 451-63.

15. McNeil and Thompson, "The Regeneration of Social Organization."

16. Ezra Stotland and Lance K. Canon, *Social Psychology: A Cognitive Approach* (Philadelphia: Saunders, 1972), p. 512.

17. Stotland and Kobler, *Life and Death of a Mental Hospital*.

Chapter 10. Social-structural Determinants of Anomie

1. Andrew F. Henry and James F. Short Jr., *Suicide and Homicide* (New York: Free Press, 1954).

2. This method of plotting interaction was suggested to me by David Phillips of the University of California, San Diego. For a theoretical model for roles and positions in networks, see Harrison C. White, Scott A. Boorman, and Ronald L. Breiger, "Social Structure from Multiple Networks: I. Blockmodels of Roles and Positions," *American Journal of Sociology* 81 (1976): 1384- 446.

3. On the importance of a complex role-set for role articulation, see Rose Laub Coser, "The Complexity of Roles as a Seedbed of Individual Autonomy," in *The Idea of Social Structure: Papers in Honor of Robert K. Merton*, ed. Lewis A. Coser (New York: Harcourt, 1975), pp. 237- 64.

4. On the "norm of relay learning," see Emily Mumford, *Interns: From Students to Physicians* (Cambridge, Mass.: Harvard University Press, 1970), pp. 163-70.

5. Karl Mannheim, *Man and Society in an Age of Reconstruction* (New York: Harcourt, 1967).

6. William Caudill found that in the psychiatric hospital he studied (also a university hospital) seniors participated more than residents, who in turn participated significantly more than nurses. Within each status group frequency of participation was directly related to position in the hierarchy. See William A. Caudill, *The Psychiatric Hospital as a Small Society* (Cambridge, Mass.: Harvard University Press, 1958), pp. 243 ff.

7. The effect of "negative democratization" on the communication system in an organization was pointed out to me by Helga Nowotny of the Institute of Advanced Studies in Vienna, Austria.

8. On the relations between authority positions and observability, see Rose Laub Coser, "Insulation from Observability and Types of Social Conformity," *American Sociological Review* 26 (February 1961): 28- 39.

9. On the mobility block in hospitals, see Harvey Smith, "Sociological Study of Hospitals," Ph.D. dissertation, University of Chicago, 1949; and Caudill, *Psychiatric Hospital as a Small Society*, p. 7 and chap. 3.

10. Alexis de Tocqueville, *Democracy in America*; and Georg Simmel, "Superordination and Subordination," *The Sociology of Georg Simmel*, trans. and ed. Kurt H. Wolff (New York: Free Press, 1950), pp. 179- 303.

11. Anne Parsons, personal communication.

12. Robert K. Merton, "The Ambivalence of Organizational Leaders," in *Sociological Ambivalence and Other Essays*, by Robert K. Merton (New York: Free Press, 1976), pp. 73- 89.

Index

Academic exercises and meetings, 28
Admissions procedures, social worker, 15–17
Ambiguity, training in, defined, xv; see also O'Brien Hospital
Ambinormative expectation, 135–36
Ambivalence: evading the issue and coping, 106–107; psychiatric practice and training, 5; structural avoidance, and coalition, 75–80
Anomie, social-structural determinants, 163–79; absence of natural triad, 174–76; flow of communication and structure of leadership, 171–74; instrumental association, 170–71; instrumental interdependence, 163–68; leadership and morning conference, 176–79; primary interaction, 168–70
Anxiety, 144, 145, 157, 160, 171
Attitudes, defined, 37
Authority holders, relations between, 45–51; conflicts and, 47–48; control over administration, 47; high-status role-partners, 48–49; role-partners, 46–47; tension and antagonism, 46
Avoidance and conflict, normative structure of, 51–57

Barber, Elinor, 40, 104, 133, 134
Bateson, Gregory, 42
Blau, Peter, xiii

Calvinist dogma, 165
Caplow, Theodore, 72, 74
Catholic dogma, 165
Clinical administration: preceptor's, 20–23; and psychotherapy, 33–34
Clinical management of patients, 9, 10–13

Cognitive dissonance, self-confidence and, 126–29
Cole, Stephen, 142
Conformity, attitudinal, 37–38
Consensus and dissensus (norms and counternorms), 120–32; cognitive dissonance and self-confidence, 126–29; discrepancies and differences (changes over time), 129–32; intellectual flexibility, nonauthoritarianism and assertiveness, 121–26
Contextual dissonance, 126–27
"Continuing case supervision," 28
Contract therapists, 21, 52–53
Contradictory expectations, 126
Contradictory norms, psychiatric residents at work, 29–32
Control and support, therapeutic triad, 37–45
Countertransference, 74

Defense, patterned mechanisms, structural ambivalence and, 98–119; comparison between activity systems, 107–19; learning through doing, 99–103; learning through treating, 103–105; social mechanisms, 105–107
Detachment, see Involvement and detachment
Domineering mother, 41
Drug therapy, 7
Dual leadership, treatment set, 70–75
Durkheim, Emile, 144, 163
Dynamics of Bureaucracy, The (Blau), xiii

Electroshock treatment, 7
Emotional support, 44
Erikson, Erik, 140–41

217

group psychotherapy, 23–24;
night nurse, 19–20; psychotherapy (and clinical administration), 33–34; psychotherapy (supervisor and administrator), 24–28;
schedule for interviews with,
184–93; workup of patients,
17–18
Psychiatric training, sociological
ambivalence in, 5
Psychiatrists, normative and self-
image scoring of (1961 interviews), 195–202
Psychiatry, rapprochement between
psychoanalysis and, 6–7
Psychoanalytic Institute, 11
Psychotherapy: clinical administration and, 33–34; differences in
self-perception as learners or
servers (by year of residency),
101, 102; group, 23–24; lack of
communication complaints,
27–28; supervisor and administrator, 24–28

Reciprocity, theory of, 44
"Regeneration of Social Organization, The" (McNeil and Thompson), 158, 160
Relational system, suicide and,
142–62; composition of staff (ebb
and flow), 153–62; direction of
change in frequency of meetings,
147–48; interaction (ebb and
flow), 145–53; participation of
residents at problems conference,
150–53; selected meetings with
residents, 145–50; sociological
studies, 143–45; tables, 147, 148,
149, 151, 152, 153, 154, 157,
158, 159; turnover in leadership,
153–58; turnover of residents,
158–62
Research (plans and vicissitudes),
2–5
Residency Education Committee, 18,
100, 170, 174
Resident therapist, status superiors,
80–85
Residents' Education Committee, 20,
24
Residents at work, *see* Psychiatric
residents at work
Role-partners, 43, 87, 88–90
Role-set, theory of, 37, 39, 44; reciprocity and, 44
Rosenberg, Morris, 126

Schwartz, Morris, xiii, xv, 144, 145,
162
Self-confidence, cognitive dissonance
and, 126–29
Selznick, Philip, xiii
Sentimental congruence, theory of,
76–77
Separation anxiety, 157
Short, James F., Jr., 144
Significant role-partners, 87
Simmel, Georg, 45
Slater, Philip, 145
Social anxiety, 145
Social mechanisms of defense,
105–107
Social worker, admissions proce-
dures, 15–17
Sociological ambivalence, 40, 118
Staff meetings, 28
Stanton, Alfred H., xiii, xv, xvii–
xviii, 144, 145, 162
Status superiors, resident therapist
and, 80–85
Status system (of O'Brien Hospital),
57–61
Stotland, Ezra, 161, 162
Structural ambivalence: avoidance
and coalition, 75–80; and pattern-
ed mechanisms of defense,
98–119; training set, 95
Suicides, 4, 14, 165; relational sys-
tem and, 142–62

Tanur, Judith, 142
Therapeutic triad, 35–61; control
and support, 37–45; normative
structure of avoidance and conflict, 51–57; relations between
authority holders, 45–51; status
system, 57–61
Therapist and patient, therapeutic
alliance between, 73–74
Thompson, James D., 158, 160
Training set, 86–97; activity demands, differences in, 90–92; conflict and tension, 95–96; distinction between high-status role-partners, 88–90; exposure to contradictory expectations, 97; related
(but distinct) tasks, 86–87; residents benefits (from adapting
behavior to demands of two activity systems), 93–95; significant
role-partners, 87
Transference, resident's, 141
Treatment set, 62–85; dual leadership, 70–75; low-status therapeutic triad, 66–70; resident therapist
and status superiors, 80–85; struc-